Willing
Oct Frees

WILLIAM A. JENKS
TEACHER, SCHOLAR, MENTOR, FRIEND

William Alexander Jenks, W&L, 1939

...Ending with a Flourish

WILLIAM A. JENKS
TEACHER, SCHOLAR, MENTOR, FRIEND

A *FESTSCHRIFT* COMMEMORATING
A MAN WHO LEFT HIS MARK
ON THE MINDS AND HEARTS
OF ALL HIS STUDENTS

MARINER
PUBLISHING
BUENA VISTA, VIRGINIA

FIRST EDITION

1   3   5   7   9   10   8   6   4   2

Library of Congress Control Number: 2007937626

...ENDING WITH A FLOURISH
William A. Jenks —Teacher, Scholar, Mentor, Friend

J. Holt Merchant, Roy T. Matthews, Parker K. Smith, Jr., editors
Includes Bibliographical References

p. cm.

1. Jenks, William Alexander, 1918-, 2. Washington and Lee University
I. Merchant, J. Holt, II. Matthews, Roy T., III. Smith, Parker K., Jr.

ISBN: 978-0-9800077-0-1(cloth: alk. paper)
        978-0-9800077-1-8 (soft cover: alk. paper)

Book Design by Patricia Gibson
Cover art: *William Alexander Jenks, Jr.*, by Christopher Johnson, original oil.

Mariner Publishing
A division of
Mariner Companies, Inc.
212 East 21st Street.
Buena Vista, VA 24416
http://www.marinermedia.com

Printed in the United States of America. This book is printed on acid-free paper meeting the requirements of the American Standard for Permanence of Paper for Printed Library Materials.

The Compass Rose and Pen are trademarks of Mariner Companies, Inc.

IT WILL BE enough for me, however, if these words of mine are judged useful by those who want to understand clearly the events which happened in the past and which (human nature being what it is) will, at some time or other and in much the same ways, be repeated in the future.

Thucydides
The Peloponnesian War

IT SHOULD BE known that history is a discipline that has a great number of approaches. Its useful aspects are very many. Its goal is distinguished.

History makes us acquainted with the conditions of past nations as they are reflected in their national character. It makes us acquainted with the biographies of the prophets and with the dynasties and policies of rulers. Whoever so desires may thus achieve the useful result of being able to imitate historical examples in religious and worldly matters.

Ibn Khaldun
Muqaddimah

THERE IS A history in all men's lives,
Figuring the nature of the times deceased,
The which observed, a man may prophesy,
With a near aim, of the main chance of things
As yet not come to life, which in their seeds
And weak beginnings lie intreasured.

William Shakespeare
Henry IV, Part 2

Contents

Preface

J. Holt Merchant
Class of 1961

ABOUT TWO YEARS ago, Parker Smith, class of 1953, went to Roy Matthews, class of 1954, with a proposal to publish a Festschrift to honor their professor, mentor, and friend, William A. Jenks. Bill's students had endowed an award in his honor in 1985 which provides aid to students who major in European history and continue to work in that area in graduate school. In 1994 Thomas Angelillo, class of 1974, established a second award to assist undergraduates who have excelled in history and have financial need. And in 2004, the class of 1954 endowed an award in his honor that will go to outstanding undergraduates regardless of major.

Parker and Roy agreed that they wanted to do still more to honor Bill, and that this time it should be a collection of essays contributed by students who had studied under him and gone on to careers such as business, education, government, journalism, and law. They also agreed that they needed the assistance of someone from the University faculty to coordinate the effort. They probably did not know that I had taken only one of Bill's courses, his survey of medieval history required of all majors in the discipline, or that I had long believed that it was the most difficult course, graduate or undergraduate, I had ever encountered. They probably did know that Bill was chairman during my first fourteen years in the Department and that he had supported and encouraged me while I taught a full load of courses and wrote my dissertation. I will always be grateful for everything he did for me, both during those early years and after.

Parker, Roy, and I compiled a list of alumni we hoped would contribute essays, first by identifying men we knew personally and then by consulting a roster of men who had majored in history during the years Bill was a member of the Department. Then with the splendid assistance of Jennifer Ashworth, the Department's administrative assistant, we drafted and dispatched letters soliciting contributions, and waited for replies. The proposals poured in, followed by contributions from alumni who continue to admire and respect Bill, and remain grateful for the role he has played in their lives and careers. We have received much needed assistance from Bill's daughter Elaine and from editors of the Calyx, who contributed the photographs illustrating his long and distinguished career at W&L, and from the editors of Mariner Publishing.

Parker and Roy have made countless trips to Lexington, and the three of us have planned, read, evaluated, edited, and at last completed work on the volume you now hold in your hands. We are grateful for the participation of all those who have helped to make this book a reality, and enormously pleased to have had this opportunity to honor Bill Jenks—teacher, scholar, mentor, and friend.

William Alexander Jenks: Teacher, Scholar, Mentor, Friend

Roy T. Matthews, Class of 1954

DR. WILLIAM A. JENKS, a native of Jacksonville, Florida, was a member of the Department of History from 1946 until his retirement in 1983. He came to Washington and Lee on an Alumni Scholarship and graduated *magna cum laude* with a degree in history in 1939. He received his M. A. in 1940 at Columbia University. During World War II he served in the U. S. Army and the Office of Strategic Service. He earned his Ph D. from Columbia University in 1949.

He rapidly rose in rank in the Department of History: Instructor, 1946; Assistant Professor, 1947; Associate Professor, 1951; Professor, 1956. His contributions to Washington and Lee and his profession were recognized in 1971 when he was named a Kenan Professor, the only Kenan chair at W and L. William R. Kenan, Jr. Professorships, awarded to individuals, not to institutions, in recognition of their achievements, are among the most prestigious honors in higher education. Dr. Jenks was chairman of the Department of History from 1970 to 1983. Under his chairmanship, the Department consistently taught more students and graduated more majors than any other department in the University. He also served on numerous academic committees and advised many student organizations.

He taught the introductory European History course which introduced many Freshmen into the complexities of historical events and thought, and conducted a Freshman seminar on modern European social and ideological movements. His many advanced classes included Middle Ages, Renaissance and Reformation, Eighteenth and Nineteenth Century European History, Imperial and Soviet Russian history, Islamic history and the Philosophy of History. Dr. Jenks also taught seminars on many topics and supervised countless Senior Honors projects. Although he was offered several opportunities to teach at the graduate level in other universities and was a visiting professor at various schools, including the University of Virginia, Duke University, the University of Maryland, VMI, and Virginia Tech, he remained committed to undergraduate education and spent his entire career at Washington and Lee.

His research in the Nineteenth century Hapsburg Empire earned him a Fulbright fellowship and many grants, including those from the Ford Foundation, the Social Science Research Council, the Fund for the Advancement of Education, the American Council of Learned Societies, and Washington and Lee faculty grants. These grants enabled him to author four books and to write numerous articles and book reviews in scholarly periodicals which earned him international recognition as an expert on the Hapsburg Empire.

Dr. Jenks' scholarly contributions also include articles in the *Austrian History Yearbook* and the *Le Baeck Institute Yearbook* plus twenty-seven book reviews in such prestigious journals as the *American Historical Review*, the *Journal of Modern History*, *East Central Europe*, and the *Slavic Review*.

Dr. Jenks' scholarship and writings have not gone unnoticed. In 1981 the president of the American Historical Association, Dr. David H. Pinkney, in his address to the national meeting, recognized Dr. Jenks for his contributions in revitalizing the study of the Hapsburg Empire, and he cited scholars in Germany who had praised Dr. Jenks' scholarship and insights into the issues of federalism. In appreciation of his teaching and mentoring history majors and undergraduates, three scholarships in his honor have been established at Washington and Lee. His reputation in history graduate departments and colleges and universities across the country is legendary as some of the most respected and noted scholars of the last forty years in European history have come out of his classes and are known as the "Jenks Mafia".

During his tenure at Washington and Lee, Dr. Jenks and his gracious and lovely wife, Jane, welcomed students into their home. Any undergraduate who was fortunate enough to receive an invitation for an evening at the Jenks's residence would always remember the host and hostess's warm reception and Southern hospitality, and being among one's peers in a stimulating and cordial environment. He has lost his lifelong companion. However, his daughter, who now lives with him, and granddaughter, who is a 2007 graduate of Washington and Lee, have enlivened his life. He has a legion of Lexington friends, and many of his former students keep in touch with him, and when they are in Lexington he welcomes them into his home.

Making a point in his Washington Hall classroom.

In his third-floor office, Washington Hall.

William Alexander Jenks As Teacher

Robert O. Paxton, Class of 1954

I ALREADY LIKED the study of history when I got to Washington and Lee in the fall of 1950. There Bill Jenks's lectures consolidated that interest. I went eagerly to Bill's classes—of course I thought of him then with some awe as Dr. Jenks—and I think I took every one of the courses he taught. He knew how to appeal to both the mind and the emotions. He would, for example, explain the issues at stake when the leaders of the French revolution were trying to construct a constitutional monarchy in 1791, and then he would tell how King Louis XVI himself blew that project by trying to escape to the Austrian Netherlands. We followed the heavy coach—the "berline"—that carried the royal family incognito eastwards until, at an obligatory rest stop in the village of Varennes, someone recognized them and the jig was up. I can remember that lecture more than fifty years later as if I had seen it on film.

Bill's lectures had shape. Unlike a lot of history professors I have heard, who tend to start each class more or less where they had left off in the previous one, in an unstructured ramble, Bill presented a beginning, a development, and an end. He announced some major historical development as his subject, discussed the human choices and general conditions that led to one particular outcome, told us how historians' interpretations had changed over time, and then enthralled us with some vivid details. The lecture always ended with a flourish.

When I became a history professor, I consciously emulated him. My syllabus laid out the lectures with a subject for each day, and I stuck to it. I tried to give my lectures shape. But I had trouble getting to that flourish at the end. One day when, as an old alumnus, I felt I could ask for his trade secrets, he told me how it was done. Simple, he said. I look at my watch and when I have two minutes to go I jump to my concluding remarks.

Bill took pains to make exams reinforce his teaching. No multiple choice or memorized facts for him. He drafted challenging essay questions that required us to analyze historical turning points and transformations. He gave our papers back with plenty of thought-provoking comments.

Some wise person has said that the best writing looks effortless, even though it probably went through many agonizing drafts. Teaching is surely the same. Bill's apparently easy fluency was the product of hours of careful preparation. He kept his scholarship up to date (his reading is still prodigious) and refreshed his lectures with current references. Good history teaching–contrary to legend—takes intensive labor.

A Letter Home – March 15, 1953

Henry Ashby Turner, Jr. Class of 1954

Charles Stillé Professor of History Emeritus
Yale University

I HAVE ENCOUNTERED a very fine gentleman in the History Department here who has given me a lot to think about in regard to life-aims and life-work. He is Dr. William Jenks, who I have for two of my history courses this semester. He graduated from here in 1939, served in the Army during the war and then, after completing his graduate studies returned to join the faculty.

I can't really explain why Dr. Jenks is so different from the other professors whom I know except for the important fact that he doesn't keep up the student-faculty barrier that most professors maintain. It's quite a refreshing experience to be able to go to someone and expect to be treated as another person rather than as just another pupil or student. I hope to see a good deal of Dr. Jenks from now on. By the way, he is giving me a inside view of the college teaching profession and there is more there than strikes the eye!

Dr. Jenks as Scholar

Henry Ashby Turner, Jr. Class of 1954

Charles Stillé Professor of History Emeritus
Yale University

WHILE HE WAS enlightening W&L students about the many and varied chapters of the past covered by his courses, Dr. Jenks was gaining international recognition in the historical profession with his scholarship on the Habsburg Empire. He authored four thoroughly researched books as well as numerous incisive articles and book reviews in scholarly periodicals.

His first book, *The Austrian Electoral Reform of 1907*, was based on the research for his Columbia University doctoral dissertation. In it he analyzed the ultimately unsuccessful effort to stabilize Habsburg Austria by instituting universal manhood suffrage for parliamentary elections. This involved, among other things, mastering the maneuvers, in complicated and protracted parliamentary negotiations, of forty political parties on behalf of a variety of interest groups and ten nationalities. The result was a revealing study of an important turning point in the history of what was one of the world's great powers until its demise in the First World War.

For his *Vienna and the Young Hitler* Dr. Jenks did trail-blazing research in the Austrian capital on the five years the future dictator spent there as a rootless young provincial who eventually ended up in a shelter for homeless men. To situate Hitler's formative Viennese experiences in context, the book provides a wealth of information about the cultural, economic, social and political life of the city Hitler later referred to as "the hardest, though most thorough, school of my life". It remains an essential source for biographies of Hitler and studies of Vienna.

In his *Austria under the Iron Ring* Dr. Jenks drew on Austrian and Imperial German documents to produce an illuminating study of high-level politics in the Habsburg monarchy. The book reveals how a canny aristocratic prime minister skillfully held together a tenuous coalition of political parties during the years 1879-1893 to give the multinational state a degree of stability that was never again achieved. Anyone seeking to understand how the late Habsburg monarchy's government actually functioned at its best must consult this book.

Based on French and Italian as well as Austrian documents, Dr. Jenks' *Francis Joseph and the Italians, 1849-1859,* chronicled Austria's loss of the control over northern Italy granted it by the other European powers following the defeat of Napoleon I. The book culminates with a close analysis of the diplomatic antecedents of the war of 1859 in which Austria's defeat by Savoy and France set Italian unification in motion. On the basis of some deft historical detective work, Dr. Jenks concluded that Emperor Francis Joseph himself bore prime responsibility for igniting that conflict.

Some years ago, I had the privilege of dedicating a book of my own to Dr. Jenks. Noticing this, a history graduate student at Yale came to me and asked how I knew him. When I explained that Dr. Jenks had been the teacher who inspired me to enter the historical profession, the graduate student replied: "Well, I hope you realize you were inspired by this country's foremost expert on the Habsburg Empire!"

A Reminiscence

Robert E.R. Huntley Class of 1950

WHEN I THINK of Bill Jenks, a flood of thoughts and memories is released.

For me, first, there was Jenks, the teacher. I was a largely un-tutored youth of uncertain motivation in 1946. Professor Jenks was the first glimpse I remember of a teacher/scholar in action. His lectures were powerful, Slowly, but eventually, exposure to such a scintillating teacher invaded and stimulated even the indolent intellect of an indifferent student. Other teachers in those years stand out in my memory in various positive ways — Pusey, Flournoy, Leyburn, for example. But none combines the qualities of Jenks.

Years later, when I retuned to teach in the law school, he became a colleague and friend. But only when I became president did I encounter the full measure of Bill's character and strength. He was a superlative head of the school's strongest department and was highly respected — even revered — by the faculty. He was repeatedly elected by them to the President's Advisory Committee, the Faculty's most important voice. That committee made or advised about all important decisions concerning faculty retention, promotion, and tenure. The president consulted it—and in my case always followed it's advice–about many significant issues he faced. Bill's counsel was wise, dispassionate, and on target.

Of the heroes of my W&L years as student, teacher, and administrator, Jenks is the one whom I identify as a precise embodiment of this school's ideal professor: an accomplished and productive scholar, a teacher who drew out the best in the young minds that encountered his, a campus citizen whose understanding of our most exalted ideals was joined with capacity for practical solutions.

My friendship and admiration for him have only grown as the years have passed. Nowadays, he and I and a few other old-timers meet for dinner most months. Always the delight of the evening for me is my conversation with Bill. His wit and intellect have not flagged.

You Can't Escape History

Roger Mudd, Class of 1950

THE CALL CAME out of the blue. Her name was Abbe Raven. She was a vice president of A&E Television, a cable company, and she said they were planning to start a new channel that did only history—documentaries, movies, short historical features— and would I be interested in signing on as the host of the documentary series? Other than Brian Lamb's C-Span coverage of Congress, I knew as much about cable television as I knew about acupuncture - next to nothing. So my response to Abbe was a flurry of questions. Would it be full-time? Who was supplying the documentaries? Could I work at home? Who had editorial control? Who else had they hired? When were they planning to start? Who owned A&E?

Over the next few weeks I got the answers to all my questions: It would take about three or four days per month; the documentaries would be supplied by a string of reliable and respected independent producers; I could work at home, writing and rewriting, plus an overnight stay in New York every other month to record my on-camera commentary; I would share editorial control with The History Channel and the various producers; they had already hired Sandy Vanocur, another network refugee from NBC, to host historical movies, and Karen Stone from ABC to do a feature called "Year by Year;" they planned to start on the first of the year and, finally, A&E was owned in roughly equal parts by the Hearst Corporation, Disney and NBC.

It all sounded too perfect—I could broadcast, I could write and I could almost be the historian I started out to be. I signed on and started that September, 1994 at $79,500 a year for 28 days of work a year.

Working at home was a new and exhilarating pleasure. My office is in the log wing of our house which had been built in 1901 by a Confederate veteran who had returned to McLean after the war to find that the house he had grown up in had been dismantled by the Union troops. They had converted our hill into one of the semaphore signal stations strung up along the Potomac River as back-up to the telegraph wires the Confederates were always cutting, sending Edwin Stanton and his War Department into a panic. Each time I wrote at home I found an excitement that comes from tapping into the lode of stories and exploits and legends that surrounded me.

Flanking me were bookcases filled with a lifetime of buying books—most of them US history. But what I found I used most in working for The History Channel were five shelves of reference books—*The Oxford Companion to World War Two*, the *Oxford Companions to American Literature and English Literature*, *Webster's Unabridged Encyclopedic Dictionary of the English Language*—the 18-pounder, the *World Almanac*, the *Encyclopedia Britannica*, two atlases, *Brewster's Dictionary of Phrase and Fable*, *Bartlett's*, the *New York Public Library Desk Reference*, the *Complete Book of US Presidents*, the *Almanac of American Politics* and Samuel Eliot Morrison's *Oxford History of the American People*. I bought a marvelous office chair with wheels and when I got really rolling I was in constant motion between the computer and the book shelves

Before long The History Channel and I fell into a pattern we could rely on. About every 6 to 7 weeks a Federal Express truck pulled up at the house with a box of video tapes—rough cuts of the documentaries scheduled for the next quarter. Over the next 10 days in bits and pieces I would watch them and take notes to get acquainted with the content, the tone and the scope. Within a week, another FedEx truck came, bringing rough drafts of the studio copy for the open and close for each documentary. The copy had been written by one of 3 or 4 New York free-lancers who had also watched the tapes and been furnished with historical background material.

Then for the next 2 or 3 days, I worked almost full-time editing, almost always rewriting the copy, even scrapping it to make sure the words were clear, inviting, and did not walk over the documentary itself.

It became a constant challenge to achieve the right balance. The copy had to be accurate but it also had to hold the viewer's attention; it had to give the program some valuable historical context but could not be so freighted with facts and figures that the viewer started sinking under their weight.

Some copy went through untouched; other drafts needed tweaking.

British General Bernard Montgomery got described as "supercilious and egotistical." Was that accurate and was it fair? I pulled down the World War Two book and read around on Montgomery. I decided the words were fair but I changed them to "divisive and egocentric" because I thought they better explained why Montgomery had such terrible relations with both Eisenhower and Bradley.

The opening copy for a show called "The Siege of Louisbourg" began this way: "The Mighty Fortress of Louisbourg seemed impregnable when the French built it in Northern Nova Scotia in 1713."

That opening left me cold. First, I barely knew where Nova Scotia was and knew less about the French and Indians Wars. So I went to the books, got out the atlas and re-wrote the open to read: "Six hundred miles north east of Boston lies Cape Breton Island, part of the Canadian province of Nova Scotia. But 285 years ago, it was French and it was here overlooking the harbor that King Louis the 14th built his great military outpost in the New World - the Fortress of Louisbourg."

I think that rewrite helped—it gave the viewer a geographic locator, it gave the viewer a time locator and it gave the viewer some historical context.

Another example was for the show titled "Decisive Weapons-The Longbow." The copy read, "At the Battle of Crecy in 1346, the Genovese, still using the traditional crossbow, found out too late that their English enemies had abandoned the weapon."

I was confused. First, if the English had abandoned the crossbow, what weapon were they using? Also, I didn't know where Crecy was. The historical atlas told me it was in Northern France. And if the French were fighting the English, what were the Genovese doing there? I looked up "Genovese." I knew enough that Genoa was a city-state but still couldn't figure why they were at Crecy. So down came my *Oxford World History—From Earliest Times to 1800*. Under the heading, Battle of Crecy, I discovered that the Genoese crossbowmen were soldiers of fortune who had been paid to fight for France.

So I changed the sentence to read: "At the Battle of Crecy in northern France in 1346, mercenary soldiers from Genoa hired by Paris were still using the traditional crossbow. They found out too late that the English enemy had switched to the deadly long bow." They were modest changes and all that effort might have been out of proportion to the result. But I thought not. I thought any effort that made history clearer was worth the effort.

Once I finished with the scripts, I FedEx-ed them to The History Channel or faxed them up if I was pushing a deadline. When the copy was cleared, it was put on prompter, proof read and set aside until taping time. I went to New York perhaps 4 or 5 times a year for a two-day stretch. We taped my copy for 12 to 15 shows on each day, beginning about 9:30 each morning and finishing before lunch because I had found over the years that my voice weakened and thinned out in the afternoons.

There was in addition a certain sequence for wardrobe changes. Wearing, say, a blue shirt, a gray jacket and red-figured tie,

I would tape shows 1,3,5,7 and 9. Then, keeping the blue shirt but changing to a striped blue and gold tie and a blue blazer, I would tape shows 2,4,8 and ten. That way nobody could write in complaining about my wearing the same tie and coat two nights in a row.

During those first years we had a dazzling variety of programs: a series on the Empires of Industry—coal, steel, textiles, ships and beer; a series on the Fifties, based on the David Halberstam book—Levittown, Elvis, school desegregation, interstate high-ways and the pill; a history of the US Marshals; five days of the Nixon impeachment hearings during the summer of President Clinton's angst and six hours with the great minds of American history: Gordon Wood, James McPherson, Richard White, David McCullough, James Horton and Stephen Ambrose.

Working for CBS and NBC over the years I became aware of the huge audiences they drew—18 and 20 million a night—but it was never quite possible on The History Channel to know what impact I was having. Even though the number of subscribers was in the multi-millions, the actual number of viewers was never much more than a million. So we never knew exactly whether we were in fact, arousing people's interest in history, causing them to think more clearly about the past. Not sure, that is, until the man ahead of me in the grocery store turned and said, "Thank God for The History Channel. It's all I watch." or the black woman at the bank who is a part time graduate student at George Mason University who gave up her place in line to say that they watched our stuff all the time in class or the 14-year-old neighbor boy who told me he used my program, "History Alive," to help with his term paper.

But there were times when a viewer's reaction left me baffled. Fran Templin of Sun City, Arizona, a woman I did not know, wrote to say:

"Dear Mr. Mudd. I am writing to apologize to you for the slur on your name many years ago when I objected to your method of commentary and I wrote that you were aptly named. For that I am sorry and hope that you will accept my apology. I do enjoy you on The

History Channel and wish you many years of health, happiness and speak. Sincerely, Fran Templin."

Or about the time I was finishing 40 years of broadcasting when a young girl from St. Paul who wanted my autograph wrote:

"Dear Mr. Mudd. You are a very competent newsman. Have you been on the air long?"

My part-time schedule with The History Channel enabled me to hold a second job—none other than Visiting Professor of Journalism at my beloved alma mater, Washington & Lee University. One of W&L's history professors, a graduate of Princeton, had spotted a piece in the *Princeton Alumni Weekly* about my teaching at Princeton and that led to an invitation to come to Lexington. On April 17, 1995, I resumed my life as a university professor, teaching a twice-a-week seminar on the Washington media with 18 students, half of them co-eds. After well over 200 years as an all-male institution, W&L, facing declining enrollments, had gone co-ed in 1985. In the late 1940's when I was an undergraduate, school tradition included a venerated and widely observed honor system, conventional dress (coat & tie), and a civil obligation to speak to the known and unknown. But this was 45 years later and only the honor code remained in place. Gone was the speaking rule, although a few continued it, and gone altogether was conventional dress. A few of my male students wore their cat hats to class that first day but not again. Regardless of their dress, the students were bright, pleased to have a teacher from what in academe is called "the real world," laid back in an attractive Southern way, responsive and as it turned out much better writers than my Princeton students. During that Spring, my classroom visitors included Bob Schieffer of CBS News, Diane Rehm of NPR Radio, Brian Lamb of C-Span and Charles McDowell, my W&L classmate and the long-time Washington columnist for *The Richmond Times-Dispatch*.

After Charlie's visit, we took four or five of the students to dinner while Charlie kept us all roaring with laughter with tales about growing up in Lexington. Charlie's best one involved a curmudgeonly professor of zoology who had grown tired of the school's worship of Robert E. Lee. He arranged to have Charlie pose as tourist guide at the stable where Lee's famous horse, Traveller, was quartered when Lee was president of the college. Traveller died in 1871, the year after Lee, and his bones were on display in the basement of Lee Chapel. Charlie was to stand next to the skeleton of a large dog the professor had borrowed from his classroom.

"Now, Charles," the professor told him, "when the tourists come and ask to see Traveller's bones, you tell them they're in Lee Chapel." And when they point to the dog skeleton and ask, "Then what's that?" you tell them, "Oh, that's when Traveller was a pony."

I was back again in the Fall of 1996 to team teach with the Politics Department a course on the Clinton-Dole presidential campaign. E.J. loved coming down for a few days every other week to stay in the house on campus the University furnished for us. It was the house Annie Jo White had once owned and where as a three-year-old she had sat on the knee of Robert E. Lee.

Each morning when I walked up the long hill to class and caught my first glimpse of the Colonnade, all that ran through my mind was the old Burt Bachrach tune, "You're too good to be true, Can't take my eyes off of you.'

Being back in Lexington after almost half a century felt as if I had never left.

An Eminent Scholar and Professor

G. William Whitehurst, Class of 1950

Kaufman Lecturer in Public Affairs
Old Dominion University

WHEN I ENROLLED at Washington and Lee in 1946, I had chosen journalism as my major. Returning from the war in the Pacific, I was still awash in memories of my experiences, of which I had written copious accounts to my family and bride-to-be. Indeed, I had chosen W&L because of its journalism program and the prospect of a career in the field.

However, in my second semester, by chance I drew Mr. Jenks (he didn't have his Ph.D. at that point) for the freshman course in European history. My first half of the course had been with an instructor who was so dull that he nearly killed my interest in a subject that I had always liked and read. From my first day with Bill Jenks, I was captivated. His knowledge and his ability to write a few subjects of his lecture on the board and then begin to speak without reference to notes left me in awe. Moreover, he brought history alive, as I have endeavored to do in the many years that I have had in the classroom, but I could never achieve his performance. He became and has remained my idol. It is to him that I credit my changing my major to history and embarking upon an academic career. In my progress towards my own doctorate in history, I had a number of outstanding professors, but none could match Bill Jenks.

From professor to student, our relationship blossomed into a long friendship. When my son Cal went to Washington and Lee, he took up the journalism major that I had abandoned, but at my encouragement, he took a course with Bill Jenks and told me that Bill was everything I had said about him, an eminent scholar and professor.

My academic life took an eighteen-year detour in 1968 when I was elected to the U.S. House of Representatives, but I kept my ties to Bill and Jane Jenks, visiting Lexington as often as my wife and I could, and sharing a dinner with them. Jane's passing grieved us as it did all who knew her, and Bill's loss is ours.

The finest legacy that any of us can leave is the impact upon the lives that we have touched. I know this from my own years of teaching and the bonds forged with my students. Bill Jenks's influence upon countless men can never be measured. Mention his name to anyone who was privileged to sit in his class across two generations, and they will immediately recall the joy of his lectures and his impact on their lives.

The first day that I walked into a college classroom to teach history, I thought, "If I could only teach like Bill Jenks," but I knew instinctively that was not possible. No one else could teach like Bill Jenks.

Our Century's Unknown Decisive Battle

Thomas C. Damewood, Class of 1950

IN SELECTING A title for my essay, I have tried to follow what I perceive as the Anvil Club's traditional criteria: choose one that, while appropriate to the subject, successfully conceals it, may pique the interest of other club members and leaves the author free to talk about whatever he wants. Thus, within the ambit of tonight's effort, I might plausibly address you on the Battle of the Salween River Gorge fifty years ago, the struggle for women's suffrage, or the victory over poliomyelitis.

Ah, you say, none of those events is "unknown." But that is a captious objection, because no battle is unknown, and certainly, if it were not at least moderately well known, I would be ignorant of it.

In this title, the adjective "unknown" does not apply to the noun "battle." Indeed, this battle is world famous; the literature on it is formidable. It will be remembered always in military annals as the end of a basic type of warfare extending back to antiquity and will forever intrigue us with the haunting fact that —as historically memorable and as epoch marking as it is—there is not the slightest possibility that any battle even remotely resembling it can ever be fought again.

No, the adjective "unknown" applies not to the battle per se, but to its character as decisive on a world scale. Indeed, as my title proclaims, I hope to persuade you that it is the decisive battle of the 20th century.

The most important war of our century—already dubbed by some historians as THE AGE OF CONFLICT—was the First World War. Today if World War I is thought about at all, it is commonly regarded as a bit quaint. In fact, its consequences were so vast that all other conflicts are dwarfed by the years 1914-1918. Originally, and appropriately, called the Great War, the First World War ended the Hohenzollern, Hapsburg, Romanov, and Ottoman Empires, led directly to the demise of Britain and France as prime powers, gave birth to the Soviet Union, and forced the United States from behind its sheltering oceans to the world's center stage, where it remains. The war revealed the ferocity of modern arms and left forever shattered the Europe of church and state, the notion that human progress was inevitable, and the belief that cultured nations would eschew any but humane methods of warfare and would seek to protect women and children from all but unavoidable harm.

Obviously there could have been no Second World War without a First. With some realignment, the principal combatants were the same: Germany, France, Great Britain, Russia, Italy, Japan, and—again after an interval—the United States. The First World War was scarcely over when one of its chief figures, the Allied generalissimo, Marshal Ferdinand Foch, foresaw with an eerie precision the coming of the second struggle. In 1919 Foch was handed a copy of the Treaty of Versailles. After reading it, Foch remarked: "Cette n'est pas la paix. C'est un armistice pour vingt annes." For those of you who don't understand French (or can't because of my inept tongue) le Marechal said of the Versailles Treaty: "This is not peace. It is an armistice for twenty years."

The guns of August 1914 thundered. Tinkering by Count von Schlieffen's successors with its conception and irresolution in its execution undid his plan for a quick German victory over

France. In the event, the German Armies ended up in front of Paris instead of behind it, and, after a "race to the sea," a Western Front formed from Belfort on the Swiss frontier to the Channel coast. In a labyrinth of trenches, guarded by barbed wire and machine guns, each side dug in and proved repeatedly to its foes that all the artillery barrages and bravery in the world could not dislodge it.

Seventeen months after the war began, the Western Front lay snow-covered in stalemate. As 1916 dawned, each of the opponents sought a solution.

Each side had an instrument at hand. Since 1805, when Nelson had crushed at Trafalgar the combined French and Spanish fleets of Napoleon, all had been "Rule Britannia," as the Royal Navy held together one-fourth of the planet in its greatest empire, ruled by an island nation of only some 40,000,000 people. Then, in 1905, the First Sea Lord, young Winston Churchill's great friend with the strange mandarin's face, Admiral Sir John ("Jacky") Fisher, unified in the single hull of a new battleship many of the 19th century's technical advances, replacing steam reciprocating engines with rotary turbines; increasing the usual four 12-inch guns in two turrets, individually sighted by gunners to ten 12-inch guns in five turrets, to be fired in salvoes coordinated by a gunnery officer using advanced range-finding optics from a lofty fire control tower; having more rational armor, including protection of the decks against plunging shells with delayed detonation fuses; having the interior divided into separate compartments that did not connect with each other but could, be entered only through a hatch on deck; and boasting a speed of 21 knots, that of a contemporary cruiser. On 10 February 1906 King Edward VII crashed a bottle of Australian wine across her bow as he proclaimed: "I christen you Dreadnought!" She made every battleship in the world obsolete. Shortly thereafter Fisher's design committee produced a similiar but faster ship called a battle cruiser, to scout ahead of the slower battleships as a sort of ocean cavalry, sweeping away threatening torpedo craft. Since their higher speed had been achieved by removing the weight of significant armor, critics feared that they would be vulnerable. "Nonsense," snorted Fisher, "speed is armor!"

Across the North Sea, Queen Victoria's grandson, Kaiser Wilhelm II, ruled Germany. Envious and imitative of his British cousins, the Kaiser wanted a comparable navy. In 1894, after reading the *Influence of Sea Power Upon History* by American Navy Captain Alfred Thayer Mahan, the Kaiser became convinced that his country had to have a powerful navy to move its status from *Grossmacht nach Weltmacht* (great power to world power). In 1897 he appointed Rear Admiral Alfred Tirpitz (he of the bifurcated beard) as State Secretary of the Navy. In the 19 years he held the post, Tirpitz proved himself second only to Bismarck as the ablest, most durable, influential, and effective minister in the 48 years of Imperial Germany. Well before 1914 the High Seas Fleet had risen from insignificance to second only to the Royal Navy in size and power. For its country's good the High Seas Fleet should never have been built, for it drove Britain away from its ethnic and royal links with Prussia, its ally against Napoleon and in the recent Boxer Rebellion, toward its centuries-old enemy, France, and that despised autocrat, the Czar of Russia.

After August 1914, except for the skirmish at the Dogger Bank in January 1915, the High Seas Fleet had avoided combat with the Royal Navy, but much against its will. Indeed, for years the standard toast in German wardrooms had been DER TAG!—the day when the High Seas Fleet would steam out to best the Royal Navy and make Germania ruler of the waves. However, contrary to popular expectation on both sides, the opposing fleets did not rush toward each other for a climactic battle in the North Sea. The Kaiser did not wish to lose any of his beautiful ships, and the Chancellor believed that the army would soon defeat France and that, even if Britain's principal armed force had not suffered, the English would make peace. The British, intent on maintaining their distant blockade that was gradually garroting the Reich, would not be drawn toward the German coast with its U-boats and minefields.

When the new year, 1916, opened, battle must have seemed remote enough to Admiral Sir John Jellicoe, Fisher's choice from years before for supreme naval command when war came, as he stood on the deck of his flagship, *Iron Duke*, and contemplated with the calm countenance of a country curate the Grand Fleet anchored north of Scotland at Scapa Flow, day by day growing stronger vis a vis the High Seas Fleet. The latter's continued passivity seemed confirmed that January when its commander, the compliant Admiral Hugo von Pohl, dying of cancer, was replaced with a Bavarian schoolmaster's son, a vice admiral 53-years old coming from command of a squadron of obsolete pre-dreadnoughts. Had the Royal Navy's chiefs looked more closely at a photograph of Reinhard Scheer, they might have seen in this brilliant officer the keen, aggressive, and bearded face of Francis Drake.

Reserved in expression and unassuming in manner, Scheer shows a capacity for dismissing difficulties as marked as von Pohl's had been for exaggerating them. Scheer believes that he can lure his opponent's capital ships onto submarine-laid mine-fields that allow his forces to pick off casualties and detached units at small cost to himself. The High Seas Fleet now has 16 dreadnoughts and 5 battle cruisers to the Grand Fleet's 28 and 9. Scheer also has six pre-dreadnoughts whose big guns can add to his firepower. The balance of force, given numbers building, cannot improve in his favor. He concludes that it is now or never for a decisive fleet action. At a February conference in Berlin, Scheer obtains the Kaiser's consent.

In the very early hours of 31 May 1916, Scheer, on his flagship, *Friederich der Grosse*, leads out into the North Sea his 27 capital ships, 11 cruisers, and 63 destroyers, hoping to inflict enough losses on Jellicoe that, in a few months, their lines of battle can meet on more even numerical terms for *der Tag* when better seamanship, stronger ships, and more accurate gunnery will give the High Seas Fleet the victory. Unknown to Scheer, 3-1/2 hours before he leaves port, the Grand Fleet, a total of 151 ships, takes to sea, partly from Scapa Flow, partly from Rosyth, and partly from

Cromarty, to rendezvous about 100 miles east of Aberdeen to await further developments. Months before, from the wreck of the light cruiser *Magdeburg* in the Baltic, the Russian Navy had recovered its code book and sent it to the Admiralty in London. The British are reading the German Navy's wireless traffic, while concealing much of their own by using land telegraph and signal flag hoists. While they don't know what Scheer's operational code word means, the manner of its transmission to all units of the High Seas Fleet make it obvious that a major operation is at hand. Scheer is unable to piece the scanty information he receives from his submarine scouts into the true overall picture. He decides that Jellicoe is still at Scapa Flow. Meanwhile, at 11:00 A.M. Jellicoe receives from his Admiralty the flat assurance that Scheer's flagship is still at its berth in the Jade River estuary. Jellicoe assumes that this German operation is another in its pattern of battle cruisers shelling English coastal towns in an attempt to draw the Royal Navy into a pursuit ending in an ambush by U-boats. Thus, both Jellicoe and Scheer move toward each other unaware that the other's main battle fleet is at sea.

The U-boats must leave the English coast as their fuel runs low, and Scheer finds that adverse winds bar his planned use of Zeppelins as long-range scouts. Scheer decides to use his alternate plan to draw out the British. He divides his fleet by sending ahead some forty vessels under another 53-year-old son of a Bavarian schoolmaster, Vice Admiral Franz Hipper, with five battle cruisers, five light cruisers, and 30 destroyers. Scheer follows some 40 miles south with 16 dreadnoughts, six old pre-dreadnoughts, six light cruisers, and 33 destroyers.

Hipper's force will go up the Danish coast, close enough to be observed and reported by spies and friends of the Allies. When a British group comes to engage Hipper, he plans to make it chase him into the jaws of Scheer's dreadnoughts.

Leading six British battle cruisers is Sir David Beatty, a 45-year-old dashing and aggressive Irishman, made a captain at 29 and a rear admiral at 39. Married to the daughter of American department store magnate Marshall Field, Beatty does not have to depend on his service pay and displays an independence open to few other Royal Navy officers. Because the outnumbered Hipper had retreated at the Battle of the Dogger Bank and Beatty had sunk the *Blücher*, Hipper's slowest and weakest battle cruiser, Beatty thinks that his ships are better and that Hipper is afraid of him. Jellicoe knows that exactly the reverse is true; he sends to follow Beatty the four most powerful battleships in the world, each with eight 15-inch guns, heavily armored and yet capable of 25 knots—the new *Barham, Warspite, Valiant,* and *Malaya*— under Rear Admiral Hugh Evan-Thomas.

About 2:20 P.M. HMS *Galatea* goes to check on the smoke of a vessel that turns out to be a small Danish merchant steamer. By coincidence the German light cruiser *Elbing* does the same. Each cruiser spots the other, immediately signals "Enemy in sight", and opens fire. Thus, at 2:28 P.M., what is to be called the Battle of Jutland begins.

Time constraints preclude more than a sketch of the ensuing action. Jutland is one of the most studied battles of all time. Those of you who want the details of moment-to-moment positions, maps, and analysis I can refer to ten closely printed pages of the *Encyclopedia Britannica* or to the less pedantic narrative in his 1988 book *The Price of Admiralty* by John Keegan, probably the world's best military historian writing today.

On receipt of *Galatea's* news, Beatty, his six battle cruisers and auxiliaries, sailing eastward in two line-ahead columns, alter course to the southeast. At about 3:31 visual contact is made between the screening forces of Beatty and Hipper, who is sailing due south, having turned to draw his opponent toward the main German fleet. As Hipper hopes, Beatty turns on a parallel course and signals by flag (not duplicated by radio) for Evan Thomas's four fast battleships (not yet sighted by Hipper) to follow. In the haze and maneuvering, they miss Beatty's hoist and persist in a prearranged turn northward to rendevous with Jellicoe. The flamboyant Beatty leads his six battlecruisers unsupported against Hipper's five. The Germans' excellent gunnery training is soon evident. Beatty's flagship, HMS *Lion*, is hit on its midship gun turret; a magazine explosion is barely averted, and a huge fire starts.

A salvo from the *Von der Tann* penetrates the thinly armored deck of the *Indefatigable*; another salvo hits near her fore turret, setting off a fatal internal explosion, and at 4:06 she turns over almost instantly and sinks with her 57 officers and 960 men. Twenty minutes later the *Queen Mary*, engaging the *Seydlitz* and *Derfflinger*, is hit by a full 12-inch salvo; two great internal explosions tear the *Queen Mary* apart, and in another moment only a pall of smoke 600 to 800 feet high marks her grave and that of her company of 1,258; less than 20 are saved.

At this juncture Beatty turns to his flag captain and makes his notorious remark: "Chatfield, there seems to be something wrong with our bloody ships today." Less quoted is his very next comment: "And something wrong with our system."

The aggressive Beatty, now aided by the four fast battleships, continues the fight. At 4:42 he sights the German main fleet approaching and at once turns north, hoping to draw the Germans under Jellicoe's big guns. Amazingly, although no British base could possibly lie due north, the Germans pursue. The bald-headed Hipper clamps down more tightly on his ever-present cigar and does send to Scheer a signal: "Something lurks in that soup. We would do well not to thrust into it too deeply."

At 6:00 P.M. Jellicoe comes in sight, his force advancing in six parallel columns. Beatty swings east and ahead of them, taking the British across the front of the German fleet and its bases. Within half an hour a general combat ensues, with British fire concentrated on the leading battle cruisers of Hipper's squadron. His flagship, *Lützow*, is put out of action, and Hipper has to transfer to a destroyer. But at 6:33 the *Derfflinger's* accurate fire hits HMS *Invincible* amidships; her magazine explodes, breaking the battle cruiser in half. Rear Admiral Sir Horace Hood and all but six men in her company of 1,034 perish. The heavy cruisers *Defence* and *Warrior*, which have battered the light cruiser *Wiesbaden* into a blazing wreck, are also sunk.

Now, however the High Seas Fleet is inside the converging arc

of the Grand Fleet and taking heavy punishment. Jellicoe's capital ships are starting across the head of Scheer's column in the
classic naval maneuver of "crossing the T" in which the British
ships can concentrate all their fire on the enemy ships forming
the "up stroke" of the T, while the Germans can use only their
forward guns. In just such a move twelve years earlier Admiral
Togo had annihilated the Russian fleet at Tsushima. The death
of the Kaiser's High Seas Fleet is minutes away. Tomorrow all
Britain will celebrate a 20th century Trafalgar!

However, for every offense there is a defense—if you have
practiced it enough. The High Seas Fleet has. Scheer has faith
in his sailors and gives the order: *Gefechtskehrtwendung nach
Steuerbord!* Starting at the rear the whole German line of battle
turns 180° to starboard in succession while destroyers screen with
smoke this intricate and dangerous maneuver (one unknown in
the Royal Navy). When the mist, smoke and cordite fumes clear,
the German fleet has vanished.

While Jellicoe does not know where the enemy ships have
gone (although he thinks, correctly, west), he realizes that he lies
between the Germans and their bases, so he continues south-
ward.

Scheer, naturally, realizes that he cannot keep on west. At 6:55
he makes another 180° turn back toward the British, thinking
that he will find only the last ships of their battle line. But he has
overestimated the speed of Jellicoe's advance and again comes
under the guns of the Grand Fleet crossing his T. In eight minutes the Germans can see so poorly in the mist and smoke that
they can score only two hits on Jellicoe's line while taking 27 hits
in return, all on the heavily stricken battle cruisers silhouetted
against the western horizon. To escape this hail of giant pro-
jectiles, Scheer orders another simultaneous turn away, sending
his light cruisers and destroyers to lay smoke and fire torpedoes.
Now comes the most splendid and most controversial event in
the entire annals of the German Navy. Scheer sends his four
remaining battle cruisers (including the *Von der Tann*, which has
no guns left in action) to charge straight at the foe. This goes

into history as the "death ride", an allusion to the last charge of Prussia's armored horsemen in 1870. Incredibly, none of the German battle cruisers is sunk in this courageous feat. The destroyers' torpedoes cause Jellicoe to turn away. By the time Jellicoe's battle line reforms, Scheer has made another 180° "battle turn" and gone westward into the dusk. The sun sets at 8:24.

Scheer knows that his fleet cannot survive a renewed general battle. He boldly turns to the southeast. He encounters a formation of light cruisers at the tail of Jellicoe's southbound fleet. Scheer finally batters through in a chaotic midnight battle of collisions, sinkings, searchlights, and gunfire. The cruiser *Southampton* sinks the German cruiser *Frauenlob* by torpedo. The British destroyer *Obedient* hits the pre-dreadnought *Pommern* amidships with a torpedo; the old battleship at once splits in two and goes down with her 844 officers and men. Searchlights of the battleship *Thüringen* catch the cruiser HMS *Black Prince*, which is sunk in four minutes.

By a miserable dawn of mist and drizzle at 2:40 A.M., Jellicoe realizes that his quarry has escaped; Scheer is shepherding his cripples toward the Jade River anchorage. Jellicoe turns back to his bases. He has forced his enemy from the field, maintained his nation's strategic position, and frustrated Scheer's plan to cut the Grand Fleet down to size. However, Jellicoe has been denied the only trophies recognized by world opinion. Jellicoe has lost three battle cruisers, three armored cruisers, and eight destroyers, with casualties of 6,274. Germany has lost one old battleship, Hipper's battle cruiser, four light cruisers, and five destroyers, sustaining casualties of 2,545.

Germany wins the journalistic war for world opinion. By midafternoon of 1 June her propagandists issue an artfully worded communique that, while never using the word "victory," leaves little doubt; citing by name seven British ships destroyed, it acknowledges a few losses (*Pommern, Wiesbaden,* and *Frauenlob*) while omitting the names of ships that the British may not have seen sink. The British communique does not appear in the newspapers until 3 June; it names eleven British ships sunk plus six destroyers unaccounted for, refers to four or more probable (un-named) enemy losses which it calls "serious," and does not characterize the battle as a success or a failure for the Royal Navy. The communique, composed not by press officers but by the First Lord of the Admiralty, the First Sea Lord, and the Chief of Naval Staff, is utterly devoid of imagination and the workings of national psychology. In my opinion, it would have made as much sense for the U. S. Navy in 1942 to have used Edward R. Murrow, Lowell Thomas, and Walter Lippmann to direct the Battle of Midway.

The Kaiser promotes Scheer and Hipper and hangs around the neck of each Germany's highest military decoration, the *Ordre Pour le Mérite*, the "Blue Max." King Ludwig of Bavaria rushes to honor his subjects. He raises Hipper to the nobility; henceforth he will be Franz Ritter von Hipper. The patent of nobility is also offered to Scheer, who, for reasons of his own, respectfully declines.

Scheer makes his official report to the Kaiser on 4 July 1916, pointing out with undeniable truth the details of his smaller force inflicting greater losses in ships and men on the foe. His report states: "The High Seas Fleet will be ready the middle of August for further strikes against the enemy." But he recognizes that the dream of *der Tag* is gone by the closing words of his report: "A victorious termination of the war... can only be attained... by the employment of submarines."

So, the Battle of Jutland (or the Battle of the Skagerrak, as the Germans call it) ends. Because the situation of the fleets reverts to the status quo ante, Jutland seems not to have changed the war. Appearances deceive, as its consequences flow, affecting us to this very moment.

Because Jellicoe did not destroy the High Seas Fleet, there will be no landings on the German coast as envisioned by Jacky Fisher, forcing back from France divisions to defend the *Vaterland* and its alarmed civilians. The few and narrow exits for U-boats cannot now be closely patrolled and mined. The Royal Navy cannot enter the Baltic to bar the Swedish iron ore essential to Germany's war industry. Nor will the Baltic be opened for food, clothing, and munitions to reach the Czar's armies, for —although the glorious successes of General Alexei Brusilov's offensive in Galicia lie just ahead—already Russia is beginning to falter, its soldiers going into battle unarmed, hoping to pick up a rifle from a fallen comrade or a pair of boots off any corpse. Next year the German General Staff will speed Lenin on a sealed train into Russia to produce civil war, effectively and then formally ending the Eastern Front, freeing many German divisions for transfer to France, and freeing Lenin to produce the USSR.

The Royal Navy's need for men, shells, money, and ordnance will continue to the detriment of the British Expeditionary Force on the Continent. Perhaps most disastrous for the United Kingdom will be the continued massive blood sacrifice of its educated youth in Flanders, young men whose brains will not be there in the 1920's and 30's to revive their nation's technology, industry, and diplomacy, whose intellect and energies will not be there to check and parry the thrusts of a Germany transformed under the swastika of an ex-corporal. France, too, will end in exhaustion, physically and morally drained by the carnage.

Correspondingly, a striking German success which broke the blockade and exposed Allied shipping to destruction by teams of German cruisers would have been paralyzing. But now Germany must turn to its U-boats, and its fate will be sealed when unrestricted submarine warfare brings the United States into the war on 6 April 1917. The inexorable pressure of the blockade continues. The shortage of rubber, cotton, nickel, oil, and many other substances essential for modern warfare sap the Central Powers' resistance, and malnutrition contributes to the ebbing will to fight. The High Seas Fleet must remain inactive in port or the Baltic, its crews the target of socialist peace propaganda, their eroding morale infecting not only shipyard workers but the friends and relatives of them all. On 2 July 1918 Scheer becomes Chief of the Admiralty Staff, and Hipper succeeds him as commander of the High Seas Fleet. In early November, when they order their fleet out "to break the blockade," the crews mutiny and raise the red flags of revolution over the docks of Kiel and Wilhelmshaven.

Seventy-five years later, World War I can be separated from the much publicized land battles that filled up its 51 months (and subsequent pages of our history books)—Tannenberg, Masurian Lakes, the Marne, Verdun, the Somme, Gallipoli, St. Mihiel, the Argonne Forest, Caporetto—and be seen as a titanic naval struggle whose outcome was determined on the oceans by three things: the blockade, the submarine, and the Battle of Jutland —Our Century's Unknown Decisive Battle.

Presented at the Anvil Club of Charleston, WV, on 1 September 1994.

Jenks and his Empire.

The Wrath of Grapes
Temperance, Morality, Prohibition and Crime

Randolph G. Whittle, Jr. Class of 1952

I. The Slippery Slope of Paradise

The Brooks High License Law of 1887

As PART OF the judicial system in each Pennsylvania county from 1887 until after 1920, there was a "license court." Every existing or hoped-for business in the manufacture, warehousing, shipping or sale—whether retail or wholesale; through stores, bars, saloons or restaurants—of spirits, including beer or wine, had to receive an annual license from the court. The license court also had to approve any transfer of a license from one owner or proprietor to another prospective one. Each applicant was required to appear before the court in person, supply detailed personal and business information and present a petition signed by twelve persons vouching for the applicant's good character and the need for the establishment.

The judge presiding had total discretion. For any or no reason, he could approve or disapprove an application. The judge was free summarily to reject every application in the entire county, as once happened in Greene County. He could quiz the potential licensee and could listen to opponents. A family business of long standing might encounter a license renewal denial. Failure to receive a renewal was not a condemnation or "taking" of private property, and there would have been no compensation. The judge of the license court was supremely powerful. There were no standards to guide a judge's discretion other than vague wording that licensees should be persons of good character.[1]

From its inception there had been constant efforts to repeal the Brooks Act. They failed. The statute remained in effect until vitiated by the Eighteenth Amendment. Even then the license courts continued functioning with little or nothing to do in hopes of Prohibition's repeal.

Newspapers often used the term "liquor-license trust." Trust being pejorative in the era, the expression referred to an informal alliance among those in the liquor trade, certain political and party faction leaders, and the several lawyers who seemingly knew the tricks and had the contacts to assure that their license-seeking clients were successful.

When A. V. Barker, a Republican, was judge, the lawyers advocating for licensees were Republicans. When Francis O'Connor became judge in 1901, they were usually Democrats, and with Marlin Stephens, applicants started using Republican attorneys once again.[2]

In 1915 (about one year after Billy Sunday's Johnstown revival sessions), the license court was accused of putting pressure on those seeking new or renewed licenses to join the Retail Liquor Dealers' Association, a group ostensibly trying to elevate the ethical standards of its membership. The judge's encouragement was seen as inappropriate. The "clean-up" campaigns of the Retail Liquor Dealers' Association were motivated to eliminate situations that might lead to hard-line temperance finger pointing and bad publicity. The association also had a hand in lobbying and passing out political campaign money.[3]

In Cambria County, the Brooks Act had the practical effect of destabilizing the judiciary. As the Temperance-Prohibition movements grew in influence, the license court judge was increasingly "between a rock and a hard place." Judge A. V. Barker had been defeated in 1901 in his bid for reelection by Francis J. O' Connor. O' Connor in turn was beaten in 1911 by Marlin Stephens. In both cases, seasoned political observers ascribed the defeats to license court issues.

A simple illustration of the twisted environment caused by the license court is revealed in an editorial of the *Johnstown Democrat* in defense of Judge Francis O' Connor, a Democrat:[4]

> The judge declared that if he were furnished with evidence that any person had declared that they had "pull" with the court, he would see that the person bringing him such evidence was protected and that the person making the claim was fittingly dealt with.

The editorial suggests some people were boasting they had influence with the court and were preying on license applicants. The court in turn was bothered by the implied attack on its judicial integrity.

Remonstrance

In addition to applicants for licenses, whether new or renewed, there was a format for remonstrance, a protest filed with the court against a specific license or against all license applications within a defined area. Any given remonstrance might be motivated by an unusual combination of temperance advocacy, greed and politics. The all-powerful judge could hear and consider or refuse to consider any or all of them.

Moxham had been a dry village from its inception and one of its developers, Albert Johnson (Tom Johnson's brother), had restricted all Moxham deeds to prohibit liquor outlets.

In 1907, the license court received a license application from David Costlow seeking to open a bar in the Seventeenth Ward. More than one thousand people signed a petition opposing the request. The application was denied.[5]

One concludes that the license court was a bottomless pit of intrigue—potential licensees deftly seeking approval of their own applications and sometimes plotting against competitors or opposing factions. The judiciary got pulled into these squabbles in an atmosphere of incomprehensible politics.[6]

Temperance Organizations

There were three mainstream temperance organizations in and about Johnstown: The Women's Christian Temperance Union (WCTU), the Prohibition Party and the Anti-Saloon League.

The WCTU was a women's organization with a number of branches or "unions" coordinated by a Cambria County WCTU organization. Its local unions were rooted in neighborhoods, smaller communities and occasionally in parishes. They met periodically and were social clubs with pro-temperance and anti-vice missions. Women could not yet vote, so the WCTU was not powerful in and of itself. The organization did influence other groups, the clergy and community leaders.

The Prohibition Party was a single-issue political party with negligible influence in and around Johnstown. The Anti-Saloon League had been founded at Oberlin, Ohio, in 1893. There was a national office by 1895. In March 1907, a Cambria County branch was established. The local organizing group was the Johnstown Ministerial Association, a Protestant group. A constitution was adopted and the new league sought to include two members from each temperance organization in Cambria County. Its first president was Calvin Hays, pastor of the First Presbyterian Church. Hayes had become a crusading temperance leader.[7] The Anti-Saloon League in Johnstown was very effective, especially after it had begun mobilizing its members politically.

The Local-Option Initiative

The first serious activity of the Cambria Branch of the Anti-Saloon League coalition was a local-option initiative, a state-wide effort to modify the Brooks Act to permit a locality to vote whether to outlaw the production and sale of alcohol within its boundaries. "Locality" meant a borough, township or city ward.

While the local option idea had been debated for years, a concerted effort for enactment began to crystallize in 1908 throughout Pennsylvania. The Cambria Branch was an active participant.

By February 1909, a bill, the Fair Local Option Act, had been introduced in the legislature by Willis Fair of Westmoreland County. The Johnstown Ministerial Association circulated petitions of support.[8]

The bill underwent legislative committee hearings on February 24. People, for and against, flocked to Harrisburg. About twenty women from Western Pennsylvania WCTU unions went about singing "Pennsylvania Shall Be Free." A delegation from the Cambria County Retail Liquor Dealers' Association also went to Harrisburg in opposition. Fair's bill was defeated.

Reverend Hays immediately began to organize for the 1911 legislative session. Cooperating through the Anti-Saloon League, Protestant churches began raising campaign funds and picking candidates for public office.[9] Although introduced in every legislative session up until Prohibition, local option was never enacted.

Billy Sunday

When the Johnstown Ministerial Association met in November 1910, its speaker was Rev. Scott Hershey. He spoke about the ex-baseball player Billy Sunday and the evangelistic revival work he had done in New Castle. Hershey described the many conversions Sunday had brought about.[10]

By early January 1911, both the select and common councils had been petitioned by forty-six churches in Johnstown favoring a Billy Sunday revival series. Specifically they were seeking the Point Park as a temporary site for a large wooden tabernacle to house Sunday's meetings.

Henry Raab, a Second Ward councilman, began lobbying both councils against the revival series. Also a wholesale liquor dealer, Raab had gone to Harrisburg in March 1909 to fight local option and knew what Calvin Hays and the clergy were seeking. Raab claimed his constituents were against "a lot of noise at the Point," and added, "Sunday has... a variety show, and it shouldn't be foisted upon the people of the Second Ward."

The capable attorney Henry Storey gave an eloquent speech

in support of the tabernacle. Although passed by the common council, the resolution was defeated in Raab's select council by ten nays to nine yeas, a single-vote defeat.[11]

Public pressures were energized following a trip by Storey and Hays to meet with Sunday at Toledo in May. Sunday told the two men that his schedule would not permit him to do a revival in Johnstown prior to the autumn of 1912. He also advised them he was coming to Johnstown regardless of the council's votes.[12]

Already the citizenry had been worked up by the council's refusal. At a mass protest rally in mid-April, speakers were voicing, "If the councils won't give Billy... the Point, we'll get rid of the councils! We'll get a commission form of government!" By the summer of 1911, petitions addressed to the Reverend Billy Sunday were being circulated among local churches begging for a Johnstown revival.

Meanwhile the statewide Anti-Saloon League continued its abortive campaign for local option.[13] In early 1913, the league had picked a new state chairman, Calvin Hays. By June 1913, city council members were aware that their tenures were being cut short. The legislature had passed the Clark Act and commission government would begin on December 1. The council was also being outdone time and again by an aggressive mayor, Joe Cauffiel, then at the peak of his roller-coaster popularity.

On June 3, 1913, Cauffiel wrote the recreation commission:

> I hereby notify you that the city will reserve enough ground at the Point for the Evangelistic Committee to erect a tabernacle for Billy Sunday.[14]

A very young Tom Nokes, commission president, knew Cauffiel had exceeded his authority. Nokes would also be running for city council later in the year. Too astute to battle a tidal wave of Sunday support, he raised no objection.

Construction of a large wooden barn-like building with a sawdust floor got underway at the Point near Main Street. Sunday insisted that the local committee install such a structure to his specifications. The tabernacle would be dismantled later and its lumber used to construct homes for the poor.

Sunday's Revival Crusade

Billy Sunday arrived in Johnstown on Saturday, November 1, 1913. His revival series began the next day and ended in mid-December.[15] The *Daily Tribune* gave front-page, upper-right-corner coverage to Sunday throughout the crusade. Attendance and collection totals were reported daily. The texts of Sunday's copyrighted sermons were also printed.

On Sunday, November 2, the attendance and collections were given as:

	Attendance	Collections
Morning	8,000	$437.91
Afternoon	7,500	$218.94
Night	9,000	$355.20
Total	24,500	$1,095.64

People remarked, "Billy came, Billy saw, and Billy conquered."

Sunday did not hold forth on Mondays, his day of rest. By Tuesday, also election day for choosing council members in the new commission government, he was going strong again in Johnstown.

By the end of Sunday's first week, it was reported:

> One week of Billy Sunday and the old town has been turned topsy-turvy in the matter of opinions about the famous baseball evangelist... One man, it is said, after hearing the sermon of "the Home"... cleared the cellar... of its store of liquors.[16]

Near the end of the second week, Sunday began asking for people "to stand four-square before mankind for God." Audience members so inclined would go forward and shake Billy's hand, a feature of each evening session. On Thursday, November 13, there were 174 conversions. On Friday, there were 193 more.

Sunday's preaching style was well known before his arrival. He would "wrestle" with the devil and make all sorts of energetic gestures. Whether revival histrionics or a near accident, he once almost fell off the platform. Sunday's teachings were based on rural and small-town values blended with evangelical, fundamentalist, Protestant Christianity. He was later seen as a spokesman for simpler virtues in an increasingly complicated era. Through Sunday, urbanizing America was searching for its lost innocence.

In Billy Sunday's credo, Satan is everywhere and uses many false gods and clever devices to lead men astray, away from the salvation of God. These include card playing, gambling, vice, love of money, dancing, the theater (including movies and vaude-ville), false teachings such as evolution, modernist theology, bib-lical criticism and anarchy. Liquor was especially a source of evil. Baseball, however, was an exception. It could even be played on Sundays.

One needed to repent, accept Jesus Christ as Savior, follow the ways of God and avoid the many devices of the devil. On December 5, Sunday held two services for women only. Attendance totaled 15,300 and 333 converts had "hit the trail." Before the afternoon meeting, a parade led by Billy Sunday and his wife took place downtown with 10,000 people in the procession.[17] When Joe Cauffiel "hit the sawdust trail" and went forward to shake Sunday's hand on December 7, the audience exploded into wild pandemonium.[18]

December 15 was Sunday's last day in Johnstown. The collection for the evangelist and his organization exceeded $16,000. The Cambria Steel Company gave $1,000. The trolley company had given $500. Other businesses and individuals made sizable contributions. Total attendance had exceeded 557,000. There were 12,320 conversions.[19]

Theaters continued to operate while Sunday was in Johnstown. Harry Scherer, the city's leading theater manager, sent Sunday a special invitation to see the religious drama, *Ben Hur*. Sunday politely declined. Something of a showdown was almost promoted when Eva Tanguay, the great comedienne, decided to attend a Billy Sunday meeting in late November. Sunday assured her she would be treated courteously.[20]

An interesting contest that went unnoticed occurred on Saturday evening, November 22. Anna Pavlova, the great Russian ballerina (many critics maintained she was then the greatest woman dancer in the world) performed at the Cambria Theater while Billy Sunday (to his followers the greatest preacher in the world and a man who viewed all dance as a device of Satan) held forth simultaneously, only a few short blocks away.

Advertisements for both Goenner Beer and the Cambria Theater's features were often placed on page one of the *Tribune* just under the Billy Sunday news items. Whether theater attendance fell while Sunday was in town is not known. Hotel business thrived.[21]

The Sunday Legacy

Early in the morning of December 15, 1913, the day Sunday left Johnstown, a rail car with forty tons of extremely hot steel got bumped and rolled down into the Conemaugh River, causing an enormous explosion. Windows were shattered for blocks and people were injured. Some thought Judgment Day had arrived in keeping with Sunday's prophecies.[22]

Sunday's next crusade was in Pittsburgh. Many Johnstowners took trains to attend the sessions. Temperance backers had received a boost. A Sunday Anti-Liquor League was founded by Jacob Murdock, who became president. Such prominent citizens as Edwin Slick, Dr. W.E. Matthews and H.M. Davies became members.[23] The group went to work filing remonstrance petitions. On January 26, 1914, seven baskets of them were presented. By early March, however, 265 licenses had been granted by the court. Others were pending.

II. Cauffiel's Republic of Virtue in His City of the Plain

Mayor Joe Cauffiel, a prohibitionist who had "hit Sunday's sawdust trail" had just been sworn in to his second four-year term (1920–23) as Johnstown's mayor. His top priority was set: Johnstown's problems would be solved by a deep pit burial of John Barleycorn. "Prohibition will begin tonight at midnight," the triumphant mayor announced at police court early on January 16, 1920. "And it is expected of the officers that they bring in all who are found with liquor on their persons. Such prisoners will come under the Prohibition enactment and will be sent to jail as bootleggers."[24]

The next day, Jacob Meyers, an elderly greenhouse worker, became the city's first Prohibition trophy. Cauffiel jailed him for "one day less than a year."[25] The absence of similar sentences over the next few weeks suggests Meyers's fate had warned others. More likely the distribution channels of illegal spirits had not yet become established.

Prohibition seemed to be working at first. The police court had light dockets. Crime was actually down.

An Imperfect World

In early April, Prentiss Herring, a black Franklin bunkhouse resident, died at Conemaugh Hospital from chemical poisoning. Another black resident, John Robinson, also a hospital patient, informed Coroner Mathew Swabb that bunkhouse residents were buying "pyro," a poisonous product, and mixing it with sodas. Pyro was found to have caused Herring's death and those of four others.[26]

A few days later, federal agents seized a three-still moonshine operation in Cambria City. By early May, alcoholic drinks and "real" beer were flowing again. Before a quality pipeline had gotten established, the beverage of choice seemed to have been "Jamaican ginger," an over-the-counter medicine containing alcohol. Jamaican ginger reputedly gave its imbibers a "hefty kick."

In May 1920, a nameless official told an inquiring newspaper reporter, "Yes, I have it from very good authority that good beer and whiskey are being sold right over the counter in Johnstown. There seems to be no great effort to enforce the federal law. Why this is I do not know unless the Democratic Administration is laying down on the job." Indications were that both moonshine and bonded whiskey had become readily available by mid-spring. A one-ounce shot cost fifty cents.[27]

Reports of extreme illness and death from illegal alcohol were common and created unusual litigation. In August, a distraught father appeared in the mayor's court telling of his son's buying two drinks at Marcella's Bar. The whiskey had made the boy so insane he had to be admitted to an asylum The Marcella case exposed a vortex of legal complexities that the aggressive mayor was not equipped to handle properly. Cauffiel's bumbling in police court often provided evidentiary and procedural defects for later judicial appeals.[28]

Cauffiel seemingly used the police court as a pulpit for pronouncements against alcohol. A recurring frustration was proving the true alcoholic content of seized substances. Cauffiel sentenced many "drunks" to jail terms. What he really wanted was to stop the manufacture and sale of alcohol, also the responsibility of federal agents. Cauffiel repeatedly instructed the police to round up the dealers selling spirits.

Gathering evidence was tricky. Both federal officers and the city made use of George Ridley. Ridley would go into a bar, buy a shot, gulp but not swallow it, leave the premises and spit the liquid into a two-ounce bottle for evidence. He once got confused and could not identify which bartenders had sold him various samples. One such proprietor was Daniel Shields.[29]

A Whiskey Ring

In late August 1920, it was reported that federal agents had seized seventy barrels of good-grade whiskey and eleven barrels of 190-proof grain alcohol from the Johnstown Drug Manufacturing Company.[30] The feds unmasked a large-scale liquor production operation disguised as drug manufacture.

On October 27, federal enforcement agents conducted coordinated raids on fourteen local hotels. Buys were made in Cambria City, on Iron Street near the railroad station and in Old Conemaugh Borough.[31] Investigation strengthened belief in the existence of a "whiskey ring." While there was no certain proof, rumors persisted. U.S. Commissioner Ray Patton Smith stated he did not believe a ring existed, but said if there were one, it did not have "pull" to delay or prevent raids or to get early warnings about them.[32]

The *Johnstown Tribune*, on November 29, asserted that a large quantity, 105 barrels of spirits, had arrived in Johnstown after shipment over the Pennsylavania Railroad. The piece stated that the local whiskey ring was stocking up for the holidays. It continued:

> That whiskey is easy to obtain is evident. It is possible to buy all that the pocketbook can afford and with little or no trouble. In fact "runners" for various "big fellows" are peddling the stuff openly, soliciting trade and offering well-known brands for sale.[33]

The Tippling House Ordinance

Cauffiel resurrected an old "Tippling House Ordinance," developed by the late W. Horace Rose after the 1889 flood when he, an attorney, had been the new city's first mayor. The Tippling House Ordinance went after the liquor dealers rather than their intoxicated or "hung over" customers.[34]

On December 15, following his police court, Cauffiel issued another lengthy public statement:

> The sale of liquor in the City of Johnstown must cease. The examination of samples taken from the various places show from thirty-one to as high as forty-five percent alcohol... There is one great mystery in my mind that the Federal agents in this locality seem to find no evidence leading to the violation of this law. They have been told and retold at various times of cargoes, truckloads, and carloads but they turn a shut eye and deaf ear.

Cauffiel then issued a call for fifty "good and able-bodied citizens" to take an oath and serve as special officers to suppress liquor violations.[35]

Just before Christmas, Thomas Clise from Hollsopple bought liquor at Shields' Café, became intoxicated, was arrested and later cooperated with police. Daniel Shields was arrested for maintaining a tippling house. His lawyer was his neighbor and friend, Percy Allen Rose, who ironically was challenging the very ordinance sponsored and probably drafted by his father. Shields did not appear in court at first but showed up after the mayor insisted he be present. Shields claimed he did not know the meaning of "tippling house," but chose to pay a fine rather than go to jail, the first skirmish in Cauffiel's war with Dan Shields.[36]

Cauffiel later sent three new "sleuths" into a bar on Railroad Street. The men flashed their badges and searched but found nothing illegal. The proprietor treated them all to a free drink of whiskey from his private stock—a gift, not a sale.[37] After Christmas, Cauffiel put into service two new "sleuths" who made buys of illegal liquor in six hotels. Each proprietor paid a $100 fine and resumed business.

The mayor next began a new strategy. After a few successful raids, Cauffiel posted a traffic sergeant in front of Shields' Café and another at Charles Kist's Barroom. When Shields's case came before the mayor, Cauffiel began by asking him how many times he had been arrested, tried and "forfeited."

"You ought to know," Shields fired back. "You are the fellow who framed it every time… My conduct in life has been more lawful than yours. You have been in the courts more than I have… I'd like to tell you what I think. Meet me out in the woods and I will tell you!"

Cauffiel answered that he would be told nothing.

Shields then shouted, "A thousand dollars, I can. Why single me out, then? You've got a personal grudge against me!"

After the mayor denied any personal feelings in his liquor campaign, he ordered that Shields' Café be closed. There would be others.[38]

Next, Cauffiel hired Walter Miles, another of his special policemen. Miles went about investigating, got drunk, was arrested and had to appear before Cauffiel in police court.[39] After Cauffiel's judgments were entered, the county court system seemingly went out of its way to overrule him on legal technicalities, which the hapless mayor provided in abundance. The cafés and hotels that he sought to close got injunctions against his tactics. The mayor then issued a new proclamation both expressing anger at the courts and maintaining that his actions to close the places were legal. Cauffiel was then advised that denouncing the injunctions might result in his being held in contempt of court.[40]

In September 1921, several clergymen were invited to police court for a view of Prohibition in action. Men were presented and charged with having been drunk. When asked where they had gotten the liquor, the typical answer was from a nameless friend in Seward or some other place. Cauffiel remarked facetiously, "We have no saloons in Cambria County, yet whiskey is being sold and sold in quantity."[41]

Cauffiel even hired special "detectives" to check up on the loyalty of his own police force. One such agent, a former police officer, told the mayor that his police chief, Charles Briney, had taken a drink at a social affair a year earlier. Cauffiel suspended the chief for ten days. Following an investigation and a hearing, Briney was restored to duty by the vote of all five councilmen including the mayor.[42]

In February 1922, two of the mayor's special police or "sleuths" accused a city policeman, Dewitt Schenck, of having "taken a drink." Schenck was immediately suspended by the mayor. A short time later his two accusers were arrested by county detectives for violations of the Volstead Act and were charged with "having intoxicating liquors on their persons."[43]

In August, Cauffiel staged another coup. Probably exasperated that alcoholic spirits continued to be manufactured and sold apparently in greater quantity than before Prohibition, the mayor called a special meeting of a large group of hotel proprietors and saloonkeepers—the regulars—at his office. Cauffiel then advised them he was through. If they would make and sell "good beer," discontinue the sale of moonshine and liquor and help him fight bootleggers, they could sell all the "good beer" they were able to sell insofar as the city was concerned.

Cauffiel was addressing two sore points at once. First, he was calling attention to the inadequate federal effort to enforce Prohibition. Second, by saying, "Good beer is better than bad water," he was attacking the Johnstown Water Company, another favorite target. Not only was the water supply being called inadequate—there had been a severe drought at the time—but according to Cauffiel the water was also contaminated.

The Cauffiel announcement got national publicity. Federal officers were put on the defensive. O.R. Stiffler, a federal district supervisor, was removed from the Johnstown area. In Washington, an assistant federal Prohibition commissioner stated to the United Press, "The sale of real beer, whether Johnstown's water is bad or not, is a violation of the Volstead Act and will not be countenanced. The mayor of a town cannot set aside the Constitution of the United States."

Cauffiel's ploy did nothing to change the sale or flow of beer. Around town it was seen as a publicity stunt that had taken place between the May primary in which George Wertz, a "wet," only a few weeks earlier had beaten Anderson Walters, a "dry," for the Republican nomination for Congress. Wertz was a shoe in and Cauffiel had assumed the seating of the politically connected new congressman would result in lax enforcement of Prohibition in and around Johnstown, no matter what he did through the city government.

Cauffiel got front-page attention all over the United States. Anderson Walters editorialized in his *Tribune* about the far-flung publicity: "Everywhere but in one city—Johnstown." The *Tribune* had put the "Good beer is O.K." news on the back page.[44]

Prohibition enforcement went on. Every indication was that liquor and "good beer" could be had in Johnstown almost as if there were no Prohibition. The idea of a "whiskey ring" persisted. The same names popped up from time to time. There were strong beliefs in payoffs, political strings and an invisible web of officials and political insiders who protected the liquor trade.

Convictions brought forth motions for new trials, reversals on appeal and clever legal maneuvers quite often resulting in guilty rulings being overturned. The accused hired the best lawyers. Impaneling a jury of temperance supporters was difficult in Cambria County where an unknown but very large percentage of the citizens were opposed to the Eighteenth Amendment and the Volstead Act that implemented it.

III. Prohibition Enforcement

The Walters-Wertz Feud Continues

Although they mixed in the same social and civic circles, Walters and Wertz were enemies of long-standing. In 1922, they had opposed one another for the Republican nomination for Congress. Wertz had won and served a two-year term.

Anderson Walters, incensed over his defeat, had uncovered another gem. The relocated federal Prohibition agent, O.R. Stiffler, had made a pilgrimage to George Wertz, presumably seeking Wertz's help in getting back his old job. Walters used this information (or fiction) to reheat a recurring editorial theme— politics is the enemy of Prohibition enforcement.[45]

In 1924, the two were at each other again, both seeking the GOP nomination. Wertz tried an interesting tactic. To siphon away some of Anderson Walters's hard-core temperance support, he accused the publisher of failing to report the news of raids and arrests against one of Wertz's well-known Republican affiliates, Daniel Shields. He also reported that Walters and Shields had met one another overseas when they had both been in Europe at the same time.

Since just about any informed Johnstowner would have assumed—right or wrong—that whatever trips Shields might have taken to Europe would have been in connection with importing alcoholic spirits, Wertz sought to plant the notion ever so cleverly that Walters and Shields, who lived across from one another downtown, were up to no good.

Walters fired back in a large political ad in the *Tribune* of April 18, 1924. The item was entitled "Merely Throwing Dust." The ad represented Wertz as being in a desperate situation. Walters wrote he had never met Shields in Europe—indeed it was stated they had never been together in the same city. The item went on to revive the old stories of Shields's place in the "Wertz-Sunshine Gang" which had been "running" the Republican Party's wet faction.

In early May of 1924, Shields was arraigned before a U.S. commissioner at Baltimore on charges of conspiracy to violate the National Prohibition Act, part of his first serious encounter with federal enforcement.[46]

Three weeks later, while Shields was still under indictment, a large crowd of Johnstowners attended the grand opening of the new Capitol Building at Franklin and Vine. The Capitol was a multi-purpose facility that housed a diverse array of separate business activities—a banquet and dance hall, a bowling alley and a street-level cafeteria and Dodge showroom. Mayor Louis Franke was a guest of honor.

The Capitol Building was owned and operated by the Capitol Real Estate Corporation, reportedly capitalized at $500,000. Its president was Daniel Shields. Other officers were J. L. Simler, Herman Widman and John Gastman. Gastman's brother, James, managed Shields' Café.

"Uncle Dan"

Daniel Shields made friends easily. In Washington he had developed a wide range of contacts including senators and, according to his close friend Perry Nesbitt, with Franklin Roosevelt while FDR was Assistant Secretary of the Navy. Shields reputedly could walk through the U.S. Capitol Building and greet people right and left.

These contacts helped him with a business venture exporting picks, shovels and hand tools to Russia, probably during its New Economic policy phase.[47] Shields apparently encountered difficulty getting paid, possibly after Stalin's take-over. At any rate, Shields's export career soon ended.

In the spring of 1923, Shields made the acquaintance of Dell Hayes, an unmarried clerk with the Internal Revenue Service in Washington. Miss Hayes handled Prohibition enforcement information regarding Pennsylvania breweries and also had access to records about licensed alcohol manufacturers.[48] Shields was seeking detailed information about distilleries lawfully producing alcohol for medicinal and industrial purposes.

When Shields had discovered that Miss Hayes had free access to this kind of information, he quickly arranged an introduction. Boxes of candy, telephone calls and both theater and dinner dates followed. The information he was seeking began flowing his way around April 1923. By April 1924, Dell Hayes had been paid about $2,100.

In connection with other investigations, Prohibition agents raided Shields's Johnstown offices and learned of his espionage arrangement with the friendly IRS clerk. Dell Hayes was now in hot water. Federal prosecuting attorneys needed to convince her to cooperate without giving Shields's legal defense team an opportunity to argue that she would be testifying against him to avoid her own prosecution.

Meanwhile, Dell Hayes had become Mrs. Dell Evans, and in 1926 had given birth to a baby girl. Shields sent an unsolicited gift of $100 to the baby. A "Dear Uncle Dan" letter followed, thanking him for the money. It had been ghostwritten by the mother for her thirteen-week-old child. Shields's attorney had introduced this letter as evidence—part of the defense strategy.

The trial in Washington, D.C., went on for several days. After being cloistered all night, a jury found Shields guilty on two counts of bribery. Shields's petition for a new trial was denied. He was fined $900 and on November 6, 1928, began serving a two year sentence at Lorton, Virginia. Shields's term was shortened for good behavior and he was released on June 14, 1930.

Shielding Shields

While Shields was being tried for bribery, other legal battles were headed his way. The former Emmerling Brewery on Baumer Street in Hornerstown was apparently a site for brewing illegal beer and distilling whiskey. In April 1925, E.C. Emmerling and Victor Schuller were charged with violating the National

Prohibition Act. It was reported that they had in their possession almost 29,000 gallons of "real" beer, 440 gallons of whiskey, various brew kettles, distilling paraphernalia, tanks and vats. They were also charged with transporting and selling illegal beer and whiskey.[49]

The case moved slowly in federal district court, a delay probably caused by an expanding investigation with more defendants and charges being added. By February 1926, ten people had been indicted and were being tried for alleged violations and conspiracy. Among them was Daniel Shields. Testimony was given alleging that Shields had received $80,515 in "protection money." Shields denied the charge but testified that as a real estate broker he had sold the brewery and received a commission. One of those charged, Julius Rodstein, who had acquired the brewery, testified he had bought both beer and "protection" from Shields. Shields in turn denied having owned the brewery in the first place and having ever operated it.

On February 15, at the end of a complicated "he-said finger pointing" trial that had produced a lot of hearsay about police pay-offs, three men—E.W. Hardison, J.L. Simler and I.E. Hunter—were found guilty on three counts each: possession and manufacture of liquor, possession of the material and implements for manufacture, and conspiracy. Herman Widman, J.M. Gastman and Daniel Shields were found guilty of conspiracy. The president, vice president, secretary and treasurer of the Capitol Real Estate Corporation had been judged guilty of a felony by the U.S. District Court at Pittsburgh. All six sought a new trial.

Interestingly, the case made it on appeal to the U.S. Supreme Court. On April 11, 1927, Chief Justice William Howard Taft ruled that the district court judge had erred when he sent messages to the jury insisting it reach a verdict. Shields and the others were not exonerated. They had to undergo a new trial in Pittsburgh.

In the second trial in mid-May 1928, Shields was found guilty. His petition for a new trial was denied. He was sentenced to one year in the Cambria County Jail and fined $2,000. By this time, however, Shields had been convicted of bribery and was serving a two-year sentence in the Washington, D.C. jail at Lorton, Virginia.[50]

President Herbert Hoover commuted his sentence in the Emmerling Brewery case on June 12, 1930. The $2,000 fine, reduced to $1,000 by the president, was paid in July. Shields never served time in the Cambria County Jail.[51]

IV. Rife Lawlessness

Around 3:00 a.m. on Wednesday, March 15, 1922, an explosion shook the Woodvale neighborhood. Dynamite had been placed at the entrance to the Antonio Gallucci and Sons Grocery Store next to Saint Anthony's Church. When it exploded, every window in Gallucci's building was broken. None of the Gallucci family or other tenants were killed, although many were thrown from their beds. A police investigation got underway.

Six weeks later, Jim Nicoletti met with Antonio Gallucci. Nicoletti informed him that many people were jealous of his success and prosperity. Gallucci was advised that he could live in peaceful comfort and enjoy Nicoletti's renewed friendship by giving him $1,500. Gallucci was warned he must say nothing to anyone about the matter. He was also told that failure to give Nicoletti the $1,500 would result in Gallucci receiving the same treatment as had happened to Nicoletti's own brother-in-law who had been murdered.

A day later, Carmelo Esposito visited Gallucci's store and told him that for $1,000 he would tell him who was responsible for the dynamiting. Esposito then departed but returned telling Gallucci that if he did not pay the $1,000, "they"—the gang—were going to bomb him again. Promising to pay more later, Gallucci gave Esposito $125, and later told his troubles to his priest. The priest apparently talked Esposito, a member of the same church, into returning the $125.

Meanwhile, Nicoletti persisted with his demands. On a September 8 visit to collect from Gallucci, an incriminating conversation was overheard by police officers hidden in an adjacent room. Nicoletti was arrested. Esposito's arrest soon followed.

The investigation led to the arrests of three other people believed to be involved in the extortion racket. The men retained Charles Margiotti, a skillful attorney from Punxsutawney and a future state attorney general. Following a trial that took eight days, Jim Nicoletti and Carmelo Esposito were both found guilty of "blackmail" and "demanding money by menace and force." Three other alleged gang members were found "not guilty."[52]

On October 7, 1925, Reverend G.K. Hetrick, a crusading anti-liquor pastor of the Conemaugh Evangelical Church, discovered twenty-two sticks of dynamite encased in a galvanized bucket placed under the porch where he slept. The makeshift bomb's fuse had somehow stopped burning. Hetrick had been receiving threats warning him to halt his anti-liquor crusades.[53]

In the early morning hours of April 9, 1926, an explosion caused extensive damage to Angelo Salvatore's barbershop at 313½ Broad Street in Cambria City. A heavy concussion shook buildings and shattered glass. No one was injured or killed. Amazingly, at that same time the same night, a bomb was exploded at Mike Lapaglia's Riverside home. No one was present. Family members refused to discuss the matter with investigators.[54]

That same week, Frank Rizzo, who operated a small store at his Prospect home, was murdered. Rizzo had been knifed a few years earlier and a later attempt had been made to bomb his business. Around nine o'clock on the night of April 12, 1926, Rizzo was called to come into the street. Two shots were fired. Rizzo died instantly.[55] About one hour later that same April evening, Frank Muro, a twenty-five-year-old coal miner, was found shot to death on the Bedford Road near Elton. Mrs. Rizzo, unaware of Muro's death, identified him as the man who had summoned her late husband into the street.

On January 17, 1927, Sam Ippolito was murdered. According to his brother, Joe Ippolito, he (Joe) had started receiving visits from Tony Arena, Andrew Gruttadano and others who told him he had to pay his brother's "bill" plus $500 to avoid being killed himself. The implication was that his brother, Sam, had refused to pay an extortion demand and was murdered as punishment.

Joe Ippolito, a Coopersdale barber, armed himself with a loaded two-barrel shotgun he kept at his shop. On March 23, Arena and Gruttadano visited the barbershop, presumably to collect. Ippolito got his rifle and killed them both. Ippolito was tried and judged guilty of manslaughter. The verdict was overturned on appeal.[56]

On October 30, 1928, George Cupp, a prominent Johnstown grocer and Harry Cupp's brother and former partner, was shot to death. Among his last words were, "I am shot. The gang got me." Testimony revealed that Cupp began fearing for his life in late May. Tony Lima and James Siciliano were charged with the murder. Lima had an alibi and was found innocent and the case against Siciliano was dropped. New evidence surfaced. Lima was again indicted but in March 1930, he was found "not guilty."[57]

These random reports of bombings, murders and threats reveal the existence of extortion racketeering in and around Johnstown during the mid- to late 1920s. Elderly Johnstowners still talk of earlier "banana wars" involving crime and extortion. What is not known is the degree to which people paid up and were left alone.

The Grand Jury Investigation

In 1929, the county judges established a special grand jury to explore crime and to evaluate the integrity of public officials, including the police. In a report made public on July 31, the grand jury did not reveal any official corruption but concluded with:

> It is felt that disrespect for the liquor laws has produced disrespect for all law... The more grave criminal offenses have been observed to have sprung out of an environment connected with the illicit liquor business.[58]

V. The Decline and Fall of "Fighting Joe" Cauffiel

On January 14, 1929, Mayor Joseph Cauffiel and Jonathan Rager were both charged with "conspiracy to do certain illegal acts." Rager had connections with several Johnstown gambling places, including one he operated in Morrellville. Rager claimed that in 1928 he had been bribing the mayor to leave his illegal operations alone. He testified later that Cauffiel had asked him to arrange with Jack Gastman, a Shields associate, a share of the gambling operation in the Capitol Building. Rager claimed Cauffiel was seeking a kickback, especially from the baseball pool operating there.[59]

Rager also claimed he had contributed money to Cauffiel's campaign for mayor. Since Rager's donation had not been reported as a campaign contribution, he concluded Cauffiel had pocketed the money. Rager was pleading guilty.[60]

Protesting his innocence, Cauffiel fought the charges. His public and private family posture was that a cabal of political, liquor, police faction and personal enemies were framing him. Cauffiel's personal public relations image was at a low state. He had been in one lawsuit after another over a stock deal involving a western mining company, which was at worst a scam or at best a fizzle. Cauffiel had been sued repeatedly by investors whose stock values had vaporized. Time and time again in these lawsuits, Cauffiel had lost and was forced to pay damages.[61]

Cauffiel Brothers Realty, Inc., had also conducted a land sales scheme. His son, Meade, vice-president of the firm, headed up a unit that had subdivided some steep hillside acreage above Moxham into lots, "on paper." There were "deeds," but the land itself was unimproved. A customer would make small monthly installment payments and in time was supposed to become the owner of his or her lot in the Buena Vista Land Development. From time to time a customer might ask to be shown his or her lot, but no one was able to point out on the ground what belonged to whom or exactly where it was. Cauffiel was cited in a 1929 grand jury report with highly questionable practices, inasmuch as there were strong indications that people appearing before him in police court got favorable treatment if they were Buena Vista customers. While the grand jury report was issued after Cauffiel's conviction, knowledge of his land sales scheme and the alleged improprieties associated with it was widespread.

Cauffiel also had another public relations problem. He had been defeated in the Republican primary by Herbert Stockton, former school superintendent, but having cross-filed to run as an "independent," Cauffiel nonetheless had become a candidate in the November "run-off" election. Cauffiel had won by a razor-thin majority. Whether true or not, lots of people believed his claim to the mayor's chair was tainted. Nonetheless he was sworn-in on January 2, 1928.

Throughout the trial, which went from March 12 through 16, there was conflicting evidence. Policemen testified that Cauffiel would call off raids they had planned. Jack Gastman swore there was nothing to Rager's claim that Capitol Building gambling was being protected by the mayor. Cauffiel maintained total innocence. Rager, in turn, had given detailed evidence against him.

After deliberating for fifteen hours, the jury found Cauffiel guilty on several counts—extortion, perjury, conspiracy and keeping a gambling house.[62] Cauffiel's attorney, Percy Allen Rose, petitioned for a new trial, citing twenty-five reasons. The three county judges *en banc* refused the motion. The case was appealed to the Pennsylvania Superior Court, which sustained Cauffiel's conviction. Two weeks later, the Pennsylvania Supreme Court declined to review the case. There were no more remedies.[63]

At 3:30 p.m. on Monday, December 30, 1929, Joe Cauffiel reported to the Cambria County Jail to begin a two-year sentence. Many people urged him to resign being mayor. He refused. By law, his conviction vacated the office.

Endnotes

1. "Old Established Liquor Places Are Refused License by Judge Stephens," *Johnstown Weekly Democrat*, March 7, 1913.

2. Political cartoon, *Johnstown Tribune*, April 26, 1905; "The Liquor Laws," editorial, ibid., December 13, 1912; "'Hogging' of License Applications Began during the Barker Regime," *Johnstown Weekly Democrat*, February 9, 1912; "Judges Laid Low By Booze," ibid., February 14, 1912.

3. "The Liquor Organization," editorial, *Johnstown Tribune*, February 5, 1915.

4. "Lying Critics Routed," editorial, *Johnstown Weekly Democrat*, February 6, 1903.

5. "Remonstrance is Signed by Over Thousand," ibid., January 31, 1907.

6. Harry M. Chalfant, *Father Penn and John Barleycorn* (n.p.: The Evangelical Press, 1920). This work, biased in favor of Prohibition, gives a good layman's summary of the Brooks High License Law of 1887 and the way it operated in Pennsylvania as seen from the temperance perspective.

7. "Organize a Cambria County Branch of Anti-Saloon League," *Johnstown Tribune*, March 18, 1907.

8. "Local Preachers to Start a Local Option Petition," ibid., February 2, 1909.

9. . "Anti-Salooners' Convention is On," ibid., March 15, 1909; "Anti-Saloon Convention Ends," ibid., March 16, 1909.

10. "Recommends the Rev. William Sunday," ibid., November 14, 1910.

11. "Councils Deny Permission to Erect a Tabernacle…," ibid., January 18, 1911; "Scores Opponents of 'Billy' Sunday," ibid., April 21, 1911.

12. "Sunday Coming Here Anyway Says Rev. Dr. Hays," *Johnstown Weekly Democrat*, May 5, 1911.

13. "Anti-Saloon League is for Local Option," ibid., February 2, 1912.

14. "Wants Point For Billy Sunday," *Johnstown Tribune*, June 3, 1913.

15. "Cohorts of Sin and Disciples of Satan Are Vigorously Denounced by Billy Sunday in Opening Evangelistic Campaign in Johnstown," ibid., November 3, 1913.

16. "Billy Sunday Turns Old Town Topsy," ibid., November 10, 1913.

17. "Evangelist Sunday and Ma Sunday at Head of Sunday School Parade," ibid., December 8, 1913.

18. "Thousands of Men Cheer When Mayor Grips Hand of Evangelist Sunday," ibid., December 8, 1913.

19. "Rev. Sunday Completes Labors and Leaves City…," ibid., December 16, 1913.

20. "Manager Scherer Has Written Billy Sunday…," ibid., October 21, 1913; "Every Courtesy Will Be Extended Eva Tanguay at Sunday Meeting," ibid., November 29, 1913.

21. "Pavlowa Gives Johnstown a Real Treat," ibid., November 24, 1913; "Many Visitors in Johnstown," ibid.

22. "Explosion Shatters Windows… Causing Near Panic," ibid., December 15, 1913.

23. "Sunday Anti-Liquor League is Launched," ibid., December 24, 1913; "Anti-Liquor Association Will Push Remonstrances," ibid., December 27, 1913.

24. "Year in Jail is Before Him Who Carries a Flask," ibid., January 16, 1920.

25. "Aged Man Sent to Jail for One Day Less Than a Year," ibid., January 17, 1920.

26. "Drank Poison as Beverage; Dies…," ibid., April 8, 1920.

27. "Openly Selling Whiskey in Johnstown for Fifty Cents a Drink; Beer Too," ibid., May 10, 1920.

28. "Two Drinks… Sends Boy to Asylum," ibid., August 23, 1920.

29. "Bottles Drinks From His Mouth to Obtain Evidence," ibid., December 10, 1920; "Three Hotelmen Arraigned; Two Fail to Appear," ibid., December 13, 1920.

30. "Firm's Officers Are Under Bail in Liquor Case," ibid., August 23, 1920.

31. "U.S. Sleuths Make Big Haul of Wet Goods," ibid., October 27, 1920.

32. "Hints of Whiskey Ring…Center in Johnstown," ibid., November 15, 1920; "U.S. Commissioner Not Sure of Whiskey Ring; Defends Federal Agents," ibid., November 16, 1920.

33. "Another Big Shipment of Whiskey Arrives," ibid., November 29, 1920.

34. "The Tippling House Ordinance," editorial, ibid., December 15, 1920.

35. "Mayor Wants Help in Fight Against Liquor Traffickers," ibid., December 15, 1920.

36. "New Sleuth Bobs Up in Liquor Case; Employed by Mayor," ibid., December 24, 1920.

37. There was no law against owning alcoholic beverages acquired prior to Prohibition. This "private stock" could legally be given as a gift but not sold.

38. "Mayor Uses Police Power to Close Up Bars…," *Johnstown Tribune*, December 29, 1920.

39. "Prohibition Sleuth Arrested by Police for Getting Drunk," ibid., January 4, 1921.

40. "Injunctions in Liquor Battle Are Continued by Order of the Court," ibid., January 4, 1921.

41. "Mayor Cauffiel Opens War on Violators of Prohibition Statutes," ibid., September 12, 1921.

42. "Chief of Police is Suspended…," ibid., February 16, 1922; "Chief Briney Cleared and Restored to Duty," ibid., February 28, 1922.

43. "Mayor's Sleuths Put Under Arrest," ibid., February 16, 1922.

44. "On the Front Page," editorial, ibid., August 21, 1922.

45. "What's Going On?," editorial, ibid., August 24, 1922.

46. "Shields Held in Bail…," ibid., May 2, 1924.

47. Perry Nesbitt, associate and a close friend of Daniel Shields, personal interview, October 2000. Nesbitt died in May 2001.

48. Beer could be legally produced during Prohibition but its alcoholic content could be no more than ½ of 1 percent. What had become commonplace in Pennsylvania and probably elsewhere was the brewing of low-alcohol beer and its alcoholic content being secretly enhanced until it could be called "real" or "true" beer.

49. "Held For Court in Liquor Case," ibid., April 9, 1925.

50. "Daniel J. Shields…," ibid., February 11, 1926; "Emmerling Case May Go to Jury…," ibid., February 12, 1926; "Three Found Guilty…," ibid., February 15, 1926; "Motion For a New Trial," ibid., February 17, 1926; "Taft Denounces Judge's Ruling…," ibid., April 11, 1927; "Court Order for New Trial," ibid., July 25, 1927; "D.J. Shields Asks For New Trial," ibid., May 22, 1928.

51. "Government Will Not Oppose Plea…," *Johnstown Tribune*, March 21, 1927; "Daniel J. Shields Case Opens…," ibid., March 29, 1927; "Main Witness in Shields Case…," ibid., March 31, 1927; "Black Hint…," ibid., April 4, 1927; "Mystery Man in Shields Case…," ibid., April 5, 1927; "Shields Found Guilty on Two Bribery Counts," ibid., April 6, 1927; "Shields Will Be Sentenced," ibid., May 24, 1927; "D.J. Shields Asks for New Trial…," ibid., May 22, 1928; "New Trial Again Refused…," ibid., July 6, 1928; "Shields Sentenced…," ibid., July 24, 1928; U.S. Department of Justice, FBI, Files 58–145 and 23–1507. Both files are on Daniel J. Shields. The former deals with the trial. The FBI apparently had been concerned that Shields would be attempting "jury tampering" and tailed him all over the place. No such evidence was uncovered. The latter file deals with Shields's petition to restore his civil rights. This was subsequently granted, but the date was not given.

52. "Dynamite Outrage Upon Woodvale Store…," *Johnstown Tribune*, March 15, 1922; "Commonwealth Rests Case in 'Blackhand' Trial…," ibid., December 15, 1923; "Two Defendants Found Guilty on Two Counts for Alleged Blackmail," ibid., December 21, 1922; *Commonwealth of PA v. Nicoletti & Esposito*, 82 PA Sup. Ct. 26 (1923).

53. Improvised Bomb Containing 22 Sticks of Dynamite…," *Johnstown Tribune*, October 7, 1925.

54. "Salvatore" was also spelled "Salbator." "Terrific Explosion Damages Building in Sixteenth Ward," ibid., April 9, 1926; "Riverside Residence Bombed…," ibid., April 14, 1926.

55. "Three Killings Are Believed Result of Feudal Grievances," ibid., April 13, 1926.

56. "Joe Ippolito, Wife, and Children Lived in Fear...," ibid., June 17, 1927; "Joe Ippolito Is Found Guilty...," ibid., June 18, 1927.

57. "Many Witnesses Called by Commonwealth for Lima," ibid., December 11, 1928; "Tony Lima Accused of George G. Cupp Murder...," ibid., December 14, 1928.

58. Is Law and Order Helpless?," editorial, ibid., March 29, 1929; "Special Grand Jury Reports...," ibid., July 31, 1929.

59. At the time of Cauffiel's dealings with Rager, Shields was incarcerated in the Washington, D.C. jail at Lorton, Virginia. Shields and Cauffiel were bitter enemies.

60. "Warrants Are Issued for Mayor Cauffiel and J. Rager," *Johnstown Tribune*, January 14, 1929; "Mayor Cauffiel is Required to Appear in Court," ibid., February 2, 1929.

61. "Verdict Against Joe Cauffiel for Copper Deal," ibid., June 2, 1925; "Joseph Cauffiel Defending Action for $2,500,000," ibid., March 24, 1927.

62. The *Johnstown Tribune* carried detailed reporting of the Cauffiel trial between March 13 and 16, 1929. There was also an editorial, "Ashamed," that ran on March 18, 1929.

63. "Motion for New Trial," *Johnstown Tribune*, April 5, 1929; "Mayor Refused New Trial," ibid., April 8, 1929; "Sentence Upheld in Cauffiel Case," ibid., November 22, 1929; "Cauffiel Must Serve Jail Sentence: Supreme Court Refuses to Review Case," ibid., December 6, 1929.

The Phantom Procession

John B. Kincaid, Class of 1953

THE NIGHT BREWED magic, I thought as I left Washington Street and walked slowly past R.E. Lee Memorial Church. Little did I know how prophetic that thought would be. The reunion had been fun, but it was over. Still—I could not resist one last look at my old school.

The corner by the McCormick Statue and the full majesty of the Colonnade came into view. Not a creature moved, not a breeze blew, as I walked slowly towards the Chapel. Somewhere in the night I heard bells tolling midnight. The full moon cast eerie shadows across the landscape. The statue of Old George glowing in the moonlight seemed alive.

What stories these historic grounds could tell if only they would speak. As I gazed at the full panorama of the lighted Colonnade, I felt rather than heard a movement and turned.

There they were in their dress uniforms marching as only V.M.I. Cadets could. I had witnessed this scene many times of cadets marching to church, but there were no services this late.

I watched the formation salute the tomb of General Lee and noticed how the moonlight danced on their blood red cape linings. The cadets seemed so young and yet strangely old. They marched silently down the path into the dark and out of sight.

I shook myself, but before I could regain my composure, I noticed a procession slowly emerging from the shadows. A chill raced through my veins as I recognized my old religion professor, Dr. Morton, known as "Snorty" Morton, still talking to himself. Another figure emerged and I recognized the venerable Dr. Bean, a tall man with a stoop that somehow made him appear even taller. I thought I heard that melodious southern voice intoning, "The test will be Wednesday week and be prepared. It will be on every detail of the Battle of Gettysburg."

Another figure and another came into view. Some I recognized, others I didn't. Then came "Jolly Ollie" Crenshaw, a wonderful man who had taught History. I remembered the evening conversation during which I had questioned, "Why should I continue in college when there was so much to do in this big world?" He had restrained his smile and explained to this naive young lad very plainly why college was essential. "It is not just common sense you need, it is the uncommon sense that is important."

Next came the kindly Dr. Moffatt, the English professor, who took pity on me when my mind had gone blank during an exam and I repressed the urge to toss the empty blue book on the table and leave. Somehow I finished that exam with answers seemingly coughed up from the ether and passed. I could still see the white mane of the man who fit so perfectly in the classroom. In ghostly silence the procession wound its way across the campus and disappeared into Washington Hall.

I stood bewitched. Then I noticed two more shadows taking form. They were together, but distinctly separate as they strolled toward Washington Hall. Dean Gillam was the glue that had held the school together, and he had possessed the vision that propelled the college forward. He had an unbelievable memory except in my case. He always confused me with another freshman and looked irritated every time he saw me that first year. Luckily the other student transferred and the Dean's countenance improved. The man was a giant in many eyes. He extended quiet helpful guidance to many a student.

The moon cast a halo-like glow over the prematurely white hair of the other man. Dean Leyburn was the newest addition to the phantom procession. His demeanor was aristocratic, his manner sharp, his speech brilliant. He mesmerized his students. The two passed through the door and were gone.

My eyes were drawn toward a familiar figure coming from the Lee House. His hat and cane easily identified him as Francis Pendleton Gaines, President of the University. He had the voice of a revivalist Baptist minister. It could spellbind you at twenty paces. I remembered during the Korean War, President Gaines had called a total University meeting. The school must have worried that the college boys would "go bonkers." His message to the student body was, "Gentlemen, there are some things you have to take on faith. For example, when you marry it is an act of faith that you know your children are your own." I smiled remembering my wife was always annoyed with that statement. I had thought it the ultimate example of true faith. With a tip of his hat Gaines disappeared with the rest.

I turned back to Lee Chapel and there boys were assembling from the various fraternities and houses. I shivered. They were as before—forever young. My former classmates, who had gone on before, were walking slowly, silently laughing and talking together. I stepped aside to let the phantoms pass. These visions of the past stopped for a moment and saluted rather than waved to me. I felt tears moisten my face as I recognized my old friends. Some I had known well and I felt regret that I had not known all of them better. The young students moved up the hill and disappeared into Washington Hall.

I was trying to understand this vision when a man appeared in the doorway of Lee Chapel and walked slowly toward me. He was somewhat obscured by the dancing moonlight, but his face was one I had seen in a hundred pictures. He paused and studied me with intense curiosity but with a kindly countenance. Then he handed me something, continued on, entering Washington Hall without benefit of the door.

The clock somewhere tolled the last stroke of midnight. Had I been here an hour, a minute, or never? There was movement and a student emerged from Washington Hall. The creatures of the night made their various noises. I thought I heard an owl and the fleeting moment was gone.

Slowly I started back toward the lights of Washington Street and the reality of life. I then noticed I held in my hand an envelope. It looked like an invitation. I opened it and read:

> *You are invited to join the Post Alumni College of Washington and Lee, but please, not before your time. There are lessons to be taught and lessons to be learned. There are discussions to be held and ideas to be explored. Here the art is long and so is the time. The sessions will be held as long as the Colonnade of W.& L. grace these beautiful hills of the Shenandoah Valley of Virginia. R.E. Lee*

Mercersburg Academy, Class of 2002

H.F. (Gerry) Lenfest, Class of 1953

I AM DEEPLY honored to have been invited by the Graduating Class of 2002 to speak here today. Over 50 years ago when I walked this campus as a student, little did I think I would be here today delivering this commencement address.

I first want to offer my congratulations to each of you on the successful completion of your studies and your graduation. I know how hard you have all worked to be here today.

I also want to welcome our faculty and the parents, relatives, and friends of the members of the Class. I especially commend the parents who are here today to see their children graduate. Will all of you parents stand up and be recognized. Seniors, please join me by standing and giving a resounding ovation in honor of your parents who have sacrificed to send you here to Mercersburg.

I have been asked to tell you how I came to Mercersburg and what Mercersburg did for me.

Until the age of 13, our family consisted of my father and mother and my twin sister, Marie. We had moved to a working farm north of Lambertville, New Jersey. Immediately after moving to the farm, my mother died unexpectedly. My father traveled extensively marketing products of a small company he had founded. With one parent gone and the other frequently away from home, Marie was enrolled in a boarding school in Maryland, and I was sent to George School, a Quaker coed boarding school in Bucks County, Pennsylvania. I was bitter about my mother's death and although my marks were okay, I didn't fit in well and didn't return after my first year.

I continued to be disoriented after the passing of my mother and was not a very good student in high school. My mother had been raised in Western Pennsylvania and had two cousins from Scotdale named Kerr, and another cousin, Jimmy Stewart (the actor), from Indiana, Pennsylvania, who had all gone to Mercersburg. I believe prior to her death, she had recommended to my father that I attend Mercersburg. Seeing that I was going downhill fairly quickly, my father sent me to Mercersburg.

Mercersburg became almost a surrogate family for me through the interaction with the wonderful teachers and students. I developed many friendships that were important to me. But more importantly, through the wonderful faculty and the academic program, the athletics and other activities, I experienced a true intellectual and educational development. I realized for the first time, because of my Mercersburg experience, that I could have a positive future and become the kind of person that I wanted to be.

Mercersburg was truly the foundation of my education and a transforming experience. I went on to college, served in the Navy, graduated from law school, and practiced law with a major law firm on Wall Street. I then went to Philadelphia to work as house counsel for Walter Annenberg's communications company that was then the most successful privately owned communications company in the United States. After five years as house counsel, I left the legal end to head a new division consisting of *Seventeen Magazine* and their cable television operations. From being an attorney I was all of a sudden in charge of a teenage girls' magazine, which was quite a challenge and certainly not anticipated when I was a student here at Mercersburg.

Walter Annenberg decided to sell his cable television operations, and although I had no money, I decided to try and purchase one or more of the television systems. In 1974, I convinced two gentlemen in Lebanon, Pennsylvania, to put up the money to purchase the Lebanon cable system from Walter's company on the promise that I would double their investment and buy them out in five years, which I did. We had 7600 cable subscribers and this was the beginning. In January 2000, twenty-six years later, we sold our cable television company, half of which was owned by myself and our three children. At that time, our cable television systems with 1.3 million subscribers extended from the west, here in Mercersburg, through Chambersburg, Carlisle, Harrisburg, Hershey, Lancaster, the Philadelphia suburbs, Wilmington, Delaware, across into southern New Jersey to the ocean in the Atlantic City area. The company was sold for over $7 billion in stock.

Without Mercersburg none of this would have happened and will, perhaps, explain the deep sense of gratitude I have for my education here.

So what have I learned that I can pass on to you? The first truth is that I was not able to achieve financial success alone. I recently had the good fortune of sitting next to David McCullough, the author of the best seller *John Adams* and other major works, at a dinner in New York. I told him that I was going to provide the commencement address to you today and asked if he had any pearls of wisdom that I could relate to you. He was kind enough to write me a seven-page letter in his own handwriting, and I pass one of his pearls on to you:

"There's no such thing as a self-made man or woman. We are all the result of any number of people who have helped, influenced, inspired, or guided us. Indeed, we ought to say a prayer of thanks every day for the parent, teacher, friend, even the occasional stranger who has taken an interest, offered an idea, given the all important pat on the back that kept us on course or set us off on a venture that made all the difference."

A second lesson is to marry well. A large part of my happiness in life and basis for my success in business is my wife, Marguerite. She has been a wonderful wife and mother of our three children. Her support of me has also been absolutely critical. As an example, when I was editorial director and publisher of *Seventeen* and headed the cable television operations, I had a nationally recognized position, had an office on Park Avenue, and had a substantial salary. I gave all this up when we bought the Lebanon cable system. When I asked Marguerite whether she would go along with this dramatic change, she said it was my decision and that she would support me, whatever I decided. As a result, I gave up the position, the salary and worked out of my basement for the next 12 years. Marguerite kept our financial records and helped in the operations of our start-up cable company. You should also know that Marguerite was totally in support of our major gift to Mercersburg. Marguerite, would you please stand up and be recognized.

The third lesson from my experience is that we have the great opportunity of living here in America. The strength of this great country since its founding is that people of all races and ethnic backgrounds have immigrated here and lived under the tenets of freedom set forth on a piece of paper—our Constitution—which has been perpetuated by our citizenry and our government. To be here, in my opinion, provides you more than any other nation with the opportunity to write the script of your own life—where to live, what profession or business to pursue, whom to marry, what to believe in—you can decide for yourself. You have the freedom in this Nation to be the architect of your own destiny.

The chapter of your life at Mercersburg is now over, and you must now look to the future and its challenges. There are three suggestions I hope you will keep in mind as you enter the next chapter of your education and your life because they are important no matter what path you take.

The first is to continue to pursue a broad liberal arts education. Increase your knowledge and appreciation of literature and the visual arts and music. If you make a lifelong commitment to growth and learning, if you develop an open, inquiring and discerning mind, you will become a more rounded person. And if you read extensively, both what you enjoy reading and a smattering of the classics, you will increase your understanding of the world around you. You will also increase your mastery of our language, which has become the international standard, and have the ability to express yourself well both orally and in writing, which is an important tool no matter what you end up doing. No life follows a straight path. The breadth of your learning will provide a broad base for any change in your journey through life.

The second is to live your life in such a manner as to be respected by your peers not only for your professional expertise in the field you eventually select, but as a person. That doesn't mean that you are perfect because no one is. It takes tremendous courage to accept our human weaknesses and limitations, to accept our failures, to learn from them and to pick up the pieces and go on. We can redeem the past by accepting it, by finding from it the courage and lessons to endure and improve it. If you believe in being trustworthy and a person of your word, and doing the right thing by others, you will gain the respect of those whose paths cross yours. You will be more successful not only in your professional or business career but also as a person.

The third is to have respect and tolerance for others. Do what you can, in your own way, to help bend the course of our world toward greater understanding and tolerance. No person is alone. We are all dependent upon others to find our own identity as a person. If we are to combat poverty, ignorance, environmental destruction and bigotry, we must all work together to increase tolerance and understanding in our global community. We must replace the past with a 21st century of compassion and understanding. We must find a way to help bridge the division of rich and poor; dark and light skins; Jewish, Muslim and Christian; male and female; American and non-American. I urge you to do your part.

I would like to mention two persons whose lives have incorporated the suggestions that I just proposed. The first is Ben Carson, an African-American, who when he was a boy in grade school fought with his brother to determine who would be the most rebellious student in the school. His mother, a single parent, got wind of their shenanigans. She called them to their home and said, "You boys are going to quit this nonsense. Each of you is going to read a book each week and give me a written report." Ben learned many years later that his mom couldn't read. However, Ben read his books, did his reports, and became a good student. After graduating from high school, he went on to Yale and then medical school at Michigan. Today, Ben Carson is the head of neurosurgery at Johns Hopkins, where he is in charge of 40 or so neurosurgeons. He also successfully performed in Africa a separation of Siamese twins joined at the head. In the medical profession, he is very famous. Ben is giving back. He has started a foundation to give college scholarships to grade school students in the hope that that scholarship will become their goal in grade school.

The second person was one of eleven children born on a farm in the South. His father died when he was 7, and he was raised along with the other children by his wonderful mother, who also adopted a homeless child. He desperately wanted to have an education and was able to go to college on an athletic scholarship where he graduated valedictorian of his class. He went on to graduate school and has dedicated his life to the education of young people. You probably know by now I'm referring to our own head of school, Doug Hale. Doug has devoted himself to the quality of education at Mercersburg as so many others have now and in the past. Will you also join with me again by standing and recognizing the contribution that Doug Hale and our wonderful faculty have made to your own education here at Mercersburg.

In closing, I make a final plea. Mercersburg has proven itself over the generations since its founding 109 years ago. And it will continue to prove itself over the years ahead with the continuing support of its graduates. This is the challenge I leave with you, Member of the Class of 2002. Look around this campus and embrace the memories of your education here, and in return, I hope, you will give back and support Mercersburg in the future, to the full extent that you can, so that Mercersburg can continue its quality education for generations to come.

Thanks for listening; again, I wish each of you all success both in your future education and career, and even more important, in your development as a person.

June 8, 2002

Dr. King Comes to Middletown, Connecticut

John D. Maguire, Class of 1953

ONE DAY DURING our sophomore year at Washington and Lee, my roommate Ruel Tyson and I read on a kiosk by the Colonnade a notice that said: "If you are remotely interested in the Christian ministry, consider coming as our guests for the weekend to Crozer Theological Seminary in Chester, PA." Since neither of us had been north of Richmond and were both from Baptist families and Crozer was paying, we both instantly became 'remotely interested' in the Christian ministry!

When we arrived there on a Thursday evening, we were billeted with Seminary students and I was assigned as his roommate for the weekend, Martin Luther King Jr. from Atlanta, GA. That fateful weekend began a 17-yearlong friendship. We remained in touch when Martin went on to Boston University School of Theology for his doctorate, met and married Coretta and moved in the summer of 1955 to Montgomery, AL, my birthplace and boyhood home. For my part I too had married – the summer following my 1953 graduation from Washington & Lee, had journeyed with my bride Billie to Edinburgh on Fulbrights, had returned to Yale from 1954 to 1960 then moved up the road to begin faculty life at Wesleyan University in Middletown, CT.

Martin and I had rekindled our friendship when Wesleyan senior colleague David Swift and I were part of the 1961 Freedom Rides, and were jailed briefly in Montgomery.

On January 14, 1962, Martin arrived on campus in mid-afternoon to preach to a packed-to-overflowing chapel that night.

During that 1962 Middletown visit, Dr. King stayed overnight at the University guest house on High Street in order to be available most of the next day to the College of Social Studies students and faculty. I recall, ruefully in retrospect, introducing him since it was his 33rd birthday—by saying, "I hope you make it through this year, Doc. The last founder of what became a worldwide movement is reported to have been crucified by the spring of his 33rd year!" How could we have known that the year was wrong but the season cruelly correct: That Martin would be slain on April 4, 1968, just six years later?

In February of 1963 I met Dr. King early on a Sunday afternoon in New Haven, where he had preached at Yale's Battell Chapel that morning, and drove him to our house at 44 Home Avenue for a nap before he preached again that evening in the Wesleyan chapel. Students clamored to be able to drive him to Bradley Field directly following the service for a late flight and four of them squeezed in the car with him that night.

Early in 1964 Wesleyan President Butterfield asked me to secure Dr. King, if I could, as the University's end-of-school Baccalaureate preacher and to receive the University's honorary doctorate degree. Dr. King agreed, with the proviso that since he was not in complete control of his schedule, there would have to be some tentativeness about the date. By April I was relieved to learn that he had a major series of commencements that weekend: Wesleyan on Sunday morning, Jewish Theological Seminary in New York late on Sunday afternoon, and back to Yale University for their degree on Monday. Imagine our dismay when on the Monday before he was to arrive on Saturday evening to launch the weekend ceremonies, Dr. King went to jail challenging violence-ridden segregation in St. Augustine, FL. Through my friend, his chief aide, Andrew Young, we persuaded

Dr. King—even though he had said he would not come out of jail until the campaign there achieved concrete success—to make bail on Saturday afternoon and fly via Atlanta to Bradley Field, arriving on Sunday morning (King jokingly justified leaving jail by pointing out that Mrs. Peabody, mother of the Massachusetts Governor Chubb Peabody, had gone to jail in St. Augustine that Saturday, "taking his place," as it were, so that he could come north for the weekend).

I took our oldest daughter Kelly with me to meet Dr. King, Coretta and Wyatt T. Walker at the airport. On the way to Middletown politically innocent Kelly, when discussion speculated on whom President Johnson might select for his 1964 vice presidential running mate, piped up, "Dr. King, why don't you become our vice president?" King wearily grinned and said, "John, why don't you explain it all to her?" After a quick breakfast at our house, we all went over to North College, Martin and I donning our academic gowns, he all the time greeting well wishers such as former Lt. Governor Wilbert Snow, a Wesleyan and Middletown worthy.

Following a triumphant address in which he used passages from his "I Have A Dream" speech of a year before (for example, "I have a dream that someday my children—all children—will be judged not by the color of their skin, but by the content of their character"), we had processed into Andrus Field from North College and from the moment the audience saw King until he arrived on the elevated stone stage, the same platform where 14 years later daughter Catherine would graduate Phi Beta Kappa from the University, there was continuous applause, virtually drowning out the processional music,

About 45 minutes after the service, when a small group had concluded thanks and well wishes, Dr. King, Mrs. King and the Reverend Walker exited up from the makeshift green room in the basement to a waiting car that would be escorted by the state highway patrol onto and down the Connecticut Turnpike toward New York. Ron Young, a student social justice leader, rode out to the turnpike with them. From the moment the Kings entered Middletown until their departure local security—campus security and MPD—was on highest alert since the barrage of threats on Dr. King's life had already begun. The moment the Yale ceremonies concluded on Monday, King flew straight back to St. Augustine and reentered jail for another few days!

In 1966 Dr. King paid his last visit to Middletown, again to preach. By then crowds were so great that the service was held in McConaughy Dining Hall and still overflowed. Once again on this occasion I met Dr. King and his traveling companion Bernard Lee at Bradley in early afternoon, brought them briefly by the house where daughter Mary, turning two and still in arms, greeted him, "Hi, King." He replied, "John, you've still got to work on these Maguire girls. Tell her that I need to be greeted at least as Mr. King!" King and Lee were exhausted and needed to sleep the afternoon and so spent the next few hours at the guest house. The manager of the house had two massive Great Danes and both Martin and Bernard were mortally afraid of dogs. When I tapped on their door to be sure they were up and ready to go, Bernard answered, still—like Martin—in his shorts and seeing the dogs racing toward them, jumped back with all their might. I laughingly told them that each of them had set a record for the backward broad jump!

That evening after chapel we had a kind of open house where hosts of people came, greeted and talked with Martin as he sat, increasingly obviously exhausted, on the sofa. As I watched his eyelids slowly closing, even as he spoke, I realized it was time for them to go and so bid them goodbye at the door to their room. Students again were to meet them at 5:15 a.m. for the airport journey. Throughout the day that Monday, upon their return, the three students who had driven them burbled about their luminous conversation.

I saw Dr. King only one more time before his assassination in 1968, and that was not in Middletown.

A kind of postscript: I had met Yale Professor John Morton Blum and Joe Duffey at a restaurant halfway between Middletown and Meriden to plan our leadership of the Eugene

McCarthy presidential race in Connecticut when a waitress, knowing my friendship with Dr. King, came to the table and said, "Your friend has been shot." I initially doubted her report (not aware that Dr. King had returned from New York to Memphis), but she insisted that I come into the bar and see the television. It was true. We adjourned our meeting, I raced back to Middletown where our house had already begun to fill spontaneously with friends and neighbors, black and white, who had known and admired King. We consoled each other throughout the night and at one point Billie and I whispered to each other, since she was pregnant with our last child, "If it's a boy, we'll name him Martin David; if it's a girl, Anne King." On August 29, when we had journeyed from Middletown to California to begin a sabbatical year, Anne King Maguire was born in Alta Bates Hospital in Berkeley.

The Wesleyan Board of Trustees, whom I was serving that year as university associate provost, was meeting, fatefully voting to make Wesleyan coeducational. President Etherington asked the meeting to adjourn early and move to the Chapel where he asked me to provide an informal eulogy for Dr. King. Knowing my desire to attend Dr. King's funeral the following Monday, he handed me the money for my plane ticket and on Saturday, I left for those somber, sad days in Atlanta. My final view of Martin came when his cortege rolled slowly past the porch of the house en route where mutual friends and I stood sobbing, bidding him farewell.

January 15, 2006
(MLK's 77th birthday)

Notes on the Classroom of William Jenks

Ruel W. Tyson, Jr., Class of 1953

I AM AT an interval in my academic career. For the first twenty years at Chapel Hill I was a teacher, chair of my department, did research as an ethnographer of religions, and helped found a graduate program in religious studies. For the last twenty years I worked to found, fund, and direct an institute for faculty research and conversation. I am now in the interval between retiring as director last June and resuming full time duties in the classroom next August. During this in between time I am revisiting my teaching, my teachers, early, middle, late, and continuing. How will my pedagogy change when I return to the classroom? Or will it? This is why the invitation to offer a comment on Professor Jenks is welcomed. What follows is a gesture of appreciation for what I learned from him, more indirect than direct, more from his style than from a particular set of ideas.

Please note the "more" in the last sentence lest it appear that my studies with Dr. Jenks were not useful. And useful they were, and in a way I had not anticipated. The spring of 1954 I was at Yale enrolled in a course in the history of the Christian churches in the West taught by the distinguished historian of the Protestant Reformation, Roland Bainton. Some of you will recall that the McCarthy hearings in the US Senate occurred that spring. These hearings were televised at an hour directly in conflict with my course with Mr. Bainton. Since he had written "the" book on Luther and since I had good notes, yes, very good notes, from Dr. Jenks's course, I avoided major disasters though I missed most of the last half of the semester. I could not bring myself to be absent from Joe McCarthy, Roy Cohn, the admirable Mr. Welch of Boston, and the commentary of Edward R. Murrow.

In the context of reflections during my current leave and as an added detail about the story of my absence from classes in the spring of '54, the title of the course I have in the eye of my memory is Dr. Jenks's "Renaissance and Reformation." These two terms, in lower case, are particularly helpful in my reflections about returning to teaching as they were of great utility to me in my studies at Yale.

Some of us had heard that we were the early inheritors of a reformation at Washington and Lee. It was called the Leyburn Plan, and Dr. Jenks was there on its premises, and we were there as its beneficiaries.

There is a small and delicious dissonance between "rebirths" and "reformations," both are currents of disturbance, Perhaps serious study of such matters, and Jenks was nothing if not a serious student of these subjects, is best done through modes of formality, discipline, distance, and in language without slang or cliché. Each of these aspects of the ethos of Jenks's classroom is a mode of respect for the subject matter, the students who are there to learn, and the professor who is there to teach.

My classmates will recall this widely repeated saying: if you dropped your pencil or ran out of lead during Dr. Jenks's lecture, you missed a significant percentage of the course. There were few pauses in the flow of his lecturing. I do not recall Jenks making use of tension relievers like jokes or comments on the news of the day. He was fully devoted to telling us the news of the Renaissance and Reformation. I do recall an occasional, if muted, display of wit and irony, always drawn from, or in close relation to, the material of the day's lecture. Except for an occasional move to the board to write proper names or dates, his posture was stationary, unrelentingly vertical as he stood behind the podium. Movement was in his eyes more than in voice or posture. The voice was steady. The posture was military, Though I never saw them, I assumed, perhaps on inadequate evidence, that his lectures were written out in detail in advance of the classes. His delivery was steady, I would say, relentless. By the end of the hour the beat of his sentences registered in the clenched and cramped hands of his auditors.

The play was in the eyes and the orchestration was a marvel to behold, that is, if you dared ease off for a moment in your note taking. While he read his lectures he appeared rarely to move his eyes from the gentlemen before him to the text below. Yet he did, but with the most deftly oblique feints. I wonder if one of his recreations was poker. You expected that there would be head movement, looking out, looking down. Instead, there were eyes behind rimless glasses moving on the sly, making quick dips while we, the assiduous note takers, kept our heads down and our fingers moving… The discipline of it was a marvel! You could not quite see, yet you were sure you had seen movement. We do not need to see all to appreciate the whole of Jenks's repertoire of gestures. It was his head that he kept in an eyes-front posture more expected down the street at VMI than in the ambience of our gentlemanly nonchalance. Of course, the ticket of admission to this course required leaving any hint of nonchalance under the columns below. Without changing his frontal orientation, assisted by standing behind the lectern, he had an extraordinary capacity to read his lecture as if he had memorized it. I inferred that there were long passages that he did command from memory. How else to account for long stretches when it was clear he was not reading below his eyes but speaking at his usual pace to us, direct and steady, with an occasional left to right scan?

His strong voice avoided monotone, yet it did not rise to any oratorical altitude, not to speak of anything approaching a flourish. Steady, on course, sentence after sentence, he was never on a roll just consistently rolling on… until precisely five minutes before the end of the class, he stopped, asked for questions. If there were none, he gave no flicker of disappointment in returning to his discourse. A few bolder members of the class risked revelations of their ignorance by asking a question that revealed innocence of the day's assignment. When this were the case, their exposure was public, rapid, chastening. Thus temptations to score points were effectively discouraged. Most of the gentlemen knew their limits. Never was a student ridiculed. The intonation Jenks employed when he addressed one of us as "Mister" was an award of respect.

The lectures were mostly in the narrative mode. Rarely did our teacher engage in dialectical play and never in excessive display. I do not recall him debating other historians. Perhaps he saved issues of historiography for his advanced courses. His vocal grammar was a model to admire if difficult to imitate. He employed his voice to lend clarity as well as stress in the course of his delivery which enhanced its passage to our notes. As some wit has noted, lecture notes, at their best, relate to lectures as skeletal remains to the once vital body.

I should pause to say here that I cannot recall ever spending time with Dr. Jenks in his office or elsewhere. This to my loss. Within the fallible sponge of my memory, my reconstructions of his teaching are based on his lectures in a certain room on the south side of Washington Hall, on the third floor, if I recall correctly. I do not recall if our class met in the class room in that building which, notoriously, had a picture of Abraham Lincoln on its walls.

While many of us were taking courses with Dr. Jenks, we were also taking courses in English where, thanks to Brooks and Warren's *Approach to Literature*, the New Criticism held sway. The New Criticism worked strictly within the context of the literary work, rarely going beyond its boundaries into the biography of the author or the history of the text's time and place. I see here that I have given a picture of Dr. Jenks's classroom as if it were what it certainly was not, namely, a text with sharp boundaries.

There is a widespread cliche still used by students: "You get good notes from Professor X." For me, William. Jenks is the paradigm case for the pedagogical practice that merits such a judgment. There are two other aspects of Jenks's teaching style I wish to note.

I learned to value the genre of the note.

We take notes as we did in Dr. Jenks's courses as a matter of course. We review them for tests. But that utility may not be the most important of their uses to us. In reviewing our notes, we revisit the course, much like retracing a trail we once walked with our trail guide. Later, we are on our own. It is during that re-visiting and re-tracing that we learn. We see connections among ideas and events which we could not see when we took the notes since the most important connections are not found in the sequences but in the patterns that may be discerned in and across them.

Learning is re-learning and the notes, like traces along the trail, teach us more than we knew when we took them down. We assumed we were capturing the real thing. But learning is not ritual recording or rote memory work. Learning is making connections among competing options and weaving plausible narratives.

While we spend a lot of time in the practice of note taking, we are, at the same time, learning to do something else with these notes, and this something else allows us to claim that along with the practice we learn an art. We learn to make notes, literally or figuratively, as we review our notes. Taking is preparation for making. We are making notes of the discoveries we made during our re-visitings and re-visions. This is one of the many transferable skills we acquire while doing the work of learning. Notes do yellow and fade while arts improve with practice. Attentive students of Professor Jenks's mode of lecturing were early initiates and fortunate beneficiaries of the genre of the note.

We undervalue formality.

There was no intimacy, even proximity, in the Jenks classroom. There were few, if any, gestures toward conviviality. Here I remind the reader that I refer to his lecture courses. I assume that he offered seminars where the table and not the lectern was the center of the proceedings where dialogue trumped exposition. There was distance in several varieties, the distance of formality, of standing upright on a podium behind a lectern, and observation of rather strict boundaries between the seated students and the standing professor. There was the distance between the subjects of our study and the location from which we were studying "The Renaissance and Reformation." There was no pseudo coziness.

While formality is not the only way to express seriousness, in our culture, which progressively disvalues formality and lacks a serious sense for the serious, a reminder of the manners we learned in Dr. Jenks's classroom is as salutary as it is welcomed.

If we renew this reminder in our diverse practices, we need to note that there is no contradiction between passion in our commitments and the observance of formality, particularly if we accompany our engagements with an occasional ironic wink lest formality be confused with arrogance.

Scribbling and Scrambling: The Publication of In Vanity Fair

Roy T. Matthews, Class of 1954

IN 1982 MY first book, *In Vanity Fair*, was published. The book was co-authored by Dr. Peter Mellini. What we both experienced during the writing and publishing of the book was summarized in a talk which I delivered to the Michigan British Historians organization in 1982. The talk has been slightly revised for these articles and essays which honor Bill Jenks. It reflects many of his ideas and understanding of history which I learned in his classroom, the lessons and advice he passed on to me as my mentor, and the standards he set for all of us who wanted to succeed whether we became teachers, journalists, lawyers, ministers, business men or what we would do with our lives and careers.

Thank you for your introduction and a special thanks to all of you for attending this session of the Michigan British Historians. I appreciate the opportunity to share with you some of the satisfactions and disappointments associated with the writing and publication of *In Vanity Fair*. In particular, I want to explain the methods my co-author and I employed and the objectives we set out for ourselves in this joint intellectual enterprise.

My talk will consist of three parts. First, I will outline the four major phases of the project. As we examine the four major phases, I will introduce and interweave the other two components of the presentation: (1) the human interest and personal involvement that widened my circle of friends and enriched my life; and (2) the intellectual challenges and responses generated and demanded in the conception, research, composition and production of the book.

However, before we begin our odyssey, a word on the title of my presentation is in order. I knew that I did not want to deliver a slide presentation on the history of the magazine or offer selected examples of its caricatures. I have done that too many times, and I guessed that some of you in the audience have already been subject to that "show and tell" format. After some deliberation I decided to reconstruct the history of the writing of the book so I might convey some sense of all that went into its many transformations and final production. How could I put those experiences into a title? Remembering some of the adventures Peter Mellini, my co-author, and I had, two words came to my mind: scribbling and scrambling. To scribble, according to the dictionary, is to write hurriedly without heed to legibility or grammatical form. Well, we often did just that as our typists would attest and as we corrected each other's grammar and spelling. The word scramble, according to the dictionary, is to move or climb hurriedly, to vie in free-for-all competition, to struggle urgently. The more I thought about these two words, the more appropriate they seemed.

From one view there is the scholar who scribbles, or, in more serene moments, writes, records, composes his or her thoughts based on diligent and meticulous research; then, there is the promoter, the one who takes a chance in the free-for-all and struggles. Writing a book, certainly one that focuses on relatively recent times, conjures up both images—the scholar in the "ivory tower" and the promoter struggling in the market place. That I would oscillate between these two worlds for ten years—from 1972 to 1982 was not what I had in mind in early 1972 when I reached a turning point in my academic career and which marked the beginning of the first phase of events.

Let us call this first phase the "Spy" phase—a series of research and writing of papers which lasted until the fall of 1974. The second phase, 1975-1976, was a relatively short transition period characterized by a shift in topics and our amateurish efforts at hawking our book in front of publishers. The third phase, from 1977 to 1979, was the most productive one for during those two years we researched the bulk of our manuscript, wrote the first draft, polished the text, designed the book, and signed our contracts. In the final phase, 1979-1981, we revised parts of the text, read the galleys and page proofs, made last minute changes, and became victims of conditions beyond our control that placed our publisher and our book now in peril and then in paradise.

As historians we now have laid out before us the chronology in the writing of *In Vanity Fair*. However, as scholars, I suspect we are more interested in the formulation of the book's text, its contents and style, and the reaching and writing of the manuscript. But before we get to those tantalizing topics, we must understand an episode of human interest and personal involvement. I have already noted that in 1972 I reached a turning point in my career. For seven years, since 1965, I had been teaching in an interdisciplinary program in the Department of Humanities at Michigan State University. Playing the role of the hopeful and dutiful young scholar, I had revised my dissertation for publication and had received a large file of polite rejection letters. While this experience was sending me a clear message, within me other transformations were taking place. I was rapidly losing interest in European diplomatic history. I found the topic to be dull and the prospects for future work and employment in the area to be limited. I realized, too, that if I were going to remain in an interdisciplinary program, I would be trying to serve two incompatible masters. A specialization in diplomatic history was becoming more and more irrelevant to my research and teaching in a program that integrated the visual arts, literature, philosophy, religion, and history. Once I realized this, I had to make a decision as to which path I was going to follow. To me, it was increasingly apparent that what I needed to do was to find some scholarly pursuit that capitalized upon my newly found interests and training in interdisciplinary studies, and, indeed, in new ways of thinking and then to relate those experiences to what I learned in my undergraduate days at Washington and Lee University and, in particular in my history classes, and, of course, to my training in graduate school regarding research methods and techniques. What historical topic would allow me to pull all of this together?

As historians, we also know that the obvious is often overlooked and that inconsequential episodes sometimes turn out to be of major importance. In my office, on the wall, had hung, for two years, two *Vanity Fair* or "Spy" caricatures: Captain Alfred Dreyfus of the famous Dreyfus trial and scandal in France, and Lord Northcliffe, Alfred Harmsworth, who founded and owned several London newspapers, including, after 1908, *The Times.* I looked at those prints and asked myself one simple question: Has any book ever been written on *Vanity Fair* and its caricatures?

During my first sabbatical leave in the Spring of 1972 I sought an answer to my question by looking for books, monographs, articles and papers on *Vanity Fair,* and I discovered that very little, if anything, had been written about the magazine. That summer I spent in London where I continued research, and when I returned to MSU that fall, I was determined to write a lengthy monograph or perhaps a biography of Sir Leslie Ward or "Spy", his *nom de crayon,* within the next eighteen months. Since that March, I had read all the secondary works on the magazine and nineteenth century caricaturing I could locate. A search for Ward's papers that summer in London led me to the solicitor who had probated the family's will and who knew Ward's single surviving daughter. But it would be another year, the summer of 1973, before I would hear from her directly. She could not tell me much about her father and did not seem interested in my proposal. I did have a copy of his memoirs which were primarily anecdotal and seldom informative or incisive. However, I had established important contacts during the summer of 1972 at the libraries and museums, especially the National Portrait Gallery. During 1973 and 1974 I delivered several papers and continued to do research in the states: at MSU, the University of Michigan, the Library of Congress, and the New York Public Library.

The "Spy" phase ended in the fall of 1974 when I delivered a paper on Ward at the Rocky Mountain Conference of British Studies. In the audience were two men who would influence my life from then on: Peter Mellini, Professor of British History at Sonoma State, and Peter Stansky, Professor of British History at Stanford University. After my talk, Peter Mellini introduced himself, and we discussed *Vanity Fair* for the next several hours. He began to convince me that I should abandon my biography of Ward and collaborate with him on a book about *Vanity Fair*. By January 1975, we were exchanging letters on the structure and organization of the book. Meanwhile, Peter Mellini was trying out our ideas on Peter Stansky and William Abrahams, Stansky's friend and then West Coast representative for Little, Brown and Company. Both men encouraged us to push ahead. We also sought advice from American and English lawyers on the copyrights of the prints. They assured us that all of the caricatures were in the public domain.

Our first venture in putting together a book proposal resulted in an eight page paper that included a provisional table of contents, categories of *Vanity Fair* subjects (*e.g.* Royalty, Women, Clergy and Dons, Sportsmen, Political leaders *etc.*) and excerpts from the as yet to be completed text (paragraphs on the format and content of *Vanity Fair)*, and the history of caricaturing. The book's style began to evolve out of this proposal. Since we wanted to write the text to reflect the witty, urbane prose of the magazine, we decided that the text should not be too academic and scholarly and that we should use as many quotes as possible from the magazine to capture the flavor of *Vanity Fair*. We also tried to identify our audience and agreed that our readers would probably be educated and well read but not primarily professors.

This conclusion reinforced our decision on the book's style and voice.

Our first scribbling was now followed by our first round of scrambling. We mailed our proposal to the leading art publishing houses, and one of these, Prager, forwarded our letter to their English partner, Phaidon Press. Soon we heard from Phaidon that they were interested and wanted to see more. In August, 1975, Mellini went to England to deliver our expanded proposal which was warmly accepted. The Phaidon representative estimated a market price at £3, or, $8.00 in the United States for a book with a few color plates, probably eight or sixteen—and about fifty black and white illustrations. That price was to rise substantially before the final product.

While in England Peter went to see one of his favorite print dealers, George Suckling who ran a print shop in Cecil Court—a short street lined with print shops and second hand book stores off St. Martin's Lane, near the National Portrait Gallery. Suckling, in his knee length soiled smock and tufts of grey hair, looked like he just emerged from a Dickens' novel. London was full of men like Suckling; another one was Finbar MacDonald who had print shop in Camden Passage. Their shops were piled high with stacks of prints, old maps, and tear sheet from magazines from which they could pull out the exact item you were seeking. Suckling told Peter about Paul Victorious, an American who had recently died and whose large stock of *Vanity Fair* caricatures had been purchased by two businessmen from Cincinnati. Peter misunderstood Suckling's accent and misspelled Morton Olman—Allman—and that threw us off track for an entire year in locating Olman and his company.

The scrambling continued that fall when we sent more material to Phaidon, including some early drafts of parts of chapters and slides. It was at this point that Peter and I learned our first lesson about how the fates play in the publishing world. We received a letter from our supporter at Phaidon, a Mr. Calmann, informing us that Phaidon Press was moving from London to Oxford and that he was resigning from the company because he did not want to leave London. He assured us, however, that we should not worry because he was turning our proposal over to a Mr. Haviland and everything would be all right. We never heard from Mr. Haviland or Phaidon, even after several letters to him.

The October 27, 1975 issue of the *New Yorker* ran an advertisement for *Vanity Fair* caricatures sponsored by four print dealers across the country. I asked Peter if he thought that this ad was a result of his learning about the sales of the prints from Suckling. My hunch later proved correct, for by June 1976, I been able to trace down the name of the company in Cincinnati. The link to Vanity Fair, Ltd. and Paul Victorious was made, and the beginning of a long friendship between the owners of Vanity Fair Ltd. and us commenced. Tom Benjamin, the partner of Morton Olman was to be a storehouse of information and a strong supporter of our efforts. With my research concentrating now on *Vanity Fair* rather than Sir Leslie Ward, I wrote three papers and delivered them at conferences in 1976. Meanwhile, *British History Illustrated* published my article on Spy which I had sent them some time ago. The article brought forth many unsolicited letters from Spy fans and collectors which confirmed our opinion about the potential audience for the book—affluent, educated, well traveled readers who collected prints or were students or "fans" of the Victorian era.

The second, or transitional phase, 1975-1976, actually ended in July, 1976, when our scrambling finally paid off—a tentative contract with Scolar Press of London. Peter and I revised our proposal in late 1975 and sent it to several English publishers in the Spring of 1976. Peter was to be in London that summer at which time he would follow up on our mailings with a personal visit and search out other publishing houses. When Mellini arrived in London he went to see his friend, Gordon Phillips, the archivist for *The Times*. He told Gordon about our project. Several days later Gordon was at the office of Scolar Press and mentioned our proposal to Sean Magee, one of the editors. Magee expressed an interest in it, and Gordon then called Peter to tell him to go see Magee at Scolar Press. After a three hour meeting between

Mellini and Magee, Scolar offered us a tentative contract and a £100 advance. Scolar asked us to send more examples of our writings and some caricatures which Scolar was to make into a dummy for circulation to United States publishers. A letter from Magee, in July, 1976, spelled out Scolar's suggestions for the book and contract: fifteen color plates, eighty black and whites, 220 pp., 9"x 12" trim size, and priced at £6 to £8. Magee's letter also revealed the warmth and understanding of a man who turned out to be a young, genial Irishman with a degree from Oxford, an uncanny recollection of Derby winners, and a weakness for the tote. By the fall of 1976, in an exchange of letters, we had worked out the details with Scolar regarding the book's contents, features, organization, and format. We agreed upon the twelve categories, or sections of the book and who would be some of the individuals in each category. For example, in the Royalty section we would have Queen Victoria, Edward VII, Napoleon III; in the arts section we would include some poets (Tennyson and Swinburne), painters (John Millais, Whistler); and, among the politicians, Benjamin Disraeli, William Gladstone, and the two Churchills—Randolph and Winston.

Having landed a tentative contract and having agreed to the contents and format of the book, Peter and I concentrated our efforts on delivering papers at conferences and writing the manuscript—back to scribbling. The spring and summer of 1977 would be a time of major turning points in the development of the book. First, I interviewed Tom Benjamin of Vanity Fair Ltd, in his office in Cincinnati who filled me in on some of the gaps in the history of the stock of the caricatures from 1940 to 1971. Second, in April we delivered a paper at the Pacific Coast Conference on British Studies that provided us with an opportunity to make plans for further researching and writing. While in Los Angeles we met with Ken Taylor, the most successful and knowledgeable dealer on the West Coast of *Vanity Fair* prints. Ken was invaluable in locating rare prints and advising us on which caricatures to include in the book. During an informal conversation at the conference, Peter Stansky and I discovered the family connection between Thomas Gibson Bowles, the founder and first owner of *Vanity Fair*, and Lord Redesdale who married Bowles's daughter. That family connection led us eventually to the Mitford clan, in particular Jessica Mitford and Lady Diane Mosley, granddaughters of Bowles. Third, in early April I received a letter from Professor Jerold Savory who informed me that he was planning to publish a book on *Vanity Fair*. His description of his book was uncomfortably close to our format. After five years of research, this was the first evidence I had of any person writing on *Vanity Fair*. Peter and I were spurred on to complete our research and to beat Savory. We were to fail in our efforts. Fourth, in June 1977, we received a formal contract with another advance, which we signed in September, after our solicitor in London worked out the fine print in our favor.

The summer of 1977 was when we wrote most of the manuscript. We divided our time between East Lansing, Michigan and Mill Valley, California. In the first part of the summer we read *Vanity Fair* on microfilm which had been purchased by the MSU Library. We photocopied hundreds of caricatures and the accompanying short biographical entries or letterpresses in addition to numerous columns and articles that revealed the magazine's style and its attitudes and views toward contemporary political, social, and economic issues and events. We also photocopied examples of advertisements which appeared in *Vanity Fair* plus word games, contests, and other features.

We now began to discover many fascinating persons whom *Vanity Fair* caricatured but were unknown today—either to Victorian enthusiasts or scholars, but who, in our opinion, brought to life *Vanity Fair*, the Victorian world, and the human comedy. Each day, as we cranked through the reels of microfilm, we uncovered characters who intrigued us, heightened our curiosity, and amused us. We also stumbled across something else—the more we knew about *Vanity Fair's* weekly "victim," the more revealing the letterpresses became for us. Thus, we started to read literally between the lines of the biographical entry or letterpress to catch the innuendoes and oblique references that told us, and those subscribers and readers who were "in the know", precisely what was occurring in the private lives of the magazine's featured celebrity.

As we chose the caricatures to be included in the book, we collected information on each individual from memoirs, autobiographies, biographies, monographs, journal articles, and the *Dictionary of National Biography*. We suffered from feast or famine. Books on Winston Churchill, Matthew Arnold, Charles Darwin, Lord Kitchener, and other famous persons were inexhaustible, and we had to limit our research to only a few sources. But who had written about others we wanted in the book? Such as S. F. Cody, the Texas aviator, Mrs. Starr, the Mother Superior at the Hull Convent who was on trial in London, or Tom Cannon, the jockey? We did find articles or monographs on many of them. For example, *Flying* magazine provided us with information on Cody; in a brief, obscure biography located after a lengthy search we found about Mrs. Georgina Weldon, one of the most charming and captivating people in our book. In the summer of 1978, in London, I traced down the reports on the trial of Mrs. Starr as recorded from the court proceedings in *The Times*.

During the last part of the summer of 1977 we wrote the first drafts of the text in California. We divided the twelve categories between us. Peter took the royalty, politicians, generals, sportsmen, journalists, empire builders, and Americans, and I wrote on the arts (painters, novelists, poets, playwrights, musicians), bench and bar (judges, barristers, and solicitors), clergy and dons, scientists and inventors, and business men. Sometimes we traded off within the categories due to our expertise or prejudices. I had already written the entire Introduction by then so that part of the book was behind us. Peter was later to write the chapter on collecting *Vanity Fair* caricatures. We made a complete list of the over 2,300 caricatures as they had appeared, by date, in the magazine that included the date, issue number, title, name of the individual, caption, and caricaturist. We also compiled an alphabetical cross listing. The next summer I corrected and revised the list in London, checking it against other listings I located in museums and libraries.

Each entry for the book was to include at least three components: biographical information on the person's career and life up to the time of his/her appearance in *Vanity Fair; Vanity Fair's* opinion of its "victim," either summarized or quoted from the letterpress; an assessment of the caricature as to its style, format, effectiveness. Sometimes we were able to incorporate anecdotes about the victim and the caricaturist. On occasion, we summarized the individual's accomplishments and career after he or she had been featured in the magazine.

In our research we were not looking for the accepted interpretations nor attempting to discover some professional thesis or evaluation written by another academic on the persons we chose for the book. On the contrary, we were hunting for that single remark, observation or episode that would provide us with the precise connection of the subject to *Vanity Fair's* opinion or caricature of its victim. For example, George Bernard Shaw's caustic observation about Sara Bernhardt proved to be the proper disparagement to *Vanity Fair's* laudatory treatment of the "Divine Sara". I studied James Tissot's caricature of Matthew Arnold for some time and looked into many biographies of Arnold before I finally located Charlotte Brontë's comment on Arnold's foppery which Tissot had captured so tellingly. After one of us wrote and revised our entry, we would exchange it for further revision. We wanted the entire manuscript to read as if one person had written it—and had written it to reflect the style of *Vanity Fair.* This nearly proved to be our undoing. Our different writing styles had to conform to a single style, and we could not always agree on how that style should be expressed and whether it was capturing the voice of *Vanity Fair.* Nonetheless, we reached an understanding and reworked each other's copy that summer and throughout the fall. But neither of us was satisfied with the tone and sound of our efforts, and we despaired that the task would never be completed. Both of us were teaching and carrying out our other academic responsibilities while we were drafting the book. We had reached the end of our rope by December, 1977. Peter then proposed that he fly to Michigan, and we would simply sit down and re-write all parts of the manuscript that did not please us. In about three weeks, in early 1978, we polished the text to our satisfaction

In March 1978, I flew to London to teach in Michigan State's Humanities Spring Program and carried with me approximately three-fourths of the completed text. The rest I would have to research and to write in England. From March until mid-June, while teaching in the program, I used every spare moment to work on the last phases of the book. In late June Peter joined me for the final editing of the text, the correcting of previously overlooked mistakes, and the entry of the last minute information and details. We turned in the manuscript to Sean Magee on August 1, 1978.

An entirely new aspect of research opened to me that spring and later to both of us that summer. For lack of a better term, I will call it investigative journalism/history. We had never been able to discover what happened to the remaining stock of *Vanity Fair* caricatures from February 1914, when the magazine ceased publication, until 1940 when Paul Victorious shipped the caricatures to his print shop in Charlottesville, Virginia. Too, we had no information on who owned or edited the magazine after Frank Harris, the controversial and colorful Irish journalist and entrepreneur, failed, in 1907, to restore *Vanity Fair* to its past glory.

Horace Walpole coined the word, and it has such a wonderful ring to it: serendipity. Barbara Tuchman was fortunate when she found, at the New York Public Library, *Sentinel*, which was a United States Army newspaper on Far Eastern affairs that contained a series of articles by the then young army officer who was serving in China—Joseph W. Stilwell when she was researching her book *Stilwell and the American Experience in China, 1911-45*. Thomas Pakenham, author of *The Boer War*, tells us in his introduction to his book how he stumbled upon the papers of Sr. Redvers Buller, the British Commander-in-Chief in South Africa in 1899. Pakenham located the papers under a billiard table at Buller's country house in Devon. Serendipity finally smiled upon us.

Soon after I arrived in London in March I went to the National Portrait Gallery, re-acquainted myself with Richard Ormond, the Assistant Director, who had been so helpful to me in 1972. He gave me his permission to go through the boxes on *Vanity Fair*. Most of the collection was familiar to me from my previous search. However, in 1976, the National Portrait Gallery had mounted an exhibit on *Vanity Fair*, and a new box of letters and papers had been gathered as a result of the show. I should note that the exhibit's catalogue and its introduction had already been of tremendous value to us because it reinforced nearly every bit of research we had done up to 1976, and it supplied us with some new insights and also some references that we had not uncovered.

As I was thumbing through the box I turned up a letter that was to provide the hint to the history of the magazine from 1907 to 1914 and the journey of the caricatures from 1914 to 1940. I could hardly believe what I was holding in my hand: a letter from a Mrs. Peggy Harvey who identified herself as the daughter of Robert Weir, the print dealer who had purchased the remaining stock of *Vanity Fair* caricatures from its last owner and had subsequently sold them to Paul Victorious. I wrote her a letter at once and followed up with a telephone call to her residence in a small town just north of London. She invited me to her home and provided me with additional information including the location of what the family had kept which now rested in the attic of her sister's antique shop in Cambridge. From her lead Peter and I, that summer, were able to examine these caricatures plus proofs (the original sketches by various caricaturists), and even handbills that described Weir's collection which he was selling. Also, from our conversations, I was able to trace back to the last owner of *Vanity Fair*.

All Mrs. Harvey could remember was that the owner was a doctor who advocated health foods and had also owned a flour mill and marketed the flour for his patients. She thought the company was still producing the flour and that the man's name was Alleson. I went to a health store and looked at every bag of flour until I discovered, sitting on a shelf, an Allinson Flour Mill bag. Again, I could hardly believe my luck. More letters and phone calls resulted in the locating of C. P. Allinson, the only remaining child of Dr. Thomas Richard Allinson, the last owner of *Vanity Fair*. Peter and I interviewed the old gentleman in a house full of cats whose presence and smell could not be avoided. Unfortunately, he could not recall very much about his father's economic adventures except to say that his father lost money, finally closed down the enterprise, and, yes, he had sold off most of the stock to a print dealer whose name he could not remember.

These transactions opened new doors for us, and throughout the summer we interviewed more persons connected to the fate of the caricatures. As we were regaled with stories and anecdotes we recorded them and when we interviewed other people, we would ask questions pertinent to those particular episodes. If the stories were verified by three sources, we decided to incorporate them into the last chapter of the book which was on collecting the caricatures. We talked to many men whose lives had been touched by *Vanity Fair*. Some had risen to the heights of power and prestige in the print world, for example Benjamin Weinreb; while others, like Ron Chappel, a poor unkempt sort had spent his life at odd jobs in print shops. I interviewed Weinreb of Weinreb and Duma in an ornate office above his shop on Great Russell Street near the British Museum. He told me about Paul Victorious as a person and business man, the price of prints, and his own life as a dealer. Peter and I met Chappel in a print shop, and when we asked him where he would like to talk—here or somewhere else—he replied that he always talked best in a pub. So, after many beers, he had supplied us with more stories and details.

To finish this saga of scribbling and scrambling on such a positive note—with a book contract, the manuscript delivered, and the missing pieces in place—would be a fitting ending. But we were far from the end. Except for some minor revising, the scribbling was over. However, from 1979 to 1981, we had more scrambling with many disappointments and frustrations. We were disappointed because many of our earlier hopes proved unfulfilled. We were frustrated because we were helpless in influencing events far beyond our control. Whether the book would ever be published would not be decided on the merits of our endeavor or the quality of our work but on economic realities, business agreements, and the policies of Maggie Thatcher.

The fall of 1978 was spent in Bologna, Italy where, on my second sabbatical, I began another research project—the origins and early stages of caricaturing. That October I was informed that 1979 as a publishing date was out of the question and that the book would appear in 1980. During 1979 Peter and I revised some last minute bits and pieces of the manuscript while Kath Davies, the copyeditor in Edinburgh, anglicized our American spellings and made some stylistic changes. Meanwhile, Sean Magee flew to the States in May 1979, on a business trip for Scolar, and we settled some minor issues that had surfaced about the format. We still had no American publisher, and it had been made clear to Peter and me that Scolar could not publish the book alone. In addition, costs for the book had skyrocketed, and the company, a subsidiary of the Bemrose conglomerate, was not fairing well. But Sean was optimistic as negotiations with several American companies were moving forward.

In the summer of 1979 Savory's book was published. He had won the race. I held my breath every time I opened the *New York Times Book Review*. No reviews, no notices, no ads. Likewise, no reviews in any other publications. While Savory's book was of poor quality in its reproductions and never received much recognition, its appearance was enough to scare off St. Martin's Press which was studying our manuscript and deciding whether to publish it in the United States.

Our nadir was reached when a letter arrived from Magee in late January 1980. Sean told us that Scolar was "really stuck for the present" and the whole situation was a "pretty big disaster". Peter called me and said that we no choice but to peddle the book ourselves. He was going to fly to London, talk to Scolar, pick up the dummy, and begin knocking on doors once again. His first stop would be the University of California Press since it was so close. Within two weeks after his return from London, by mid-February, he reported that the University of California Press seemed mildly interested in his presentation and would let him know by mid-April. We both shrugged our shoulders and agreed that we had been this route before. Neither of us was very optimistic.

That Spring (1980) I was in Florence teaching in the MSU Humanities-Romance Language program. On April 18 I received a telegram that read: "Hooray, UC will co-publish". I hugged all my students, shouted for an hour, and that evening the students threw a party for me with chocolate cake and asti spumanti. The book, we were told, would be out for the 1981 Christmas market.

Scolar mailed the manuscript to California, and in the fall of 1980 galleys began to arrive. That Christmas was spent reading the bulk of the galleys. We worked out a procedure for reading the galleys. Peter and I received sets from the printer in Berkeley. Each of us would proof them. I would call Peter, and we would go over my corrections and compare them to his. Then we would reverse the procedure. AT&T did very well by us.

All seemed to be going very well, but the Iron Maiden's economic policies in England would not allow us to rest easily for very long. In September 1980, Peter and I were informed that Scolar was going to be closed down. Bemrose was losing money and wanted to get rid of Scolar. Several employees had been dismissed or were made redundant, as they put it, and Sean was frantically looking for another position. These developments raised the unpleasant but obvious question of the future of *In Vanity Fair*. More scrambling.

Peter flew to London in early 1981. He and Sean went over the manuscript one more time. He returned with the entire manuscript, layout, and caricatures chosen for the book. From now on, the University of California Press would supervise the publication and final printing of the book. But what was to be the fate of Scolar Press and, of course, our relations with the company? In March, Bill McClung, the editor of the Humanities Division of the UC Press assured us that his organization would take care of us and our book. And then one of those ironies, those twists of fate. McClung, who was also an entrepreneur, and James Price, the chief editor and manger for Scolar, bought Scolar from Bemrose. By April, Scolar's future was secure under new ownership and personnel. Sean still had his old job, and we had our contact in London.

The summer of 1981 was getting closer, but Peter and I had not yet received the page proofs by the late Spring, and we were, once again, becoming a bit suspicious. Our suspicions were confirmed in June when we were told by McClung that there was no possibility of getting *In Vanity Fair* out by the Fall. The layout and design, with the colored plates and black and white illustrations, were just too complicated to risk the errors that might result from a rushed effort. Spring 1982, would be the publishing date. McClung stuck by his word, and from that date until late 1981 everything ran on schedule. We soon had the page proofs and quickly returned them. We expanded the Preface to thank everyone who had worked with us at the UC Press. The general index was completed in late 1981. But it was not finally over. In October and November 1981, we hurriedly went through the color plates to reduce their number because Scolar calculated that they could not pay the cost for so many color prints. A series of transatlantic phone calls and memos settled the number of color plates to be included. *In Vanity Fair* went to press in January 1982, and was in our hands by September.

Postscript *In Vanity Fair* received many laudatory reviews in the public press and scholarly journals. Its 3,000 copies sold out quickly, but UC Press was not interested in another run. We scrambled in the late 1980's to find another publisher. In 1997 I finally found another publisher, Quiller Press (London). With some minor scribbling to correct and update the text, *In Vanity Fair* was republished in 1999, and, again, quickly sold out.

From the Archives to the Courtroom

Robert O. Paxton, Class of 1954

WHEN I WAS preparing under Bill Jenks' mentorship to become a history professor, I expected a fairly quiet life in the classroom and the archives. I had no inkling that one day I would be called upon to testify in a trial in France for crimes against humanity.

As it happened, my work swept me up in "the Franco-French Wars," the battles that the French people have fought among themselves about how to think about their years under German occupation, from 1940 to 1944. France was more divided by its World War II experience in than any other occupied nation, except perhaps Yugoslavia. Whereas most occupied European peoples closed ranks around their head of state, whether in exile like Queen Wilhelmina of the Netherlands or at home like King Christian X of Denmark, the French had two rival governments after the defeat of June 1940. Marshall Philippe Pétain, a hero of World War I who wanted no more war, collaborated with the German occupation from his temporary capital at Vichy, the French equivalent of White Sulphur Springs. General Charles De Gaulle, a hitherto little known tank officer, led the Free French from London in an effort to ensure that French troops would participate alongside the Allies in the Liberation of France.

De Gaulle's Free French were on the winning side, of course. Their Second Armored Division was the first Allied unit to enter Paris in August 1944. Marshal Pétain was sentenced to life imprisonment for treason. That has not prevented him from retaining fervent supporters among French people who consider him a patriot who spared them from worse. They call him the shield that complemented De Gaulle's sword. I chose the Vichy collaborationists as my subject when I began research for my doctoral dissertation in 1960. My W&L classmate and fellow Jenks student Henry Turner '54 offered decisive help: he called my attention to the abundant German archives concerning the occupation of France. While the French archives were still closed and most writing about Vichy was limited to self-serving memoirs, I had in hand the actual minutes of meetings where Vichy French officials sat down to haggle with German officials.

The German archives revealed what the Vichy regime actually did. Instead of limiting itself to trying the fend off German initiatives, as its defenders claimed, Vichy actively sought to make a place for France in Hitler's Europe (it was Hitler who fended off French initiatives), and took advantage of the defeat of the Third Republic to transform France into an authoritarian traditionalist dictatorship. The archives also made it clear that until the tide turned in late 1942, a large number of French people supported Vichy. Only later did many French people come to accept the rebel General De Gaulle.

My second book, *Vichy France: Old Guard and New Order*, containing these views hitherto unheard of in France, was translated into French in 1973. It aroused a furor. The president of the Association for the Defense of the Memory of Marshal Pétain, an admiral, called me a liar to my face before millions of television viewers. Critics and supporters of my scandalous book filled newspaper double spreads.

At the moment my book reached French bookstores in 1973, the French were already undergoing a fundamental shift in their approach to the awkward memories of World War II. This was certainly not my doing alone. The student rebellion of 1968 had raised up a new generation who rejected their parents' opinions on most things. They doubted the standard view, shared by both Gaullists and the Left, that most French people had always been resisters, at least in their hearts. Marcel Ophuls' celebrated documentary film, *The Sorrow and the Pity*, also came out in 1973 and demonstrated how widespread collaboration had been.

Since the 1970s, far from covering up the awkward wartime past, French young people, journalists, jurists and teachers, have embarked on a nearly obsessive reworking of it. The Jewish issue came to dominate this reworking. I and others found in the German archives that Vichy had initiated its own anti-Jewish program in the summer and fall of 1940, at cross purposes to the Nazis. Vichy excluded Jews from employment in the public services and intellectual fields and seized their property, while the Nazis wanted, in 1940, at least, something quite different: to expel German Jews into France. Two years later when the Nazis began to apply the Final Solution to the Jews of Western Europe, they found Vichy's discrimination measures, internment camps, card files of names and addresses, and cooperative police an indispensable help in locating, arresting, and deporting the Jews of France.

Reworking the Vichy past also took judicial form. An active judicial purge of collaborators had followed the Liberation of 1944. About 1600 of them had been executed after trials, about 40,000 sentenced to prison, and another 100,000 demoted or dismissed from jobs. The postwar purge had been uneven, however, and a number of collaborators—often those involved in Vichy's anti-Jewish program had been only lightly punished in 1945.

Uniquely among the European states once occupied by the Nazis, France embarked on a second series of prosecutions of collaborators after the 1980s. Foot-dragging by leading French political and administrative figures delayed them for many years. Since in France murder charges face a statute of limitations and cannot be prosecuted after 25 years, the prosecutors used the new charge of crimes against humanity developed in the Nuremberg trials of the Nazi leaders in 1945. In the 1980s, French prosecutors charged several former Vichy officials with crimes against humanity for abetting the Nazi deportations of Jews. They were elderly men by then, and most of them died during the indictment process. The biggest target—former Vichy Police Chief René Bousquet, whom the German archives show offering to help the Nazis deport Jews from France but who had been lightly punished in 1945—was assassinated in 1993 before his trial could begin.

That left among the indicted only Maurice Papon, who had been, from 1942 to 1944, a young official in Bordeaux whose responsibilities had included, among other things, the Jewish population of the region at the moment when the Nazis were trying to deport them all to death camps. As a mere executant rather than a policy-maker, Papon was indicted only for complicity in crimes against humanity. But if the Vichy regime's anti-Jewish measures were ever going to be the subject of a legal judgment, Papon was the only accused left. By the 1990s, Papon had become a powerful public figure in France, a senior civil servant and sometime cabinet minister. To put such a prestigious person on trial for actions taken fifty years earlier was a measure of the extraordinary determination of some French leaders to arrive at a legal judgment on Vichy collaborationism.

And so on October 31, 1997, I found myself in the handsome 18th century courthouse in Bordeaux swearing before a panel of French judges to tell the truth, all the truth, and nothing but the truth. But what exactly was I supposed to do in that courtroom? Technically, I had been summoned as a witness. But in 1942-1944 I had seen only Lexington, Virginia, and never Bordeaux. What I had learned in the German archives would have been considered hearsay in an Anglo-American court.

The chief judge in this case had telephoned me in New York before the trial opened and asked me to help explain the historical context of Maurice Papon's actions in 1942-1944 to the court. He had discovered that eleven of the twelve jurors had been born since 1945. He wanted them to receive a history lesson when the trial began that would make more comprehensible the disparate fragments of testimony they were going to hear. I was not alone: two French scholars and a Swiss were also summoned. Despite some reluctance—Papon's personal responsibility was less clear than that, for example, of former Police Chief Bousquet—I decided the judge's request was reasonable. A seat on the Concorde helped persuade me.

My two hours on the stand were stressful. As a witness, I was not allowed to have any notes. I presented my statement from memory in French, as the resentful and formerly powerful Papon glared at me. I essentially presented a history lecture. I laid out the interpretation of Vichy that my books had contained. I stressed that the German occupiers had depended upon French administrators and policemen to carry out their policies, and that some French civil servants had refused to comply and survived..

When I had finished, the defense attorney asked me how it felt to put my scholarship at the service of the public prosecutor. The chief judge intervened at once to explain that it was he, not the prosecutor, who had invited the historians. I was the court's witness, not the servant of either side. Maurice Papon had the last word, in accord with French legal procedure. He observed that historians are always revising the previous generation's interpretations, and he was confident that my interpretation of Vichy would soon, in its turn, be revised.

The court found Maurice Papon guilty of complicity in crimes against humanity on April 2, 1998 and sentenced him to ten years in prison. After three years, the old man—now 92—was released because of age and declining health. I was firmly convinced that Papon really had helped the Germans deport Jews, and that his sentence was just. A narrow majority of French people agreed, though many did not, and my role was vigorously criticized. Some high French civil servants argued (forgetting the Nuremberg judgment) that they were bound by duty and could not be prosecuted for obeying orders. Some historians, too, thought I had allowed myself to be used.

I stick by my participation. Professional historians should be willing to contribute their learning to court cases where a historical judgment and the interpretation of historical documents are involved. But they can expect to become controversial. Historical scholarship is not just about the past.

Franz von Papen
Two Days in a Room with a Man who Boosted Hitler Into Power

Henry Ashby Turner, Jr., Class of 1954

FOUR YEARS AFTER graduating from Washington and Lee with a thirst for historical knowledge instilled by my courses with Professor Jenks, I spent most of the summer of 1958 in the German city of Koblenz, where my wife Jane and I were honeymooning while I conducted research for my Princeton Ph.D. dissertation. Each weekday, we walked to the West German Federal Archive, then located in temporary quarters directly on the Rhine River. There I read my way through stacks of German documents from the period of the Weimar Republic that was established after the First World War and succeeded by the Third Reich. Since we could not afford the price of photocopies in that pre-Xerox age, Jane sat beside me, making handwritten copies of documents whose exact texts I needed.

One morning while we were at work in the small room assigned to researchers, the door opened and a man I immediately recognized entered. Well known to me from countless photographs, he was unmistakably Franz von Papen, a reactionary Catholic politician who had briefly headed the German government as Reich Chancellor in 1932 and who bore greater responsibility than any other single person for Adolf Hitler's appointment as

Chancellor at the end of January 1933. Seventy-eight years old in 1958, spry and dapperly attired, von Papen arrived at the researchers' room accompanied by a considerably younger man and a woman and escorted by a bevy of solicitous archivists.

My astonishment could not have been greater. By coincidence, I had before me that morning a letter von Papen had signed during his chancellorship, and now there he was, in the flesh in the same room with me. Moreover, he and his two companions were assigned seats at a desk directly in front of the one where Jane and I were working, no more than five feet away. When the archival files von Papen had requested were delivered to him, I could easily see from their labels that they consisted of the correspondence of none other than his erstwhile patron, nemesis, and victim: Kurt von Schleicher.

Von Schleicher was the politically influential army general who successfully promoted von Papen for the chancellorship before bringing about the latter's fall from power a half year later and taking his place at the head of the government. Seeking revenge, von Papen then successfully used his personal influence with the elderly President of the Republic, Paul von Hindenburg, to bring about the downfall of Chancellor von Schleicher. He then successfully conspired with Adolf Hitler to form a new cabinet headed by the Nazi leader, assuming that he, as Deputy Chancellor, would be able to control Hitler. Although that proved to be one of the most disastrous political blunders in history, von Papen made his peace with Hitler and was rewarded with ambassadorial posts. After the Second World War, he was put on trial before the international tribunal at Nuremberg but was acquitted on the grounds that he had not been directly implicated in the crimes covered by the indictment. Kurt von Schleicher, for his part, was shot to death at his home by Nazi thugs the year after von Papen had conspired to bring him down and replace him with Hitler. There I sat in 1958, a novice historian, a few feet behind a man who had played a major role in events of world-historical significance. But for von Papen's actions a quarter of a century earlier, there might well have been no Third Reich, no

Second World War, no Holocaust. Needless to say, I was bursting with curiosity about the man seated in front of me and longed to ask him a host of questions. But under the circumstances, that was just not feasible. It was an unwritten rule of German archives that researchers did not intrude upon each other's privacy, and von Papen was of course no ordinary researcher, as the assiduous attention he received from the archival staff left no doubt. If I, a lowly graduate student, had presumed to approach him, I might well have incurred the wrath of the archivists and jeopardized my access to documents that were essential for my dissertation. I had, in short, no choice but to look on in silence while von Papen and his two companions attentively read through the correspondence of Kurt von Schleicher, the man who had elevated him to the chancellorship, then brought him low, only to be felled in turn by the conspiracy in which von Papen played a crucial role, thus clearing the way for Adolf Hitler's rise to power with all its dreadful consequences.

I was naturally curious about the identity of the man and woman who had arrived with von Papen and were now seated on either side of him. My curiosity was increased when I noticed that they were speaking with each other in English. That quickly changed, however, when they overheard Jane and me exchanging words in that language, at which point they put their heads together and began to speak French. I thereupon decided to make matters difficult for them. Working at the desk behind Jane and me was a Canadian historian who spoke fluent French, so during the lunch break I arranged for him to lean forward after we returned to the research room and ask me, in a voice loud enough to be overheard by von Papen and his companions, a question in French to which I could respond with 'oui' or 'non'. When he did so that afternoon, the threesome in front of us immediately fell silent and thereafter communicated by passing written messages among themselves.

The following day, von Papen and his companions returned to the research room and resumed their perusal of von Schleicher's correspondence while Jane and I were again at work behind them. When they departed for good that afternoon, the identity of von Papen's companions remained a mystery to me. It was not until twenty-nine years later, in 1987, that I finally discovered who they were. In that year a voluminous biography of von Papen appeared under the imprimatur of a 'vanity' publishing house that printed, for authors willing to foot the bill, manuscripts spurned by regular publishers. In this case, the authors were two Americans, Henry M. Adams and Robin K. Adams, the first of whom was identified as having been in 1958 an associate professor of history at the University of California at Santa Barbara, the second as his wife. As a little research quickly revealed, Professor Adams' scholarly attainments were, at best, very modest, his wife's non-existent.

How these two Americans came to accompany Franz von Papen to the Koblenz archive in 1958 is revealed in their book, parts of which consist of reminiscences by Henry Adams about his own experiences. As a student at Georgetown University in 1930-31, Adams had befriended von Papen's son, who was also studying there. The following spring, while auditing lectures at the University of Berlin, he met the elder von Papen through the intermediacy of the son. After the war, his cordial relations with the younger von Papen resumed, and he and his wife embarked upon their biography of his father, having enlisted the latter's assistance in their research. Their travels together with him in pursuit of his past took them to the Koblenz archive for two days in late July 1958, as is duly recorded in their book. The final product of the Adams' labors was a biography so adulatory, naïve and uncritical as to make the pejorative adjective 'apologetic' totally inadequate. Von Papen is characterized as a man whose "forthright honesty, courage, self-confidence, idealism, loyalty to his country and trust in others played him false, leading him to underestimate the ruthless character of power seeking revolutionaries from another world than his..." The flavor of the book may be gauged by the heading of the chapter that deals with von Papen's role in bringing down von Schleicher and conspiring to install Hitler as Chancellor: "Prelude to the Vice-Chancellorship."

It is, in short, one of those fortunately rare books that literally subtract from the sum of human knowledge.

I might add that in the course of my own subsequent work as an historian I reached the conclusion that interviews with participants in past events are of little or no value for getting at the truth. Even with the best of will, human memories are selective and fallible, and the temptation to indulge in self-serving revision of the past record is often irresistible. My own later attempts to elicit historical information by means of interviews would prove very disappointing. Far more revealing are those traces of the past left on paper at the time. The two days I sat frustrated behind Franz von Papen at the Koblenz archive were thus best spent, as they were, reading the historical documents I had before me. In the light of what I subsequently learned about that suave, crafty gentleman from other documents, I am sure that if I could have spoken with him in 1958 he would have very charmingly told me a pack of lies.

The Jenks Mystique

Robert Fishburn, Class of 1955
Former Editor, *Roanoke Times*

I RECENTLY RAN across a massive pile of my class notes from 1953. They were neatly bundled, like love letters, though secured by dried rubber bands instead of ribbons.

In one sense, they were love letters, written in a tiny, tight hand: scribbled tributes to a history professor, William Jenks, who somehow made me strive to get down his every word, every allusion, every nuance. Of course I didn't and couldn't. His lectures were jewels, the brilliance of which was simply not transferable to paper. But I tried harder than I did for any other professor to capture the essence of his words, though my grades were no indication of the intensity of my struggle.

I was to learn over the years that I was only one of many dozens, perhaps hundreds, of students who fell under the spell of the "Jenks Mystique," a compound of humaneness, erudition and mystery. I never joined the widespread speculation, now so fresh in my mind, that he had led another life, perhaps as a secret agent in WWII. It was quite enough that he was the best lecturer I encountered during my years at W&L and Columbia University. That was what he did superbly and publicly; and as I look back on it, it was no small miracle that he was able to sustain such a high level of communication of and commitment to scholarship, day after day, year after year.

The question tantalizes all who have had good (and sometimes, great) teachers: What made them good, what unique combination of talents made them great? For me, it was always the awed recognition that Dr. Jenks had somehow managed to shape the tumult, gore, glory and confusion of European history into coherent, graceful forms, even if I never could get them on paper.

Looking Back...

Samuel A. Syme, Jr., Class of 1956

REFLECTING UPON MORE than fifty years of assorted associations with Bill Jenks, a wide variety of images emerge. There are the familiar scenes shared by all who studied under him. Should we laugh—or just stare at one another—when he offers one of his acerbic asides on the first day of a new class? In addition to all of the Jenksisms we transcribed, did we really record enough of the lecture to see us through the tests & exams? And how often, right after submitting one of the numerous short papers he required, did we finally remember the clever sentence we had meant to include, but didn't?

Then, there were the wonderful meals & receptions at his home when we returned to Lexington over the years. The company was always good, & invariably included former faculty, friends from town & occasionally, someone who probably wondered why he was there. The food was beautifully served by the ever-gracious Jane, who became a part of our lives with Bill. If we were lucky, the menu included thinly sliced properly cured Virginia ham, & all of the things that went with it.

One of my fondest memories of Bill & Jane was a tour to Eastern Europe shortly after Christmas 1984. The majority of us had ties to various Virginia schools, & some friendships formed then continue now. The trip took us from Vienna to Budapest (where we welcomed the new year) Prague, Dresden & the two Berlins. Our local guides were quite good, but it was important to watch Bill as they talked. Those of us who remembered his expressions—or lack thereof—knew there probably was more to the story than we were being told. As we walked together afterward, the record often was set straight.

Finally, the trip to Europe brings to mind Bill's fondness for a particular red wine which was unavailable in Virginia stores. It was *Bull's Blood of Eger* or, more correctly, an Hungarian product called *Egri Bikaver*. It had powerful characteristics as you might imagine, & was somewhat rowdy. I located a source in Myrtle Beach & when I delivered the case on one of my trips to Lexington, it seemed to hit the spot. I learned later that it was not offered to the casual visitor & that it lasted a reasonable amount of time.

Bill's devotion to his profession is carefully measured in his output—not only in his scholarly achievements, but in the number of us who followed in his path. And the sum must include the love & concern which both Jane & Bill continued to share throughout the years that followed our undergraduate relationships at Washington & Lee.

Women as Strongest

William R. Goodman, Jr., Class of 1958

THE STORY OF the three bodyguards and the riddle contest held at the Persian court of Darius in 1 Esdras 3:1-5:6 is the only distinctive passage in a book that is otherwise a rather free Greek version of materials that closely—though not exactly—parallel 2 Chronicles and Ezra-Nehemiah. In this important composite tale, each young man tries to best the other's statement of "What one thing is strongest" (3:5). They put their answers under the pillow of the king, who, they believe, will reward the wisest with gifts and honors. Upon waking, the king summons an audience and requests each youth to give a public defense of his answer to the riddle. The first two argue that wine and the king, respectively, are strongest. But the third wins with his witty defense of women and truth (3:12, 4:13-32, 34). The king grants the winner's request that the exiled Jews be permitted to return to Jerusalem, that the city and the temple be rebuilt, and that the vessels be returned. This third youth is identified in an obvious gloss as Zerubbabel (4:13), the illustrious leader of the second temple, making this an deifying legend about an important leader of the Jews during the Babylonian exile.

The view of her, from a male perspective, is that women have the most power in the world sexually, economically, and socially, and therefore are the strongest. Simply put, "men cannot exist without women" (4:17). While the king and all people who rule over the sea and land are powerful, it is women who are most powerful since they give birth to these leaders (4:15). Women raise the men who plant the vineyards that produce wine, also a powerful—but not most powerful—force (4:16). Women make clothes for men and bring them renown (4:17). Female form exercises direct power over men: "If men gather gold and silver or any other beautiful thing, and then see a woman lovely in appearance and beauty, they let all those things go, and gape at her, and with open mouths stare at her" (4:18-19).

Restating Genesis 2:24, the third youth claims that a man will leave his father and country and live out his days with his wife, and then adds the negative assessment that relationship with a woman causes a man to forget both parents and country (1 Esdras 4:20-23). The young man tells the king and his nobles that all this proves "women rule over you" (4:22a), a reversal of Genesis 3:16 in which a man rules over the woman. He argues that men will do anything for women—give them all the fruits of their labor, rob and steal for them, face lions, walk in darkness, love them more than their own parents, lose their minds because of them, and even become slaves on their account (4:22b-26). The third youth concludes, "Many have perished, or stumbled, or sinned because of women" (4:27).

To clinch his argument, the third youth cites an incident (4:29-32) that occurred at another (unnamed) king's banquet when Apme, the king's concubine, sitting in a place of honor at the king's right hand, took the crown from the king's head, slapping him with her left hand. That the king allowed her these liberties and was willing to do anything to make her happy proves, according to the third youth's logic, that women are strongest. His listeners—all males—appreciate these ideas about gender and male-female relationships.

Apparently favoring the third youth's argument for women as strongest, over the arguments for wine and king, the king and nobles look knowingly at each other (4:33). Just then the riddle contest takes an unexpected turn: the third young man begins to speak again, now defending truth as strongest (4:33-41). No doubt an addition to the original folk tale, this enigmatic addition displaces women as the winning answer. Ironically, the third youth wins by cheating; he introduces a second entry, while the other youths got only one. "Gentlemen, are not women strong:" he begins (4:13). Then, adding an ethical dimension to the original secular story, he argues, "Wine is unrighteous, all human beings are unrighteous, all their works are unrighteous, and all such things. There is no truth in them and in their unrighteousness they will perish. But truth endures and is strong forever" (4:37-38). When Zerubbabel prays, "Blessed be the God of truth!" (4:40), all the people acclaim, "Great is truth, and strongest of all!" (4:41).

Truth *(alētheia)* is a feminine noun, and the description of truth in the youth's defense bears great similarity to the power of the Egyptian *Ma'at,* the Greek *Sophia* (Wisdom), the Hebrew *hokmâ* , and the Persian *Arta,* all feminine in gender and all subjects of hymns of praise extolling their cosmic and earthly powers.

In the end, women are not considered the strongest; they are labeled as unrighteous (4:37); they cause men to stumble and sin (4:27); they make men forget their fathers and country (4:21). The third youth voices negative views regarding women that were likely reflections of popular culture in the Persian or early Hellenistic period. This story makes Zerubbabel an important person in the postexilic era. It objectifies and ultimately denigrates women of the same period.

Do-Gooders in the Caribbean:
Franklin Roosevelt, Anti-colonialism, and Anglo-American Relations During World War II

Thomas C. Howard, Class of 1960

I. Introduction: Franklin Roosevelt, Molasses, and Colonialism

WHEN REXFORD TUGWELL, one of the most energetic and controversial academic advisors in Franklin Roosevelt's original New Deal brains trust, resigned from his post as head of the Resettlement Administration in December 1936 he had molasses on his mind. Rather than returning to his academic post as professor of economics at Columbia University he announced that he would at once assume the position of Executive Vice-President of the American Molasses Company run by his friend Charles W. Taussig, who had become an advisor to FDR on Caribbean affairs. Critics of the administration who had referred to Tugwell as "Rex the Red" now settled for calling him " molasses man." It surprised observers on both the right and left that someone who appeared to be among the most progressive "anti-business" members of the circle closest to Roosevelt had decided to go into business. In November Tugwell bantered with Roosevelt about the move and, according to his account, when FDR speculated that he might also be looking for a new job in 1941 Tugwell suggested that he ought also consider going to work for Taussig because "no other businessman would have either of us". The President agreed and added jokingly that now neither of them could be professors after, as he put it, "our unorthodox behavior."[1] Either prospect conjures up some intriguing images: one of Roosevelt working his way up the corporate ladder in the sugar business, another of Professor Roosevelt lecturing his classes on the virtues of the New Deal. Both are far removed from what FDR envisioned on other occasions for his eventual retirement from office. He speculated on occasion about his return to Hyde Park where he could receive visiting world leaders and delegations from the new United Nations headquarters that eventually came to be located not far down the Hudson Valley in Manhattan.[2] Instead he might have spent his final days locating new markets for "Grandma's Molasses," the leading brand of the American Molasses Company during the thirties and forties. Today "Grandma's" is the best-selling molasses in the United States, now distributed by a subsidiary of British-based Cadbury-Schweppes.[3] Churchill would have been pleased.

Of course it turned out differently. On April 12, 1945 Eleanor Roosevelt met at 3:00 in the afternoon in the Red Room at the White House with Charles Taussig to discuss his forthcoming role as one of the State Department advisors to the American delegation soon to depart for the United Nations Conference on International Organization scheduled to convene in San Francisco on April 25. The previous month Roosevelt had appointed Taussig as an advisor mainly concerned with the question of international trusteeships and related "colonial" questions.[4] A few minutes into their conversation Mrs. Roosevelt was called to the telephone to speak with Franklin's cousin and confidante Laura Delano who informed her that the President had collapsed at the Little White House in Warm Springs, Georgia. Mrs. Roosevelt excused herself from her meeting with Taussig to inquire further about her husband's condition. Although she wasn't to receive the news directly until later in the afternoon, FDR was pronounced dead at 3:35, just about the time she excused herself from her meeting with Taussig.[5] At Warm Springs Roosevelt was working on the draft of the speech prepared by

Archibald MacLeish that he planned, against doctor's advice, to travel to San Francisco to deliver at the opening of the United Nations conference. Instead many in San Francisco were to invoke his memory while they drew plans for a post-war world that often blurred and dimmed his vision. This was perhaps most clearly evident during deliberations on the issue of international trusteeship. On this as on other questions related to the future of "dependent" and colonial territories, the final settlement departed significantly from Roosevelt's wishes, especially those he expressed at the height of his anti-imperialist convictions in 1942 and 1943. He often spoke of the need for a postwar system for the international supervision of all colonial territories, not only those of the former mandated territories of the League and those taken from Japan and Italy. As it turned out Charles Taussig was going to be one of the few in the American delegation to speak out on behalf of this earlier vision and, with a little help from Eleanor Roosevelt, to continue a campaign on its behalf in the months following San Francisco.

This story helps to illustrate one of purposes of this paper, which is to contribute a small piece to the puzzle of United States foreign policy during the war years of the Roosevelt presidency concerning the future of the European colonial empires, especially the British Empire, and the influence of developments in the Caribbean on the shaping of this policy.

II. Changing Interpretations of Franklin Roosevelt's Anti-Colonialism.

A surprisingly large number of historians and a few other curious souls have struggled to understand Franklin Roosevelt's complex attitudes and policies toward European, especially British, colonialism. What exactly he wanted to be done about the "colonial world" after the war will always remain something of a mystery, largely because FDR wanted it this way. As he famously put it himself, he never let his right hand know what his left hand was doing, and he doubtless would have enjoyed tremendously the efforts of later battalions (well, perhaps only a company or two) of historians to try to decipher his hand signals. The arguments have changed over time and of course they vary according to the color of the ideological spectacles worn. They range from those who view FDR as an uncompromising champion of independence in the near future for all colonial peoples to those who contend that his anti-colonial rhetoric was little more than hypocritical blather and a cover for the expansion of American commercial interests at the expense of Britain and other colonial powers. Others have stressed the compromises they consider Roosevelt to have made, especially during the last year or so of his life, to insure Anglo-American harmony for the final war effort or to prepare the way for his larger international agenda, including gaining support for the creation of the United Nations organization. Some have charged him with succumbing during the final months of the war to the need to appease more conservative centers of power in the administration, especially the Joint Chiefs of Staff, and most especially the Navy Department that wanted to prevent the Pacific islands of Micronesia captured from Japan from falling under the uncertainties of international supervision.[6]

Nevertheless, out of the many differences there appears to have emerged broad agreement on at least two points. First, there is widespread acknowledgement of the deep conviction of Roosevelt's anti-colonial beliefs; he expressed them ardently both publicly and privately throughout the years considered in this study. Second, most who have written on this subject accept Roosevelt's genuine dedication to improving the plight of colonial peoples in a way analogous to his efforts domestically to improve the lot of the poor and the disadvantaged. As mentioned, some have noted what they regard as a marginal retreat from his anti-colonial position toward the very end of his life, accompanied by more muted and qualified language regarding the trusteeship question and colonialism in general. This paper takes some issue with this interpretation and argues that not only did Roosevelt's fundamental commitment to decolonization never alter, but that to the end of his life he expressed his conviction to others who continued to take him at his word and to act on it. In this way his anti-colonial agenda was extended through the final months of the war and into the postwar world by advisors and confidantes such as Taussig and Tugwell, and even more powerfully by his wife Eleanor.

Throughout his presidency Eleanor Roosevelt urged FDR to take stronger stands and to act more forcefully on issues involving racial discrimination and other social, economic and political inequities. Similarly Taussig and Tugwell at times recommended to the president that he take more visible, effective actions on such problems within their areas of activity. They were friends who frequently kept in touch. They both generally had access to the president when they wanted, and they influenced his thinking and actions on colonial questions in numerous ways. They viewed themselves as loyal adherents of the Roosevelt vision. They were, in other words, New Deal liberals with a decided do-gooder bent who, while they were not averse at times to doing well by doing good, their conscience and social activism were genuine. In what they did, tried to do, and even in their mistakes, they provide important insights into the character—and the limitations—of the international liberal imagination.

Franklin Roosevelt was by no means a social or economic revolutionary, and much that made up the New Deal was his own effort to bring together many of the progressive programs of the past in a different form that would make the system fairer for all. He improvised. Although he had a huge personal impact on United States foreign policy, especially as wartime leader, many of his words and actions were derived from earlier traditions. During the 1930s New Deal foreign relations focused mainly on Latin America and the reformulation of the Monroe Doctrine into what came to be called the Good Neighbor Policy. Perhaps the description of Roosevelt in foreign affairs that works best is that of a Wilsonian internationalist tempered by lots of pragmatic expediency. But his idealism was real. FDR came to believe, and later to preach, that the Good Neighbor Policy provided a model for other regions of the world. He genuinely believed that the best of American ideals and institutions would spread naturally to the South to Latin and Central America and the Caribbean—without the need for anything like the harsh hemispheric interventionism of the past.

Roosevelt believed in the active export of the New Deal, of the best of American social and political liberalism—of "American-ism" —to the rest of the globe. This was, of course, inseparable from economics, and US foreign policy aimed at the breaking of economic barriers, including imperial preferential systems of any sort. From at least the Atlantic Charter in August 1941 through the Bretton Woods Conference in July 1944—and beyond—the aim of the United States to gain commercial access to the British Empire, to all colonial empires, was evident. Throughout the war it sought to gain equal American access to the trade and raw materials of the world. As the United States increasingly dominated the war effort, especially in relation to Britain, the reality of an economic global order dominated by the United States became clearer.[7] Much of this had already happened in Latin America before 1941, and during the war special efforts were made toward its realization in the Caribbean basin. Underlying this paper is the contention that United States foreign policy in the Caribbean during the war years provides a highly useful but seldom used window on the closeness and the competitiveness of wartime Anglo-American relations, on American anti-colonialism, and on colonial issues far beyond the region. [8]

III. The Caribbean: An American Window on Colonialism

Developments in the Caribbean region served as a significant but widely unrecognized influence on the thinking of Franklin Roosevelt regarding global colonial issues. During World War II they contributed to his growing negative attitude toward the European colonial empires and his belief that these "relics of the past" represented some of the greatest threats to the establishment of a peaceful and prosperous global order after the war.

By 1941 the remaining European possessions in the Caribbean

represented some of the oldest remnants of the European colonial empires, but where modern nationalist movements were late in coming. Despite outbursts of anti-colonial sentiment earlier in the twentieth century, it wasn't until conditions created by the depression in the 1930s caused tensions to erupt in a succession of riots and strikes throughout the area, including the British West Indies. British colonial authorities were increasingly conscious of American influence on the growing discontent According to the report of the 1938 Royal Commission that investigated causes of the unrest, a significant stimulus behind the demands for better conditions were the activities of West Indians who worked abroad, especially in the United States.[9] But direct American involvement didn't occur until the years following U.S. entry into the war, the same years that witnessed the emergence of more mature West Indian nationalist movements. The war dramatically heightened the presence of the United States in the region and created a unique arena for the playing out of the often-conflicting forces of British colonialism, American anti-colonialism, and nationalism. American activities served to weaken British authority, to prod them toward further regional development, and, often unintentionally, to contribute to the emergence of the much more activist nationalism of the postwar era.

The Anglo-American agreement announced in September 1940 transferring fifty aging destroyers to Britain in return for United States rights to ninety-nine year leases on bases in five British West Indian islands, the Bahamas, Jamaica, Antigua, St. Lucia, Trinidad and Tobago (as well as British Guiana, Bermuda, and Newfoundland) represented not only a significant step by the United States in its undeclared resistance towards Germany, but began a chapter of intensified regional interaction with Britain.[10] In the Caribbean there were now to be what amounted to colonies within colonies—American bases, air strips, and service facilities constructed on British colonial soil, all with vast potential for tension and the spread of American influence. For Americans this provided nearby examples of what they regarded as British colonial neglect. For Britain it became an area where it might spruce up its colonial image through economic development schemes. In short, Britain felt the impact of intensified American anti-colonialism in the Caribbean before it became a major factor in Asia, Africa, the Middle East, and elsewhere during and after the war.

IV. The Anglo-American Caribbean Commission: "Special Relations" in the Midday Sun

Two months after the Bases-for-Destroyers Agreement was announced, President Roosevelt appointed a commission to study social and economic conditions in the region. His action was the outgrowth of a memorandum from Charles Taussig who, in addition to his business activities in the Caribbean, was the chair of the President's Advisory Committee of the National Youth Administration.[11] Taussig's memo stressed that because Britain and the United States had such an important stake in the Caribbean, it would be advisable that a joint study be made "with a view to improving the economic and social conditions in the islands."[12]

The recommendations of this commission led by the fall of 1941 to the creation of a new Caribbean office in the State Department which, after close consultation with Taussig, was instrumental in the creation of the Anglo-American Caribbean Commission (AACC) in March 1942.[13] This new commission, with its origins in an American initiative, and with Taussig as its American co-chair, now received enthusiastic American promotion. It quickly launched an ambitious program focusing on emergency food supplies and transportation, research plans, health issues, and the creation of a regional broadcast service.[14] It pursued a mainly American agenda. From the start the stature of the American permanent members reflected the greater importance accorded the commission by the United States. In addition to Taussig, they included Rexford Tugwell, by then Governor of Puerto Rico, and Coert Dubois, the chief of the new Caribbean Office of the State Department. Taussig and Tugwell enjoyed direct access to the President, a comparable advantage never enjoyed by their British counterparts. This relatively high status and the enthusiasm of the Americans was unsettling to the British commission members, in part because 1942, in addition to being the high point of closeness in wartime Anglo-American cooperation, was also a time of general intensification of American criticism of British colonialism. In January 1942 Winston Churchill sent a memorandum to Roosevelt reminding him of his promise to make some statement that "there is to be no question of the transfer to the United States of the British West Indies Colonies either under the Bases Agreement or otherwise." He added that this was an action he considered especially important in light of the anxiety "likely to be revived by the proposed communiqué about the Anglo-American Caribbean Commission." [15]

Roosevelt gave the assurances Churchill requested, but tensions over the future of the region continued. Had officials in the Colonial Office been aware of the tenor of a number of the communications between the President and Taussig, they would have been more alarmed. One revealing example is the long personal report (the AACC submitted a later formal report) to Roosevelt in June 1942 after Taussig's return from a fact-finding trip to sites where American bases were under construction. He cited a number of concerns regarding political tensions and nationalist aspirations before listing a number of specific recommendations, including changes of policy for the administration of Puerto Rico such as popular elections for governor. Taussig's speculations about the region as a whole are worth quoting at length:

> I received the impression that the people of the Caribbean are looking toward the United States for progressive leadership and that colonial governments, while not looking for such leadership, will accept it if only for the reason that they realize their physical safety is entirely in the hands of the United States. The Caribbean perhaps is the only area of the world where it is possible during the war to give a preview of what the post-war world may look like. Within this area are represented independent

republics, colonies of three European powers, and the possessions of the United States. Major problems of regional, hemispheric and world trade are involved. Political aspirations of subject peoples are being pressed. Racial problems exist in an aggravated form...Obviously the Caribbean represents opportunities for constructive statesmanship.[16]

He then elaborated on the sort of statesmanship he believed was needed:

It seems to me the time is at hand when by using our possessions in the Caribbean as the springboard you could pave the way for a 'charter' granting more political freedom to all colonial people. Just as our changed policy toward Cuba and the abrogation of the Platt Amendment in 1933 became the keystone of the 'Good Neighbor Policy' so could a Second Caribbean Emancipation bring hope to all subject peoples of the United Nations.[17]

Taussig's strong advocacy of some sort of colonial charter places him in the midst of the debate then taking place in the State Department over the desirability of issuing a statement of principles applicable to all dependent areas. In May 1942 the Far Eastern Division of the Department, guided by the wishes of Secretary of State Cordell Hull, drafted a proposal for a "world charter" that would broaden the scope of the Atlantic Charter to include the concept of international trusteeship for all subject peoples.[18] As a member of the Department Areas Committee of the State Department, and in private discussions with Hull and others, Taussig contributed to these deliberations.[19]

Throughout the remainder of the war, Britain was uncomfortable with the concept of trusteeship as it seemed to be applied by the Americans. Roosevelt increasingly viewed trusteeship through an international organization as the best means of promoting self-determination and insuring ultimate independence for colonial territories. The British generally viewed this "internationalized" trusteeship as little more than a vehicle for the spread of informal American political influence and a mask for American commercial covetousness, though this sort of venting remained behind closed doors. As Taussig noted, they realized their dependence on American assistance and tried to keep such resentment to themselves.

Of the two major State Department wartime initiatives dealing with the colonial world, namely international trusteeships and the creation of regional commissions, only the second held any appeal for the British, beginning with Churchill himself. For them regional commissions were more realistic and might also hold out the chance of assuaging American skepticism through close cooperation on colonial questions. They believed that practical experience with the difficulties involved could temper American hostility, or at least rein in their rhetoric. At first reluctant and defensive, the British became determined to make the best of the Anglo-American Caribbean Commission. They might even turn the tables a bit on the Americans by themselves promoting the commission as a model for regional cooperative ventures elsewhere in the world.

The dynamics within the AACC turned out to be a fascinating microcosm of that intriguing construction known as the "Special Relationship" between Britain and the United States. It is the mythic dimension of the study of Anglo-American relations during and since World War II about which so much has been written and so little in the final analysis subjected to concrete historical analysis. It's just too slippery. But insofar as it may be possible to discuss the specialness of the relations between these two nations, the sunny Caribbean is as good a place as any to try. All the clichés that come to mind were here in the perceptions of the commission members: brash, overfed, big-talking Americans and deceitful, patronizing Britons—infants playing with dangerous toys and effete dilettantes. It was invariably polite because there was generally grudging admiration on both sides. It was close, intense, and highly competitive. It all boiled down to the question of "our" way of doing things as opposed to "their" way. In the words of one of the most popular Broadway musicals of the 1940s: "I'm superior, you're inferior. /I'm the big attraction, you're the small. / I'm the major one, you're the minor one, /I can beat you shootin', that's not all. / Anything you can do, I can do better. / I can do anything better than you."[20] Who won most of the time? Surely we know the answer.

The AACC assumed a major role in the attempt to coordinate regional problems and to push for more integrated approaches to issues involving labor, health, agriculture, communication, education, and much more. Areas that, despite the long historic shadow of the United States in the region, had not been greatly touched by the United States were now confronted by newcomers with their money (including higher wage scales); their grand schemes; their popular culture ("Rum and Coca-Cola," sung by the Andrews Sisters, was a revealing popular song of the time that rhapsodized about the "Yankee dollar"); and their own special brand of racism. Racial tensions heightened, especially in areas where the new American military installations were constructed, and brought to the attention of many in the region the realities of racial discrimination on the mainland.[21] On the other hand, the Americans on the AACC pushed to demonstrate the more liberal racial policies of the Roosevelt administration, especially in contrast with what they saw as the entrenched, politely deferential racism of the British colonial system and the white settler communities in the islands of the West Indies. Two notable examples of this involved the appointment of one African-American and one West Indian to positions on the AACC. The American, William H. Hastie, civilian aide to the Secretary of War, was appointed as an advisor to the commission in the early stages of its work. Hastie was not controversial aside from his color, though this was sufficient to heighten the differences between the American and British delegations. Taussig attributed in reports to the President the excellent local reactions when the commission went on tour to the fact a non-white had been included., if even in an advisory capacity. He speculated that because of this the British might seriously consider the appointment of a "colored West Indian" to the commission.[22] As it turned out, such a person did receive an appointment through the commission, although it was made against strenuous British objections. Taussig happily, one might even say gleefully, supported the appointment of Eric Williams to a position with the commission.

After the war Williams became one of the most celebrated Caribbean nationalist leaders, and ultimately the first Prime Minister of independent Trinidad and Tobago. An Oxford graduate, Williams had been teaching at Howard University in Washington since 1939. In 1942 he published a book that established his reputation in many quarters as the foremost West Indian scholar on Caribbean issues. The book, *The Negro in the Caribbean*, was a frontal attack on colonialism in the region. Although the book earned much applause for Williams in West Indian and American black communities, it created quite the opposite reputation for him in British colonial circles. It was in part because of this that Taussig pressed for his inclusion in some capacity with the commission. As Williams later described it, he had applied unsuccessfully for a job with the commission through Sir John Huggins, Taussig's British counterpart, before he met Taussig who was, in his words, the "live wire" of the commission. Taussig was "a man of great personality, and withal a very pleasant and likable person," wrote Williams. He added that Taussig, "who knew all about *The Negro in the Caribbean*, decided that I was to be associated with the Anglo-American Caribbean Commission. And then the fun began."[23] Well, not for everyone. Following his appointment Williams used the commission, and the American delegation used Williams. In the course of his years of association both with the wartime commission and its postwar successor, Williams was able to travel, lecture, and write, most all of it aimed at undermining the colonial establishment. In general Taussig and the other Americans supported William's' work, and laughed with him at some of the more foolish examples of British intransigence. But the time came, as Williams put it, when the Americans didn't laugh.[24] They were not amused when he wrote of racial problems in Puerto Rico, or criticized aspects of the naval bases agreement, including the racial tensions created in the vicinity of the bases. As Williams put it, the Americans "just did not want to acknowledge that there was a race problem in their possessions. They could see the mote in other people's eyes, but would not see the beam in theirs." [25] Taussig, Tugwell, and other American officials were actually acutely aware of the racial tensions in Puerto Rico and elsewhere where Americans lived and worked, but they believed that they were more qualified to deal with the problem than were the British. "Anything you can do, we can do better." Under Governor Tugwell Puerto Rico was, in fact, often held up as a model of enlightened administration. Both Taussig and Tugwell impressed on Roosevelt the need for reform, for movement in the direction of greater self-government, and indigenization of highly visible posts in government, education, and other areas. Taussig showed photographs of Puerto Rican slums to Roosevelt who reacted with dismay and urged that more effective reforms be undertaken. Roosevelt was especially sensitive of such criticisms for they were strikingly similar to ones he was accustomed to leveling at Churchill about conditions in the British colonies. It's hard here to resist including one of the most entertaining of these exchanges. It occurred after two of FDR's stops to and from the Casablanca Conference with Churchill in January 1943. The stops were in Bathurst (now Banjul), then the administrative capital of the British colony of Gambia in West Africa. On his return stay-over he suffered from a fever and sinus problems, though he exaggerated his condition when he wrote to Churchill, "I think I picked up sleeping sickness or Gambia fever or some kindred bug in that hell-hole of yours called Bathurst."[26] FDR did not forget his "colonial nightmare" experience in Bathurst, and used it on numerous occasions to illustrate his contention that the British Empire should be phased out of existence. At a press conference in early 1944 his anger was still evident. After describing the squalid nature of conditions he had observed, he continued: "And I looked it up, with a little study, and I got to the point of view that for every dollar that the British, who have been there for two hundred years, have put into the Gambia, they have taken out ten. It's just plain exploitation of those people." [27] But making such gibes could be risky. There were skeletons in the American colonial closet that could also be rattled—even in the White House. At a dinner there soon after FDR returned from Casablanca he described seeing children on rubber plantations with legs about two fingers in circumference. Mrs. Roosevelt asked: "Did you tell Winston?" When he answered that he had, she responded, "Well, are ours any better?"[28]

V. The United States and Puerto Rico: Having It Both Ways

The embarrassing fact was that Puerto Rico during the war remained a colony of the United States, although it was an embarrassment mitigated by its usefulness as an example of enlightened rule for other colonial powers. The neat trick was that Britain and the others were expected—indeed urged—to move toward the granting of full independence to their possessions while the United States temporized over the eventual status of Puerto Rico.

Puerto Rico had occupied an ambivalent status from the time of its acquisition from Spain in 1898. Unlike Cuba and the Philippines, the other two territories taken from Spain, Puerto Rico existed in a condition of colonial limbo where, in various forms, it has remained ever since.[29] As Britain began gradual military withdrawal from the region after 1903, the Theodore Roosevelt administration asserted a doctrine of preventive intervention, the famous "Roosevelt Corollary" to the Monroe Doctrine, that was applied to the whole of Latin America. [30] The increased military presence in the region meant that Puerto became more strategically important and the location of a number of naval facilities. Washington gradually liberalized colonial rule, including allowance of a greater level of self-government and a single member in the U.S. House of Representatives with the right to speak and introduce legislation, but not to vote. Poverty and unemployment, aggravated by the collapse in sugar prices in what amounted to a one-crop economy during the depression of the 1930s, and growing nationalist demands, led to instances of violence similar to those in the British West Indies. There were demands for independence in some quarters, though many in positions of influence also feared loss of tariff protection and other economic advantages.

Franklin Roosevelt took a special interest in the problems of Puerto Rico and a number of New Deal social and economic relief programs were extended there. The Puerto Rican Reconstruction Administration was especially important in promoting agricultural diversification and public works. Tugwell promoted similar programs after he became governor. In his inaugural address on September 19, 1941 he spoke at length about the fundamental need to confront the causes of poverty. "To bettering the condition of the poor I shall bring every resource I am able to find in the Governorship. I will be the friend of every man or woman who helps." He went on to address various issues and how he planned to deal with them:

> The time is past when absentee capitalists can expect to extract extravagant percentages of gain, using the people's need and their own monopoly to force the acceptance of usurer's terms. To the other kind of capital—investment— we can offer the security of our basic riches, certainty of return, and the good faith of a government which has never broken its word. But that kind of capital will appreciate the absence of speculation and concentration on the tasks of production... What is the way into this future? Through constant improvement in administration, through research, through education, through the work of a deepening social conscience... In bettering public health, in educating children, in bringing power, light, sanitation into people's homes, in building more homes for the underprivileged, in providing all kinds of public works, in the conservation of soil and other resources, in replanting forests, in the use and tenure of the land, in the search for higher wages and greater social security—in all

these we shall find work enough in the years to come…
To talk largely of freedom, of security and of individual
rights without finding ways to translate these words into
action will no longer suffice.[31]

Nor was the university to escape scrutiny:

The university must find closer and more intimate
relations with industry, agriculture, with government,
with the suffering and hope of our people. The theory of
an institution set apart on a little island of scholarship,
ignoring the confusions of the world must be given up.
There individual ambitions must be transmuted into
effort for the common good; there technical excellence
must be created and turned to the combating of poverty,
disease, and the inefficiencies which lie behind them.[32]

It was the New Deal in a cocoanut shell. Tugwell wrote a letter to Roosevelt on November 3 in which he outlined his own
private version of his plans. He described how he and his advisors and supporters were viewed with dismay and distrust by the
old guard who "suspect that you send me secret instructions in
every mail!" He urged FDR to make a statement in the near future about the desirability of Puerto Rican cooperation with the
greater Caribbean initiatives then in the works: "It is my hope
that you will make such a statement when the Commission on
the Caribbean (AACC) is announced." He went on to mention
his recent correspondence with Taussig and Harold Ickes, the
Secretary of the Interior. He ended his letter by writing that he
was doing only "the things which I think you would have me
do if you had the time to direct them in detail and that I regard
myself merely as an officer in what has come to be literally a
rather large army." [33] It was an army that was to become larger
than either could have ever imagined within the following year.
Roosevelt responded on November 7 with encouragement and
support for his plans and the difficult job he was undertaking.
He agreed to make the statement on the Caribbean "as soon as
the set-up is ready to be announced." He reported that he had

recently told Bolivar Pagan, whom he considered one of the ob-
structionist Puerto Rican politicians, that he shouldn't oppose
the plans for the AACC because it promised to help Puerto Rico
economically and socially." [34]

The programs pushed by Tugwell, and even more the wartime
economy, brought much greater prosperity to Puerto Rico. The
new excise tax on rum from the island sold—and promoted—
on the mainland that was returned to the Puerto Rican government didn't hurt. Even with the hugely expanded responsibilities
of the war Roosevelt continue to take a personal interest in all
that happened. One of the programs, the Development Corporation, that attempted to promote local investment and drive
"absentee" investment away led to the revival in some quarters,
including Congress, of the old "Red Rex" epithet. Tugwell was
also successful in helping to create a new generation of political
leaders, including Luis Munoz Marin who was to become the
first Puerto Rican to be elected governor in 1948. Jesus T. Pinero
was appointed the first Puerto Rican governor by President Truman following the resignation of Tugwell in 1946. Pinero was
recommended to Truman by both Tugwell and Charles Taussig.
In 1947 Truman signed the legislation that gave Puerto Ricans
the franchise in gubernatorial elections, the culmination of the
recommendations of a presidential commission in 1943. In short,
Tugwell, Taussig, and others were remarkably successful in promoting progressive change in Puerto Rico and, more broadly, in
other areas of the Caribbean. But their work was also an important factor in assuring that Puerto Rico would not veer very far in
the direction of independence. Tensions and violence continued
into the postwar years, including an attempt to assassinate President Truman in 1950 and shots fired at members of the House
of Representatives from the visitor's galleries in 1954. There were
those, both in Washington and San Juan, who promoted independence, but the ties and advantages were too strong by this
time for such a move, and in 1952 Puerto Rico was proclaimed
a "Commonwealth." It was a designation vague enough to have
different meanings for different people, but one thing was clear:

it didn't include independence. The British would have loved to be able to work out something similar in the West Indies, to say nothing of other areas around the globe. Eventually independence did come to most of the British Caribbean, in no small measure because of the momentum created by the American presence during World War II—and the marvelous model of the colony—the "Commonwealth"—of Puerto Rico." [35]

VI. San Francisco: "Let's all work together in the memory of the President."

Four days after President Roosevelt's death, Charles Taussig called Edward Stettinius who the previous November had replaced the ailing Cordell Hull as Secretary of State. Stettinius was angry. He had heard "through the grape vine" about Taussig's conversation with Mrs. Roosevelt the afternoon the President died and now wanted an explanation. According to Taussig's memo of the conversation Stettinius had said: "Charlie boy, I thought we were a team," and asked for his word that in San Francisco he would consult with him before he did anything there. The conversation ended on an ostensibly friendly note with Stettinius saying, "Let's forget it and work together in the memory of the President." [36] It was not to be.

During the months immediately preceeding and following the death of the President, a succession of decisions were made which would permanently shape the contours of the postwar settlement regarding the colonial world. By 1945 Britain had successfully ridden out the worst of American anti-colonialism, though there remained serious differences when Sir Oliver Stanley, the Secretary of State for the Colonies, visited President Roosevelt at the president's request and at Taussig's urging in January 1945 to discuss the future of the Caribbean Commission and, by extension, other colonial issues. In consultation with Taussig the State Department prepared a long briefing memorandum for the president outlining the main differences between the United States and Britain on colonial policy. [37] One key section dealt with differentiating between trust territories and colonies. As the memorandum phrased it, "in our usage, 'trusteeship' has an international significance whereas the British apply it in a national sense, with themselves as trustees."[38] The memo also emphasized the American position on the need for requiring some sort of "international accountability" for the administration of all dependent territories and the desirability of declaring that independence, rather than self- government, was the ultimate goal for all dependent peoples.[39] Actual conversations between Roosevelt and Stanley skirted many of these issues, leaving Stanley with the impression that the American position on the matter of international supervision of dependent areas was flexible and open to negotiation.

By the time of the Yalta Conference the next month Roosevelt had at least for the present modified somewhat his position on trusteeship in response to the objections of the Joint Chiefs of Staff—especially the Navy. Their concern over the need for continued United States control over captured Japanese Pacific islands and other strategic considerations led to a new working definition of trusteeship. But he considered this to be no real compromise of his basic vision for greater internationalization of global problems, including his support of independence for all colonial peoples as soon as possible. When he met for the last time with Taussig on 15 March, he reaffirmed his desire for a broader concept of international trusteeship at San Francisco, despite certain concessions in the name of military security in the Pacific. He joked with Taussig about the Navy's concerns not only about trusteeship but also the entire proposed United Nations organization. On the question of administering territories he told Taussig that neither the Navy nor the Army "had any business administering the civilian government of territories."

FDR also expressed his hope that the British were moving in the direction of more liberal policies under people like Stanley whom he thought was "more liberal on colonial policy than Churchill." And so it went, FDR assuring Taussig that his position on trusteeships and colonial issues were the same as ever.

At the same meeting he agreed to include Taussig in the San Francisco delegation as an advisor because he felt Taussig would be "extremely useful on matters pertaining to negotiations on colonial matters."[40]

Taussig lived up to the trust Roosevelt placed in him. In the debates over the establishment of the United Nations trusteeship system may be observed early signs of subsequent bitter disputes over the decolonization of the European empires and the increased tendency to cooperate with the colonial powers rather than stand as a champion of anti-colonialism. There had been efforts from the military to keep the issue of trusteeships from coming up at all in San Francisco, though this had little support, including from Stettinius.

After a number of compromises on the structure of the Trusteeship Council, the critical issue was the determination of the true purpose of trusteeship. Should it clearly and explicitly aim toward independence? The American delegation was divided. One key delegate, the Republican Harold Stassen whom Roosevelt had included as part of his bipartisan effort to gain support for the United Nations organization, took the position that the word "independence" was provocative, and that "self-government" would be sufficient. "If one goes beyond that phrase," declared Stassen, "there was danger that we would be interpreted as butting in on colonial affairs."[41] Taussig, who had already expressed himself several times in writing to Stassen, was the chief advocate of the opposite view and pushed for the inclusion of an express commitment in the UN Charter to move toward independence for all colonial territories. He maintained that to repudiate it would be nothing less than a repudiation of the ideals of Franklin Roosevelt. On 18 May he circulated a memorandum stating several reasons for supporting the goal of independence for all colonial peoples. It included his concerns that the Soviet Union would be able to capitalize on the refusal of the United States to do so and suggested collaboration with the old colonial powers. He went on to declare that independence "as a goal for all peoples... has been the traditional and sacred policy of this Government... it has been reiterated on numerous occasions by President Roosevelt." He added it would also be a gesture on "behalf of the peoples of the Orient as well as those in Africa and the Caribbean."[42] It was a powerful statement, but the battle was lost at least for now in San Francisco.

Soon after returning from California Taussig met with Eleanor Roosevelt at her apartment in New York; she was interested to hear the "inside story of the Trusteeship fight." He told her how little influence the memory of FDR seemed to have with the US delegation, but that it "had much influence with the delegations of the smaller countries." She wasn't surprised and offered to help with opinions in her columns and radio program.[43] It was the sort of issue that she would incorporate into her greater struggle for human rights during the public career in her own right that she was just beginning. She remained in touch with Taussig, though his increasing isolation in the Truman administration was evident.

It is clearly possible only to speculate on how different the postwar world might have been had Roosevelt's hopes been fulfilled. Most likely his pragmatic side would have led him to modify his anti-colonial stance in view of strategic considerations and the speed with which the colonial world was subjected to nationalist explosions in one territory after another. It is tempting, however, to believe that Roosevelt would have remained as basically committed as ever to the principles he so long maintained, especially his belief in the right of all peoples to choose their own form of government. Roosevelt had learned much about the colonial question around the globe during the war, in part through the prism of the Caribbean. He almost certainly would have tried to place the United States more forcefully on the side of nationalist movements demanding independence. We know what did happen. We know that as the tensions of the Cold War intensified in the months and years following San Francisco the United States was increasingly stigmatized by both the Soviet bloc and the new, developing nations as but another colonial power, determined to maintain the status quo wherever possible. The fears and paranoia of the postwar world led the United States into the contradictory policy of avowing support for colonial independence while often simultaneously propping up the old colonial powers. In the Caribbean the United States provided ambivalent and selective support for West Indian independence. Puerto Rico, of course, remained American.

VII. Coda

In May 1946 Rex Tugwell drove with Charles Taussig to Hyde Park for the simple ceremony at which Eleanor Roosevelt turned over the estate to the Department of the Interior as a national monument and for the dedication of the new presidential library and museum, the first of its kind. Tugwell had resigned as Governor of Puerto Rico, and was soon to move to a new teaching post at the University of Chicago. In a description of the day written soon afterward he reflected on memories of when both he and Taussig had been guests at Hyde Park. He wrote of their discussion of various times spent with FDR and how weightier matters had been apt to be mixed with the trivial, with speculation about the way the world was going, and how FDR's "comments on the past brought out of that strange rich miscellany with which his mind was stocked."[44] Their conversation turned to how Roosevelt's many critics had charged that he was confident beyond his capacities. They agreed on his great confidence, but they saw it as one of his most profound strengths:

> Even the issues that faced him, and about which he was not able to find a policy, never kept him from feeling confident those solutions would turn up. He felt so much at one with history, so much the agent of benign progress, that even mistakes were not great worries. The average would be good. And I heard him suggest more than once that mistakes might have their uses too.[45]

"The average would be good." Do-gooders. Operating according to the virtuous principles that the United Stated has always claimed for itself. Such an enterprise can lead to serious mistakes

in foreign policy, but are they more serious than those committed in the name of realism and expediency? Roosevelt made
mistakes of both sorts, but the grand sweep of his vision was
founded in that sense of himself as an agent of humane progress
for all the peoples of the world. It was a vision shared by many
of those around him who, like Tugwell and Taussig, regarded
themselves as officers in his army during his lifetime and advocates of his legacy after his death. It was, of course, also the vision
of Eleanor Roosevelt, perhaps the most clear-eyed and effective
international do-gooder of her time. With perhaps only slight
hyperbole Kofi Annan has referred to The Universal Declaration of Human Rights, adopted by the General Assembly in 1948
which owed so much to her leadership, as "a yardstick by which
we measure human progress."[46] She and her small group seized
the moment in the fading glow of the Roosevelt vision to give
it universal form that may eventually be seen as one of the most
benevolent achievements in human history.

Notes:

1. Bernard Sternsher, *Rexford Tugwell and the New Deal.* (New
    Brunswick [MI Rutgers University Press, 1964), 322-23. Tug-
    well did not remain with the company long, returning to
    public service as head of the planning department of the New
    York City Planning Commission where he remained until he
    briefly became Chancellor of the University of Puerto Rico
    in 1941 before his appointment as governor later the same
    year. Tugwell had studied at the University of Pennsylvania
    where he was influenced by one of his economics professors,
    Scott Nearing, who later became one of the nation's most in-
    fluential radical thinkers. As assistant secretary of agriculture
    under Secretary Henry A. Wallace Tugwell played a major
    role in drafting the Agricultural Adjustment Act of 1933. In
    1948 Tugwell supported Wallace's bid for the presidency.
2. In the months following FDR's death the new president,
    Harry Truman, corresponded with Eleanor Roosevelt

about numerous subjects, including the feasibility of locating the new United Nations headquarters next to the Hyde Park mansion on the Rogers estate that had been leased by the War Department during the war. See Truman Correspondence, 1945-60, Eleanor Roosevelt Papers, Franklin D. Roosevelt Library (FDRL), Hyde Park, NY, Box 4560.

3. Tugwell was amused that the leading brand of Molasses made by his new employer was "Grandma's", with the slogan "Look for Grandma on the Can." The label, now owned by Mott, Inc., was acquired in 1982 by Cadbury Schweppes. For another account of how FDR saw his role after the war see Warren F. Kimball, *The Juggler: Franklin Roosevelt as Wartime Statesman* (Princeton: Princeton University Press), 100.

4. Although Taussig has been described as "the White House's leading adviser on colonial issues," his name infrequently appears in the published literature on FDR and decolonization. See, for example, Paul Orders, "FDR and European Colonialism" in David Ryan and Victor Pungong, eds. *The United States and Decolonization* (New York: St. Martin's, 2000), 76.

5. Jim Bishop, *FDR's Last Year* (New York, William Morrow, 1974), 535-40. For his personal files Taussig wrote a memo of his conversation with Mrs. Roosevelt in which he commented on the timing of their meeting and its coincidence with events in Warm Springs. See "Memorandum of Conversation at the White House with Mrs. Roosevelt 3 pm to 3:30 pm in the Red Room, April 12, 1945," Taussig Papers, FDRL, Box 66.

6. The most important single study of this question remains William Roger Louis, *Imperialism at Bay: The United States and the Decolonization of the British Empire, 1941-1945* (New York: Oxford University Press, 1977). Other major contributions to the discussion of Roosevelt's thinking on colonialism are Kimball, *The Juggler*, especially the essay (with Fred E. Pollock) "'In Search of Monsters to Destroy': Roosevelt and Colonialism" and the essays in Ryan and Pungong, *eds., The United States and Decolonization.* For an economic inter-

pretation of New Deal diplomacy see Lloyd Gardner, especially his *Economic Aspects of New Deal Diplomacy* (Madison: University of Wisconsin Press, 1964).

7. There are many studies of the Good Neighbor Policy; one solid and irreverent example is Fredrick D. Pike, *FDR's Good Neighbor Policy; Sixty Years of Generally Gentle Chaos* (Austin: University of Texas Press, 1995). For the use of the Good Neighbor Policy as a model see "Baffled Virtue… Injured Innocence': The Western Hemisphere as Regional Role Model" in Kimball, *The Juggler,* 107-125.

8. For general studies of Caribbean history in a wider context see Stephen J. Randall and Graeme S. Mount, *The Caribbean Basin: An International History* (London: Routledge, 1998) and Robert F. Smith, *The Caribbean World and the United States* (New York: Twayne, 1994).

9. Lord Moyne [Walter Edward Guineas, 1st Baron Moyne], *West India: Royal Commission Report* (London: HMSO, 1945).

10. Fitzroy Andre Baptiste, *War, Cooperation and Conflict: The European Possessions in the Caribbean, 1939-1945* (New York: Greenwood, 1988), 51-61. Also see Philip Goodhart, *Fifty Ships that Saved the World: The Foundations of the Anglo American Alliance* (New York: Doubleday, 1965).

11. Aubrey Williams, who was closely identified with the New Deal's Left Wing, headed the National Youth Administration. It was committed to racial justice and developed a special Negro program headed by Mary Bethune. Mrs. Roosevelt took a special interest in its work

12. Memorandum concerning the Caribbean Commission. No date, but handwritten notation, "Memo sent to President," Sep., 1940—also Sec. Hull, Taussig Papers, FDRL, Box 35.

13. Draft letter from Sumner Welles to Roosevelt, 24 Oct. 1941, FW844,00/7-1244, Decimal Files, Department of State (USDD), National Archives, Washington, DC. The Commission was formally created on 9 March 1942. The only book-length account of the work of the AACC and its suc-

cessor organization remains Bernard L.Poole, *The Caribbean Commission: Background of Cooperation in the West Indies* (Columbia: University of South Carolina Press, 1951).

14. Recommendation of AACC, First Meeting of AACC, 26-31 March 1942 (typescript) Taussig Papers, FDRL, Box 33. Also file on "Radio" in Box 34.

15. Copy of Memorandum left by the Prime Minister with the President on 14 January 1942, 844.00/26, USSD.

16. Letter from. Taussig to Roosevelt, undated but marginally noted 22 June 1942, Taussig Papers, FDRL, Box 34.

17. Ibid.

18. Cordell Hull, *The Memoirs of Cordell Hull* (New York: Macmillan, 1948), 1234-37.

19. Memorandum of Conversation with Cordell Hull, 30 Nov. 1942, Taussig Papers, FDRL, Box 46.

20. The lyrics are from the Irving Berlin musical *Annie Get Your Gun* that opened at the Imperial Theater on May 16, 1946.

21. The American comedian Morey Amsterdam wrote the lyrics to the pop song cited here. They tell the story of the new Americans on the islands, especially the G.I.s and their romances with the locals. The refrain is: "Rum and Coca Cola/ Rum and Coca Cola/ Workin' for the Yankee Dollar". For an innovative study of the impact of race on American foreign policy during World War II see Justin Hart, "Making Democracy Safe for the World: Race, Propaganda, and the Transformation of U.S. Foreign Policy," *Pacific Historical Review,* 73 (February 2004): 49-84..

22. Letter from Taussig to Roosevelt, 22 June 1942, Taussig Papers, FDRL, Box 46.

23. Eric Williams, *Inward Hunger: The Education of A Prime Minister* (Chicago: University of Chicago Press, 1971), 81.

24. Ibid, 84.

25. Ibid.

26. Warren Kimball, ed. *Churchill and Roosevelt: The Complete Correspondence,* 3 Vols. (Princeton: Princeton University Press, 1984), 2:156-57. Quoted in Jon Meacham, *Franklin and Winston:*

An Intimate Portrait of an Epic Friendship (New York; Random House, 2003), 214.

27. Franklin D. Roosevelt, *The Public Papers and Addresses of Franklin D. Roosevelt, with A Special Introduction by President Roosevelt, 1944-45* (New York: Random House, 1938-50), 68, quoted in Louis, *Imperialism at Bay*, 357.

28. Jason Berger, *A New Deal for the World: Eleanor Roosevelt and American Foreign Policy* (New York: Social Science Monographs/Columbia University Press, 1981), 36.

29. Two standard works on Puerto Rico are Raymond Carr, *Puerto Rico: A. Colonial Experiment* (New York: Vintage, 1984) and Gordon Lewis, *Puerto Rico: Freedom and Power in the Caribbean* (New York: Harper and Row, 1963). For Rexford Tugwell's long involvement with Puerto Rico see his study written soon after stepping down as governor, *The Stricken Land: The Story of Puerto Rico* (New York: Doubleday, 1947) and Francesco Cordasco, ed., *Puerto Rican Public Papers of R.G. Tugwell* (New York: Arno Press, 1975). The last is a reprint of the 1945 Government of Puerto Rico edition.

30. For a critical study of the history of United States relations with Latin America since the American Revolution see Lester D. Langley, *America and the Americas: The United States in the Western Hemisphere* (Athens: University of Georgia Press, 1989).

31. Cordasco, *Puerto Rican Public Papers*, 8-9.

32. Ibid.

33. Letter from Tugwell to the President, 3 November 1941, President's Secretary's File, FDRL, Box 48. As governor Tugwell reported directly to Harold Ickes.

34. Letter to Rex [Tugwell] from the President, 7 November 1941.

35. For an excellent examination of American influences on the emergence of West Indian nationalism see Cary Fraser, *Ambivalent Anti-Colonialism: The United States and the Genesis of West Indian Independence, 1940-1964* (Westport [CT]: Greenwood, 1994).

36. Memo of conversation with Secretary of State Stettinius, 16 April 1945, Taussig Papers, FDRL, Box 66.

37. Memorandum for the President: The Forthcoming Conversations with Colonel Stanley, British Secretary of State for the Colonies, 13 January, 1945, FW844.00/1-134, USSD.

38. Ibid.

39. Ibid.

40. Memorandum of conversation, President Roosevelt and Mr. Taussig, 15 March 1945, Taussig Papers, FDRL, Box 52.

41. Louis, *Imperialism at Bay*, 535. Also see Memorandum, Taussig to Commander Stassen, 1 May 1945, Taussig Papers, FDRL, Box 66.

42. Louis, *Imperialism at Bay*, 537.

43. Memo of conversation with Mrs. Roosevelt at her New York Apt, August 27, 1945, Taussig Papers, FDRL, Box 521

44. Tugwell, *The Stricken Land*, ix. Abe Fortas, an old New Deal hand, accompanied Tugwell and Taussig when they drove to Hyde Park.

45. Ibid.

46. Brian Urquhart, "Mrs. Roosevelt's Revolution," review of Mary Ann Glendon, A *World Made New: Eleanor Roosevelt and the Universal Declaration of Human Rights* (New York: Random House, 2001) in *The New York Review of Books*, 48, (April 26, 2001):7.

William B. Wisdom, Sr. and Jr.
A Letter and a Reminiscence

John R. Pleasant, Jr., Class of 1960

SOON AFTER THOMAS Wolfe died on September 15, 1938, William B. Wisdom, a New Orleans advertising man and book collector, initiated a correspondence with Maxwell E. Perkins regarding the purchase of Wolfe's literary estate. Enamored with Wolfe's prose in *Look Homeward, Angel* (1929), Wisdom had collected the author's work throughout the 1930's and had visited with Wolfe during the latter's trip to New Orleans in January 1937.[1] Perkins, Wolfe's literary executor and chief editor at Charles Scribner's Sons, had served as editor, mentor, and confidant for not only Wolfe but also F. Scott Fitzgerald and Ernest Hemingway. Both Wisdom and Perkins agreed that Wolfe's literary materials should be kept intact and preferably donated to a university. Wisdom purchased the estate for approximately $3000 in 1940, and Harvard University's Houghton Library accepted the donated materials in 1946.[2]

By 1943 the correspondence between Wisdom and Perkins regarding the disposition of Wolfe's literary corpus had become sufficiently intimate that the two men exchanged family photographs. On June 14, 1943, Perkins, father of five daughters, returned Wisdom's pictures, expressing feigned jealousy over Wisdom's six-year-old son, Bill Jr.: "I am returning the pictures with envy and covetousness. I think your daughter is a most charming-looking girl, and one can see right off that she is unusual in imagination and intelligence. As for the boy, I won't mention him."[3] Fifty-three years later I would like to "mention" that "boy," my late college fraternity brother, William B. Wisdom, Jr., and share an insightful letter I received from his father in July 1964. In that letter he speculates on Wolfe's connection to the Nashville Agrarians and on the reasons for the Wolfe-Perkins professional separation.

I graduated from Washington and Lee University in 1960 with a B.A. in history and was privileged to be a Beta Theta Pi fraternity brother of Bill Wisdom from 1956 until his graduation in 1958. In those days W&L was an all-male school with about ninety-five percent fraternity membership, made necessary by the absence of dining facilities and of housing, except for a freshman dorm. Most Louisiana boys during the 1950's sought haven in the Beta house, located across the street from Lee Chapel. We Louisiana Betas, close to a dozen in any given year, were defined against our more "preppy" brothers from the North and East; but among the Louisianians a slight cultural gap also existed between the somewhat provincial Shreveport (my home town) and Monroe "good old boys" and the more sophisticated New Orleanians. Bill belonged to the latter group, but his leadership ability, combined with his natural warmth and wit, allowed him to transcend regional differences and be elected president of our chapter his senior year.

Legend has it that when Robert E. Lee was president of Washington College, from 1865 till his death in 1870, a student asked him-for a book of rules. His reported reply was that "We have but one rule here, and that is for every man to be a gentleman."[4] Although I did not know Bill well personally and admired him from a distance, I can say that he epitomized, in every respect, the Washington and Lee "gentleman."

What I remember as most characteristic about Bill was his central place in every fraternity "bull session" of an intellectual nature. In the sessions I attended I don't recall references by him to Wolfe, but I did hear about his admiration for Hemingway, especially the latter's heroic code. When William Faulkner spoke at Lee Chapel on May 15, 1958, he invited questions after reading from *The Town*, the last novel in his trilogy about the notorious Mississippi Snopes clan. Bill Wisdom revealed his knowledge of Southern writers that day by asking Faulkner how, despite his criticism of the South, he accounted for the wealth of good writers from that region. Faulkner's drawled and dry reply was to this effect: "Well, I don't know about the other states, but in Mississippi there's so many folks who can't read I guess some of us have to write."[5] All of the Beta brothers had nicknames in those days. Bill's moniker was "Rughead," inspired by the somewhat matted texture of his hair. Mine was "Rocky," a name brought to Lexington by my Shreveport brothers who would not let me forget my brief amateur boxing career, which came to an abrupt halt when I was knocked out in thirty seconds of the first round by a lefthander. A mutual friend of Bill's and mine is Campbell C. "Hutch" Hutchinson III, from Shreveport, a Beta brother, classmate, and former law partner of Bill's. A testament to Bill's modesty is that "Hutch" told me recently that, to his knowledge, neither he nor his classmates at W&L in the 1950s knew of the famous Wolfe-Wisdom-Perkins connection. Many of us did know of Bill's prominent uncle, John Minor Wisdom, judge of the U.S. 5th Circuit Court of Appeals in New Orleans, who would soon render landmark desegregation rulings in Louisiana at some risk to his personal safety.

After his graduation from W&L, Bill received an M.B.A. from the Wharton School and a law degree from Harvard. He then returned to New Orleans to begin a distinguished but all-too-brief career as an attorney, investment counselor, and civic and social leader. After several years of law practice, Bill organized and became president of his own investment company, The Boston Company of New Orleans, Inc. He also served as chairman of the executive committee of the board of directors of the First National Bank of Commerce of New Orleans, served on the board of directors of several other businesses, held leadership positions in medical and environmental civic organizations, and belonged to prominent social clubs. Wisdom died tragically of cancer on May 26, 1981, at age 44, just four years after his father's death. Mr. Thomas G. Rapier, president of First National Bank of Commerce, eulogized his colleague in the New Orleans *Times-Picayune* the next day: "He was an outstanding man. I relied on him very heavily for advice."[6] It is indeed tragic that Bill died so young. It is also a pity that his death coincided with the inception of the Thomas Wolfe Society. As a well-read, cultured man, he would have surely been proud to see his father's legacy carried to fruition; and, just as surely, he, like his sister Adelaide, would have contributed significantly to that legacy.

I entered graduate school in the L.S.U. English Department in September 1962, after eighteen months of extended "Berlin Crisis" duty in the U.S. Army. Because of my undergraduate history major, I had English hours to make up and was unable to take a seminar from Dr. Lewis P. Simpson on Southern literature, my main interest, until spring 1964. Having been born a month after Wolfe's death and claiming "Tar Heel" paternal ancestors, some from Asheville, I suppose that I romanticized a personal Wolfe connection and chose his relationship to the Nashville Agrarians as the subject for my term paper, which Dr. Simpson suggested I expand for my required M.A. thesis.

Needless to say, as soon as I began serious Wolfe scholarship, I discovered my fraternal connection with the son of the man responsible for preserving Wolfe's literary estate. That summer I wrote Bill explaining my research project and inquiring about the possibility of a contribution from his father to my thesis. The full and cordial response I soon received from the senior Wisdom exceeded my expectations. Not only did he offer his views on the Agrarian relationship; he also speculated about the Wolfe-Perkins split and even invited me to his home to peruse his *Table Talk of Thomas Wolfe*, which the Thomas Wolfe Society published in 1988.

Mr. Wisdom's comments in his letter are indeed insightful.

In retrospect, however, I wonder if his emphasis on the political differences between Wolfe and both the Agrarians and Perkins might have been colored by the heated rhetoric of the Goldwater–Johnson presidential race that summer, as well as by a Republican tradition in the Wisdom family. Wisdom's opinion that Wolfe considered the Agrarians "precious" is supported by Wolfe's satire of them in *The Web and the Rock* as "the refined young gentlemen of the New Confederacy" (242). I doubt, however, that Wolfe saw them as "half-baked socialists, smeared with the blood of bleeding hearts." (I'm sure that World War I vets John Crowe Ransom and Donald Davidson, author of *The Tall Men* and *Lee in the Mountains*, and pugnacious Allen Tate would have considered those as "fighting words.") In fact, Thomas A. Underwood, in his thorough treatment of the Wolfe-Agrarian relationship, finds a note in the novelist's diary suggesting that Wolfe saw their ideas as fascistic: "the Allen Tates, etc. want a form of high-toned fascism which bears the high-toned name of Southern Agrarianism" (38).[7] Wisdom's explanation of the political differences leading to the professional split between Wolfe and Perkins, however, is an accurate summary of Perkins' letter to Wolfe on January 16, 1937. In that letter Perkins explained his objections to Wolfe's attempt in the 1930s to impose social consciousness on his autobiographical persona during time periods chronologically disparate from Wolfe's own politcal awakening *(Editor to Author* 122). William B. Wisdom's kind letter to me of *July* 27, 1964, follows:

Dear John:

Bill has handed me a copy of your letter of July 5 in which you speak of your work in English literature at L.S.U, toward an M.A. and the subject of your thesis which is Thomas Wolfe and his relationship to the Nashville Agrarians.

I fear that I share the generally accepted attitude that Wolfe was not influenced by this School. I believe that

Wolfe regarded that group as "precious" from a literary standpoint and half-baked socialists, smeared with the blood of bleeding hearts. I think that Wolfe regarded their outlook as immature and their output as jejune. I agree with you that Wolfe was too complex to ever be categorized within one literary movement.

At the time of Wolfe's own life described in the pages of *Look Homeward Angel* and *Of Time And The River*, one can discern very few socialistic tendencies or political awareness. His heart bled at evidences of poverty and at the struggle of earnest young students striving to get an education. These were simple reactions with no political overtones. Often as an instructor in New York, these same faces and bodies irritated the hell out of him.

There are no socialistic feelings in the Wolfe that went up to his friend's house on the Hudson where he was amazed and pleased at the opulence of the manner of life, the magnificence of the kitchen and the abundance of the viands. In that section there is a derogatory reference to Franklin Delano Roosevelt under the name of Frank, before he became President, in which the father of Wolfe's friend speaks of the views and ideas of this neighbor named Frank.

In my opinion, the main reason for the break between Wolfe and Maxwell Perkins lay in the fact that after publication of the first two books, Wolfe, now in his late twenties and early thirties was beginning to have real social consciousness. He wanted to introduce this feeling into *The Web And The Rock* and *You Can't Go Home Again*, both composed of biographical material of prior years in which social consciousness in a political way had never troubled him, Perkins objected to this. Perkins said, "look Tom. You did not feel that way in the time period covered by these books. You happen to feel that way now. It would be wrong for you to superimpose these current views of yours upon the mind of Eugene-Monk Webber.

Wait until you are writing about these last four or five or six years in which your views have changed, and then introduce the social consciousness into these new books that lie ahead, because they will cover the time period in which these views developed." Wolfe did not agree with Maxwell Perkins and thought Perkins was trying to influence his political views and utterances in novel form because of Perkins' natural hard-core conservatism.

Believe me John, I had no idea of getting mired down in such an explanation of a point only tangential to your thesis. As far as letters or conversations go, all the letters I collected are at Harvard and my personal conversations with Wolfe are covered by a very hastily written, sloppily written, subjective monograph of about 20,000 words, which I call "The Table Talk of Thomas Wolfe." This opus covers just about everything that Wolfe said when I was with him during the eight days he stayed in New Orleans. I have a copy of it which I will be happy to have you examine at my home, but not outside, if you would care to look at it.

I don't know how much I could tell you about Wolfe that has not been already said in the spate of biographies, critical evaluations and reminiscences which have been published.

If you do come to New Orleans I shall be very happy to make an appointment convenient to both of us and talk as long as you like.

With best wishes, I am,

Sincerely,

William B. Wisdom

WBW: rd

P.S. I am trusting only to memory but it seems to me that you may obtain some of the material you are looking for out of Maxwell Perkins' book, *Letters To An Editor*. [*sic*]

Two days later I received a follow-up letter from Bill, in which he sent greetings from "Hutch" and encouraged an early visit to New Orleans because his "Pop" was leaving town for three weeks that August. He expressed his hope that *Table Talk* would "enliven" my thesis but thought that his father's letter was only a "partial answer to some of your questions." That phrase suggests to me that Bill sensed a deeper connection between Wolfe and the Agrarians, one going beyond political ideology.[8]

As I recall, I mailed a polite declination to Bill's invitation. I had a two-week National Guard encampment scheduled for August and was also planning my wedding for the first week in September. I can now say that there were other personal reasons for my not actively pursuing the opportunity to meet with William B. Wisdom. I probably felt something like the "provincial complex" of my undergraduate years; and, at that stage of my professional career, I did not really feel competent to carry on a "literary" conversation with a person of Mr. Wisdom's stature. But over the past thirty-two years, I have frequently regretted my missed opportunity of engaging in "table talk" about Thomas Wolfe with those two distinguished representatives of an exceptional family.

Notes

1. For Wisdom's account of that visit, see *The Table Talk of Thomas Wolfe*, published in 1988 by The Thomas Wolfe Society, edited with an introduction by the late John S. Phillipson and a preface by Wisdom's daughter, Adelaide Wisdom Benjamin.

2. For a full account of Wisdom's negotiations with and impressions of Perkins and the Wolfe family, see William B. Wisdom, *My Impressions of the Wolfe Family and of Maxwell Perkins*, ed. Aldo P. Magi and David J. Wyatt (Athens, Ohio: The Thomas

Wolfe Society, 1993). In their "Foreword," the editors pay this tribute to Wisdom: "Had William B. Wisdom not acquired and subsequently donated Wolfe's literary remains to Harvard University, Wolfe scholarship and research and, quite possibly, the Thomas Wolfe Society, would not exist today, at least in the form that they do" (i).

3. Maxwell Perkins to William B. Wisdom, June 14, 1943, *Editor to Author: The Letters of Maxwell E. Perkins* (New York: Charles Scribner's Sons, 1950), 223. The "daughter" Perkins refers to could have been Wisdom's daughter Elizabeth or his daughter Adelaide Wisdom Benjamin, who has contributed so much to the Thomas Wolfe Society.

4. This legend is, to my knowledge, undocumented but receives credence in this passage from Ollinger Crenshaw's *General Lee's College: The Rise and Growth of Washington and Lee University* (New York: Random House, 1969): "Of the many changes in the College during the Lee regime, probably none was more significant or lasting than the permanent imprint of the general's own character upon the institution. A gentlemanly, lofty code of conduct replaced the narrow regulation of an earlier era" (156-57).

5. Frederick L. Gwynn and Joseph L. Blotner, in *Faulkner in the University*, record Faulkner's visit to W&L as "Session Thirty-Five," 281283, but omit this question and response.

6. "William B. Wisdom, Jr. dies; rites today." New Orleans *Times–Picayune* 27 May 1981, 3.

7. In retrospect, Wisdom can be forgiven some confusion as to the Agrarians' purpose. As John L. Idol, Jr., has noted, after Wolfe met several Agrarians at an MLA conference in Richmond in December, 1936, he expressed confusion about their identity in a letter to Dixon Wecter (March 1937): "In fact I did almost everything except become a Southern Agrarian. I suppose I don't know enough about that" (3). Perhaps the clearest statement of the Agrarians' purpose is by Louis D. Rubin, Jr., in his "Introduction" to the Torchbook Edition of *I'll Take My Stand: The South and the Agrarian Tradition*. Rubin says that their book is "not a treatise on economics; it is not a guide to political

action; it is not a sociological blueprint. It is a vision of what the good life can be" (xv).

8. Thomas Underwood has fully explored the differences and similarities between Wolfe and the Vanderbilt group. Wolfe, says Underwood, rejected what he perceived as their cultism and "dangerous political ideology" (38); they disliked Wolfe's apparent rejection of his Southern heritage and his unstructured, autobiographical, epic impulse (37). But their "common denominator" was "his and their view that mindless progress led to anomie…" (38)

A passage which I think places Wolfe squarely in the Agrarians' "spiritual camp" occurs at the end of *Of Time and the River* when Eugene has a deja-vu experience in the town square of Dijon, France. The square evokes the sights and sounds of his Altamont boyhood, and he contrasts "the quiet, leafy streets and little towns of lost America" to "an America that had been lost beneath the savage roar of its machinery, the brutal stupefaction of its days, the huge disease of its furious, ever-quickening and incurable unrest…" (898).

Works Cited

Crenshaw, Ollinger. *General Lee's College: The Rise and Growth of Washington and Lee University.* New York: Random House, 1969.

Gwynn, Frederick L. and Joseph L. Blotner, Eds. *Faulkner in the University: Class Conferences at the University of Virginia, 1957-1958.* Charlottesville: UP of Virginia, 1977.

Idol, John L., Jr. "Wolfe in Richmond: A Great Story That Never Happened" *The Thomas Wolfe Review* 10:2 (1986): 3-4.

Perkins, Maxwell E. *Editor to Author: The Letters of Maxwell E. Perkins.* Ed. John Hall Wheelock. New York: Scribner's, 1950, 1979.

Rubin, Louis D., Jr. "Introduction." *I'll Take My Stand: The South and the Agrarian Tradition.* By 12 Southerners. New York: Harper and Row, 1962.

Underwood, Thomas A. "Autobiography and Ideology in the South: Thomas Wolfe and the Vanderbilt Agrarians." *American Literature* 61:1 (March 1989): 31-45,

Wisdom, William B. *My Impressions of the Wolfe Family and of Maxwell Perkins.* Ed. Aldo P. Magi and David J. Wyatt. The Thomas Wolfe Society, 1993.

Wolfe, Thomas. *Of Time and the River.* New York: Scribner's, 1935.

—. *The Web and the Rock.* New York: Harper and Row, 1939.

A Teacher of Olympian Stature

Richard Hoover, Class of 1961

WHAT FOLLOWS IS taken from my boyhood, my Army days and from my early Foreign Service postings. I hope it will give young aspirants some flavor of life abroad in the service of the United States.

Dr. Jenks is responsible for much of what made these little tales possible. After all, his teaching determined where I wanted to live (I served at eight military and diplomatic posts abroad), how I was to make my living (by diplomacy), how I was to look at things and, in many cases, what I was to remember. I learned it is possible, for example, to wring historical value even from the ordinary events that unfold right under one's nose!

He also imparted his passion for medieval and baroque architecture, to the point that I have photographed hundreds of churches, inside and out, as he did, and lectured on them.

I tried hard to make my life a continuation of Freshman European History, of Medieval History and of Renaissance and Reformation History—the three Jenks courses I took at Washington and Lee. In vain, I strove to match his elegance, eloquence and understated humor.

For us students, Dr. Jenks was a teacher of Olympian stature. I have no idea whether the best of the Olympians know the profound impact they make upon the young and, in time, upon the old. Maybe it's not important that gods know such things. Nevertheless, his old students want him to know.

In Shaker Heights, Ohio, I belonged to a gang of heartless little squirts. Tormenting Mr. Brown was their stock in trade. Mr. Brown drew the scrutiny of little boys because: (A) he was very short and, in fact, appeared something of a milquetoast; (B) he had a fancy accent; (C) living up to his name, Brown always dressed in browns and (D) the Browns cherished their front garden and didn't want little folks tramping on it.

As Mr. Brown walked home from work, the boys pelted him with snowballs. They switched to water bombs in summer. I was deeply puzzled by Brown's total self-control. How could he not help but chase down one of those little bastards and shove him, head first, into a snow bank?

Years later, over a Washington and Lee spring break, I was put on edge to learn that the Browns were giving a cocktail party and I was invited.

Shrinking with embarrassment, I entered Brown's house for the first time. There he stood, grinning and dapper in an elegant jacket and paisley ascot. He thrust a whiskey in my hand.

I escaped to the library only to find a room filled with cased military decorations. Ancient propellers and fragments of airplane canvas hung on the walls. Some bore painted iron crosses and death's heads, Edith entered. Sensing my amazement, she asked: "Why, Richard, didn't you know?"

"Know what, Mrs. Brown?"

Suddenly, between my ears, things started coming together: Brown's slight physical stature, his fondness for brown clothing, his cultivated accent, his phenomenal self-control and, even—as I had just witnessed—his ascot and jaunty manner. Also taking shape, for me, were several big lessons about making judgments!

"Know what, Mrs. Brown?"

"In the Great War," she said, "David was one of Canada's most decorated aces."

In early '62, straight out of Washington and Lee University, I arrived in Ulm, Germany, for a two-year R.O.T.C. stint as an armored rifle platoon leader. One evening, I wandered into a watering hole near the Cathedral. The dark, paneled interior was pure Wilhelmine. Old Nazis sat around drinking—something special for this European History major.

Next morning, I told Old Top, Company First Sergeant William Taylor, about this historically evocative pub. "Lieutenant Hoover," he said, "an officer doesn't belong in that dump. It's not only dangerous, it's off-limits."

"Top," I said, "relax!"

I returned April 20, and struck up a conversation with a middle-aged man whose face suggested he had once lived a hard and wintry life out-of-doors.

"*Herr Leutnant,*" he said, "do you know what today is?"

I didn't.

"It's the *Führer's* birthday."

Casting Hitler as a poor, misunderstood genius with a few "unfortunate enthusiasms," he declared that the *Führer* had only wanted what was good for Germany.

While he rambled, eight of the largest lads I ever saw came through the door, wearing *Lederhosen*, suspenders and little alpine hats. The neck of one seemed nearly the circumference of my own waist. They escorted a fabulously beautiful blond in a frilly, scarcely-buttoned Mozart blouse. All sat down on one side of the long *Stammtisch*—the table reserved for the family of the proprietor.

"*Und Herr Leutnant,*" the old fellow blew on, "let us never forget that the *Führer* built the *Autobahn*, put Germans back to work and, you know, restored our pride in being German."

But, looking past his shoulder, I beheld seven or eight Turkish workers, *Gastarbeiter*, coming through the door. Dark, with moustaches, they had one thing in common with the Germans, across from whom they took places at the *Stammtisch:* they, too, were strapping lads. I also thought: these fellows don't know what they're doing; they don't belong at the *Stammtisch.*

The old man then dilated upon the *Führer's* great love of animals and the tragedy for us all that he had never had children of his own, to have assisted him and curbed his "unfortunate enthusiasms."

At this point, I observed one of the Turks rise slightly off the bench in order to obtain a better view, straight down the *Mozartbluse.* The blond glanced to the lad on her left. In a flash, he brought down his beer stein—right on top of the offender's head. Germans and Turks dived for each other over the table.

Following what, I bet, was ancient custom, loungers in the rear began breaking bottles on the edge of the bar—only time I'd seen that outside of the movies.

Stepping on blood and beer, over bodies, I ran into the night, thinking: Old Top certainly knew what he was talking about.

Returning several nights after the *Führer's* birthday, I walked through a doorway with no door. In the dark, I could see plaster walls. I was standing on a dirt floor. The Hitler pub no longer existed.

For me, this event had been a close personal call with the authorities, mine and theirs, and served as excellent instruction in the swift and cataclysmic consequences of law-breaking in a foreign land!

In 1970, a junior Foreign Service Officer, I arrived at Embassy Bonn, assigned to the Four-Power Negotiations on Berlin. In June, I was tapped to substitute for the vacationing chief of Consular Affairs. His parting advice: "Should Americans pose problems, get them out of your consular district and pointed toward the United States; problems solved!"

Taking this on board, I thought: What can ever happen in sleepy Bonn, the smallest U.S. consular district in the world?

The consul wasn't gone two hours when the phone rang. Americans were getting out of hand at the airport. I raced over to find 300 students, part of the some 10,000 who had been stranded in Europe when World Academy Tours went belly-up. A few yards away, a 747 was cooling its jets, so to speak, wondering when it might take off.

I stood on a chair in the departure lounge and listened to the roar of angry young people. Diddled out of their European tour, as they saw it, they refused to board the plane which World Academy Tours, in its dying throes, had just managed to provide in order to get them home. They were heated and growing surly (this against the background of a raging war in Vietnam and the previous month's Kent State massacre). They said their parents had taught them to think for themselves. They knew their rights: either the tour continued, or they got their money back!

Standing on the chair, I observed about twenty smiling and overly-large Nordrhein-Westfalen cops reeling through the lounge door, nightsticks in clenched fists. I remembered what I had seen at the old Hitler pub. I remembered the advice of the American Consul: "get them out of your district!"

If I couldn't do that, if they missed the plane and were stranded, the Embassy would be tormented forever by parents and congressmen demanding the full range of consular protective services. Believe me, to the State Department mind, such a prospect is nearly as horrible as bloodshed itself! It looked like I was about to get both!

TRULY INSPIRED, I called for silence and gave the speech of my life: "My Fellow Americans: You think you're standing on the United States Constitution here. In fact, you're not standing on anything. This is Germany, for Christ's sake. You have no rights. And what do you think these fellows in the green jackets and white caps are about to do with those sticks? Now," I said, "get your ass on the plane!"

And they did.

In the Foreign Service, foreign language proficiency is nearly everything. I spent a year studying Czech at the Foreign Service Institute under Jiri Cernik, a brilliant refugee from Communism. We even took up profanity. An elementary example: a man on the Prague street might utter a "Jesus!" when pressed. If more than pressed he might cry: "Jesus-Mary!" Only in extremis, I learned, when all was lost, might one hear a complete "Jesus, Mary, Joseph!" In three years, as we shall see, I heard the full rendition only once.

As it turned out, Cernik became a fellow Civil War enthusiast. We took field trips—once to Harpers Ferry and Charlestown, and once to Antietam. I explained it all to him, in Czech of course. Those were school rules. Cernik even bought a Remington cal. 44 Black Powder Army revolver. I taught him how to load and care for it—all in Czech.

But, for the life of me, I couldn't say, in Czech, "Never, ever, rest the hammer on the percussion cap." As a result, Cernik fired the last shot of the Civil War. It blew a hole in the holster and buried itself in his right leg. He told me later, in Czech of course, that he had not known what to do first: tend to his wound or put out the fire in his pants.

You must know that, even as American Consul in Prague, age 33, I was still a baby. Notably, I had known hardly anyone, near and dear, who had actually died. In my gut, I almost believed, as I prayed, that none of mine ever would. By extension, I dreaded the thought of being called upon to break the news of the death of a loved one.

I would have made it safely through but for an American tourist who dropped dead in a Prague department store the last week of my consular assignment. The Czech police telephoned the bad news and provided the hotel where the deceased's wife was believed to be. And you must know that, even in 1974, we were growing accustomed to using the term "Ms." when addressing ladies.

A lady answered the phone cheerily. "Helloooo."

"Ms. Smith?" I asked.

"Yeeees," she sang in reply.

"This is Richard Hoover, the American Consul in Prague. I have very sad news concerning your husband, Charles. He passed away this morning in the Central Department store."

The poor lady screamed and sobbed. Breaking such bad news was just as unsettling as I always imagined it would be.

Then, collecting herself, she said: "Mr. Hoover, I am Charles's sister. Mrs. Smith has just walked in the door. Let me pass you to her."

To my horror, for this first time, I found I not only had to break the bad news once, but twice!

American tourists to Czechoslovakia received an entry visa stamped right in their passport. A separate exit visa, stamped on a little chit, was paper-clipped to the passport. Without the exit visa, one simply could not leave the country.

Friday, closing time; a New England schoolteacher showed up at the consular section in tears. She had lost her exit visa and was prevented from boarding her flight home. She had no hotel vouchers and no cash (credit cards were a thing of the future). Nor could we raise her family in the U.S. via long distance. And, unfortunately, a dead beat tourist had failed to repay his loan, thus depleting the slush fund which every consular officer keeps in his safe, just for the purpose of helping innocents in distress. How could I protect this gentle lady?

So, I brought her home for the weekend. Home Care is the consular officer's last resort, a palpable admission that he lacks the resourcefulness, influence and funds to protect his countrymen. We had a large dinner party that night and my disgrace, sweet as she was, was there for all my colleagues from other embassies to see.

Worse, I had to throw myself on the mercies of Dr. Cervenka, Chief of Consular Affairs at the Ministry of Foreign Affairs. He was about the most America-hating Communist imaginable.

For example: when President Nixon resigned, I was instructed to inform Dr. Cervenka that it was business as usual in Washington. Instead of keeping his mouth shut or, even, commiserating, Cervenka gratuitously offered that a Watergate disaster could never happen in the Czechoslovak Socialist Republic inasmuch as the people so loved and trusted their leaders!

Monday morning, sitting with my schoolteacher in front of Dr. Cervenka, I asked for immediate issuance of a new exit visa. Smiling, he replied that the paperwork might take some weeks. Getting excited, I pointed out that the damn thing was only held in by a paperclip and was easily lost. Cervenka shot back that the procedures of his government were none of my concern. I gave back that, in the United States, nobody needed an exit visa anyway, that anyone could leave at anytime!

Cervenka suddenly stood up and went right to the schoolteacher. "May I?" he asked, picking up her enormous handbag and dumping its contents on the top of his desk. After rooting around in the pile, and flashing one of his malevolent grins, Cervenka triumphantly held aloft the missing exit visa.

This was the low point of my entire Foreign Service career, a self-inflicted humiliation caused by my lack of thoroughness.

I feel sure the Old Communist Boy's Club still meets regularly and that Cervenka, justifiably, has told this story many times.

I transferred from consular to political affairs at a time when "Human Rights" was becoming the Washington watchword.

Accordingly, I tried for months to obtain an interview with the Deputy Minister for Religious Affairs in the Ministry of Interior. Essentially, this fellow presided over religious persecution in Czechoslovakia and was my personal nominee for Antichrist.

But there were other problems: I could not get our maid, Jana, to quit packing, for lunch, the most revolting mayonnaise-laced, under-cooked egg salad sandwiches. She put them in little brown paper bags. I sometimes threw them in my briefcase just to get them out of the way.

Finally, on my return to Prague from several weeks' vacation, I received hearty congratulations; I had ten minutes to get over to Interior—the appointment with the Antichrist had just come through! I grabbed briefcase and notepad.

He was a tough guy, a chain smoker with dark lines all over his dark face. He puffed away as we talked. I brought up appalling examples of his Ministry's crackdown on religious believers. I asked why he didn't leave these harmless people alone. Why, I asked, did clergymen need permission to travel outside Prague, and why were they forced to register their every whereabouts with the Ministry?

The Deputy Minister replied that he knew me to be less than respectful of Socialist institutions. But even I must recognize that everyone in Czechoslovakia had rights, including the right not to believe in God, to enjoy one's atheism in peace. Therefore, unbelievers had to be protected against wily clerics who, if unregulated, would run amok. He pointed wearily to a large stack of case files. Many of these, he said, documented "unspeakable" instances in which priests had actually tried to convert small children and other innocents to Christianity!

Clearly, I wasn't making much headway with the Antichrist. When I stood up to go, I opened the briefcase to toss in my note pad. Exposed were all of Jana's egg salad sandwiches, a-moldering. The office filled with vile, sulfurous gas. The Antichrist blurted out in shock: "Jesus, Mary and Joseph!"

In '76 I flew straight from Prague to Gaborone, Botswana, in southern Africa. The head of state was Sir Seretse Khama, one of the best and wittiest men I would ever meet. I was asked to accompany Sir Seretse to the Fair Grounds to view the National Youth Exhibition of Arts and Crafts. We marched from booth to booth, inspecting baskets, walking sticks, jewelry, textiles and the like.

At the Francistown District booth we were met by the parliamentary deputy from Francistown, who was also Minister of Education. The display was very substandard; aluminum Coca-Cola cans whose sides had been slit so as to produce various shapes when stomped upon by little boys and girls.

President Khama looked displeased and muttered something in Setswana. Turning to me he said: "I was just complimenting the Minister of Education; of all the displays at this show of primitive arts and crafts, those from his District are the most primitive."

When I was chargé d'affaires, Sir Seretse returned from the first conference of the "Front Line States"—those countries directly bordering apartheid South Africa. His participation was bold, considering that land-locked Botswana depended on the Republic of South Africa for the necessities of life.

A massive airport welcome was planned. Schools were let out and Ambassadors and chargés lined up, on an enormously long red runner, to greet the hero. When Khama appeared at the airplane door, thousands sent up a deafening cheer. Sensing something familiar, I turned around, and was bowled over by a sight to warm the heart of any One-World champion: there, squashed flat against the barricade, were my four children, all in their blue school uniforms, screaming at the tops of their little lungs and waving madly the blue, white and black flag of Botswana!

Not long after, some 20 troopers of the Botswana Defense Force were gunned down, ambushed by the Rhodesians. It was a national calamity. The Embassy requested a condolence message from President Carter.

Obtaining presidential condolences was far from certain. In

1977-78, many in Washington saw Rhodesia and South Africa as bulwarks against Communism. Many felt that antagonizing these star importers of American goods was not good for business, not worth the loss of a single American job.

With the funeral moments away and no message having arrived, our chargé d'affaires, Frank Alberti, left the Embassy for the cemetery, empty-handed. I stayed behind, just in case. An hour later, the clerk ran out of the message center waiving a message from the President. With car and driver, I raced to the cemetery. It was sweltering, well above a hundred.

We drove up to the rear of the dense crowd. Hysterical girls were legion, some rolling in the tall grass, others stacked up in first aid stations—casualties of heat and of emotional turmoil. Some would attempt to throw themselves into open graves, to be interred with the slain soldiers.

A full 10,000 surrounded the speakers' platform. From the periphery, I could see Sir Seretse, flanked by diplomatic representatives. The Soviet Ambassador was reading from a sheet of paper. Frank appeared to be next in line and he, of course, had nothing.

Resolved to push my way to the front, I charged several times straight into the crowd. It was hopeless.

Determined, I waived my telegram and yelled: "Help! I have a message from the President of the United States of America."

At this, I was picked up bodily and passed, hand over hand, to the front. As I traveled, I could now hear the Soviet Ambassador running on about international worker solidarity with the Defense Force and with the bereaved families. Over to the left, I could see the 20 coffins ready for burial, each topped with the blue, black and white, a photo of the deceased, a military cap, and an Enfield automatic rifle. Sailing over the heads of thousands, I was handled with respect, even tenderness.

Just as I was deposited on the platform, feet first, Sir Seretse turned to Frank. "Mr. Alberti, what comfort do you bring us from Washington?"

"Frank, here it is."

Back in the State Department, as Officer in Charge of Berlin Affairs, my Soviet Embassy counterpart paid a formal call to complain about a truly nasty incident. I met him at the Diplomatic Entrance. I was in the "Why can't we all just get along" frame of mind. This was normal for those of us charged with protecting Berlin. After all, the Allied Berlin garrisons were hopelessly outnumbered by surrounding Soviet and East German divisions.

When I gushed how nice and quiet things had been, and downplayed the "little misunderstanding" which was bringing us together, the Soviet just laughed. Moscow, he said, might decide to make "a real rumpus just so the Americans in Berlin won't get stale!" He was enjoying that little joke.

I waved him through my office door. Instead of taking a visitor's seat, he walked right over and sat down behind my desk. Here was a threatening picture: the drooling Russian bear sitting behind the State Department's Berlin Desk, a provocation if there ever were one. What could I say and remain conciliatory? I had no idea. I quickly racked my brains. Nothing! And then the words came, Divinely inspired, I later thought:

"Bapic (that's Boris)," I said, "Get your ass out of my chair!" He leapt up.

In the fall of '83, some months after we arrived on Cyprus, the Turkish Cypriots declared independence by forming the Turkish Republic of Northern Cyprus. This blunted Greek Cypriot hopes of returning to their homes, businesses and hotels in the northern part of the island. The Greek Cypriot army was mobilized. Passions soared. This was on a Friday.

Saturday, I was tooling around the Turkish Cypriot north in the back of an old Land Rover, trying to figure out what the hell was going on. With me were officials from the suddenly-created

Turkish Cypriot Ministry of Foreign Affairs. A full Colonel, the Military Attaché from the suddenly-created Embassy of Turkey, was also along. He was a tough cookie and everyone's adrenaline was flowing.

Out of the blue, the Colonel proclaimed that, back in 1821, old Kyprianos had really had it coming.

I couldn't believe my ears. Kyprianos was the Archbishop of Cyprus who, together with all his bishops and about 400 others, had been garroted, strung up on his own palace gates by the Ottoman authorities.

I suddenly remembered I had first learned of this heinous act as a graduate student, sitting in the famous course on Orthodox Church History taught by Dr. Glanville Downy at Indiana University. Ah, I reflected, another proof of the value of a liberal arts education! As Downy described the gruesome details, two students, both nuns, crossed themselves.

The Turkish Colonel continued that if other Ottoman governors had been as smart—*i.e.* had hanged all the Orthodox prelates and priests they could find—"we wouldn't be in this mess today!"

Choking with emotion, he wheeled about and looked straight at me. "Hoover," he said, "when you go back south, tell your friend, Lysseridies"—that was the Turkophobe leader of the opposition Socialist Party, who had just called for an invasion to recapture the North—"tell your friend, Lysseridies, to do it now. You see, I'm going back to Ankara in two weeks. Please, Richard," he begged, "tell him to invade now. I don't want to miss it!"

That was the mood on Cyprus when, Sunday morning, Embassy Athens phoned up. "Hoover, take cover! You're all over the papers, tagged as the CIA Chief for the Eastern Mediterranean, the architect of Turkish Cypriot independence, and the man who advised Denktash (the first Turkish Cypriot President) how to bring it off!"

Believing I was good as dead, I asked myself: "Why me—a perfect innocent?!"

Monday morning, the Greek Cypriot papers headlined the

Athens story. Colleagues, even a few from other embassies, turned up at the political section to lend moral support. As they filed past my desk, I had the peculiar sensation of lying in state. Was that a slight smile playing on the lips of a colleague, the one who would move up if anything happened to me? Yes, I believe it was.

I went to the one Embassy officer who was paid to take this kind of heat and asked for his advice. He recalled that, a few years earlier, a nasty story had been published about his deputy. That young man, his wife, children, pets and household effects were out of Nicosia, and back in Washington, within 48 hours.

"Of course," he added, "the guy was a real p__y!"

I was determined not to be remembered that way!

Eventually, it all came out in the wash: years before, at a former post, I knew a powerful and vindictive diplomat. Back in his capital, he became even more powerful. As coincidence would have it, I married the woman who happened to have been the love of his life. Like I said, I was a "perfect innocent!"

Apparently, planting stories in the press was the only way the poor fellow knew to have us all rubbed out.

Lads from the Embassy's Marine Security Guard Detachment bunked at the Hoover home. It all blew over in a month.

But other dangers cropped up to threaten the Embassy and our homes.

Trying to head-off the likelihood that Islamic countries would recognize the infant Turkish Republic of Northern Cyprus, the Greek Cypriot Government opened itself up as a rest and recuperation spot for Palestinian guerillas and other fractious groups. Often, these wound up fighting each other.

One of their houses was located about three doors behind the Hoover home. One night, about three, there was a wrenching explosion. By the dim night-light I could see my beautiful wife, Catalina, asleep on her side, perfectly straight, with head gently resting on folded hands. All was normal, but for the fact that she was levitating nearly three feet in the air!

Dr. Jenks, thank you for everything!

A Reminiscence

Jack Vardaman, Jr., Class of 1962

I am happy to participate in this project to honor Dr. Bill Jenks. Thinking back to his classes over 45 years ago brought back many memories. It caused me to reflect on the importance of what we learned, and how we learned, in Dr. Jenks' classroom and how it has impacted my life. Writing this has been a long, pleasant trip down memory lane.

I had never visited Washington and Lee before I entered in 1958. My arrival could not have been more different than the way freshmen arrive today. Most have had extensive college tours before deciding on W&L and afterwards they arrive with parental escorts who make sure that they are comfortably situated in spacious dorms. I, on the other hand, arrived at the Lexington bus station around midnight the first week of September 1958. My trip started when I hitched a ride with a friend from my home in Anniston, Alabama to Chapel Hill, North Carolina. From there, I boarded a Greyhound for the remainder of my journey. Once in Lexington, I trudged up the hill to the only dorm on campus, then the Freshman dorm, and found a bed for the rest of the night before locating my assigned room the next day.

I was not well traveled before entering Washington and Lee.

There had been no trips to Europe and only a couple above the Mason Dixon Line. One, however, was important, in a strange way, to my decision to go to W&L. I was a budding young golfer and in 1957 qualified to play in the National Jaycee Junior golf tournament, held that year in Columbus, Ohio. It was the biggest junior tournament in the country and the clear favorite was Jack Nicklaus, already a golf phenomenon. The rest of us wanted a look at him to see if he was as good as they said. I played a splendid opening round and tied for the lead—two shots better than Nicklaus, producing a prized press clipping: "Vardaman 73, Nicklaus 75". But Jack was the real thing and he went on to win the tournament. After watching him play, with his towering tee shots and deftness around the greens, I knew my future lay not on the golf course. My father was a lawyer and I had always thought that if I didn't make it as a golfer, I would practice law. I remember telling myself after seeing Nicklaus that "it's law school for you, old boy." So instead of pursuing a golf scholarship at one of the Florida powerhouses, I decided to come to Washington and Lee—and how lucky for me.

While I felt prepared for college before I arrived, I can still recall a certain shock at its demands once I was there. I knew little about Europe and nothing about its history. But the freshman curriculum included a full year of European history—History 1, European Civilization 1500-1815; History 2, European Civilization 1815-present—and it was there that I had the good fortune to encounter Dr. Jenks. During the year I not only learned about this new world, but I began to appreciate what an impact a single professor could have in generating an interest in a subject. Dr. Jenks made the history of Europe come alive. He also made his students want to learn it. Because of him, and only because of him, I decided to major in history and concentrate on European history.

I had no classes from Dr. Jenks my sophomore year, and I must say that my other professors suffered by comparison. Junior year, I had him for the French Revolution and Napoleon in the fall and the History of the Islamic Peoples in the spring. I wish that I could recall his observations about Islamic history. I wonder how differently that course is taught today.

What I remember most about Dr. Jenks, however, is not so much what he taught but how he taught. Despite our status as lowly and naive freshmen, he taught as if we were sophisticated in the ways of the world and budding Phi Beta Kappas. He lectured with a crispness and precision that foreshadowed his expectations of us at exam time. Surely, he must have been bored to teach an introductory survey course to freshmen, but you would never have been able to tell it by his work. He conveyed that his expectations of you were high—higher than your own—and that if you failed to meet them, you were wasting his time and your potential. His ability to motivate and challenge students was a wonderful quality, and one that transcended the subject matter of his classes.

To this day, over 45 years later, I can still remember one day on which I did not meet his expectations—clearly, it had a lasting impression. We had a "quiz" that covered several hundred pages of reading. The last two pages of the material concerned a discrete subject, unrelated to all that had gone before. My recollection is that the topic had not been covered in class. I paid little—more likely no—attention to those pages in preparing. But when the quiz came, there it was, bigger than life, a short question about nothing other than the two pages. I had no idea what to say. I could not even think of how to make anything up. The best that I could do was to convert the question into a declarative sentence and rephrase it a time or two. When the paper came back, in Dr. Jenks's distinctive handwriting was the phrase "Practically nothing here" and he could easily have omitted the "practically". They say that it is not uncommon for people to have dreams —nightmares—about facing exams for which they are totally unprepared. I don't know what causes other people to have such dreams, but for me the cause has always been clear—Dr. Jenks's "quiz" about those last two pages. But it taught me a valuable lesson—one that I obviously have never forgotten.

My senior year, Dr. Jenks was off to Vienna to continue his research and writing. While we missed him in the classroom, we were proud of his work and his publications.

I also saw Dr. Jenks occasionally at my fraternity house—Sigma Nu. That had been his fraternity when he was at W&L and he was, as I recall, our faculty "advisor." However, he showed the good judgment to keep his distance and to show up only for special occasions and with plenty of advance notice. One of my fraternity brothers and good friends, Jack Barnes, two years my senior, was one of Dr. Jenks's best and favorite students, and Dr. Jenks had no bigger fan than Jack. Barnes made sure I appreciated my good fortune in having Dr. Jenks as a professor.

Looking back after all these years, I would have thought that I had Dr. Jenks for more than four courses. And that is surely because his influence extended far beyond what was taught in the classroom. He taught you to appreciate the past, to study hard, to learn and understand it. And he motivated you to meet the high standard that he set for himself and his students.

When it came time to apply to law school, I needed a faculty reference for the University of Virginia. While it would have been much more convenient, and easier, to secure the help of a professor on campus, I wanted Dr. Jenks weighing in on my behalf. So I wrote to him in Vienna and asked if he would provide the necessary recommendation. He did, and confirmed that he had done so in a letter to me dated 27 May 1962, which I have kept all these years and which is attached.

Clearly, this is a communication from a different time. It was typewritten on onionskin paper, no doubt to save on air postage, and punctuated with strikeouts and strikeovers. Hopefully, this letter will bring back to him pleasant memories of his stay in Vienna, his strolls through the parks and the freedom from, as he says, "the inevitable paperwork and strain of everyday preparation." Those were burdens of teaching that were little known and little seen by us as students. Dr. Jenks always spoke in perfect paragraphs and one had the feeling that his lectures were coming straight from a deep reservoir of accumulated knowledge that he maintained at his fingertips. Like the great ones in any field, he made hard work look easy.

He refers in his letter to hearing "all too much from Washington and Lee... even trans-Atlantic telephone calls on occasion." The reason, he says, is to "stay somewhat *au courant* to protect one's interests, which have a way of getting lost in absentia." To this day, I wonder how the interests of a professor such as Dr. Jenks could get "lost in absentia". But I suppose it would be naive to think there were not issues and disputes in academia then, even though they might involve the school's all-stars. Today, we hear a lot about the teacher-scholar model and a lot of debate about whether scholarship comes at the expense of teaching or adds to one's teaching ability. There was no question where Dr. Jenks came out on the issue. As he said to me, "I do think that a sabbatical is a good idea for men who are interested in research and writing, and I trust more of my colleagues will take time off in the future."

I don't recall that I heard from Dr. Jenks again—not the 99 questions he mentioned in his letter—but knowing him, they would have been good ones. His letter was very important to me at the time, much more than just a confirmation of a reference. I am happy to have kept it. Perhaps to a historian, it will seem of recent vintage, but I doubt that today many of us have correspondence that old. And, of course, with e-mail, cell phones, and text messages, people simply do not write letters like this anymore.

Despite Dr. Jenks's help at Virginia, I chose Harvard Law School and entered in 1962. It was as different from W&L as day is from night. W&L was at the time a small, quiet, Southern, homogenous, genteel and conservative school. Harvard, on the other hand, was big, loud, hyper-competitive and diverse, at least among white males. (There were few African Americans in our class of 550 and only the quota of 25 women.) It was filled with academic all-stars. I will never forget my seat-mate in one class who was raised in Brooklyn, and who, I am sure, found my southern accent as hard to understand as I did his Brooklyn dialect. The professors were frequently "in your face" and made most of us think that it would be a miracle if we survived their class and graduated. But I told myself frequently that if I could meet Dr. Jenks's standards at W&L, I could make it at Harvard.

After law school, I served as a law clerk for one year to Justice Hugo Black of the United States Supreme Court, one of the real giants of the judiciary. Then, I began to practice law in Washington, where I have been now for 41 years. Most of that time has been at the firm of Williams & Connolly, founded by Edward Bennett Williams, one of the great trial lawyers of our lifetime. So I have had the good fortune to work with two of the giants in the field of law.

Justice Black was not only a great Justice and Ed Williams not only a great trial lawyer, but they were, like Dr. Jenks, great teachers. The methods of each may have differed, but they all had a passion for their work and a personal commitment to excellence. One thing I learned from all three is that there are no "naturals" who do it on talent alone. The best combine natural talent with passion and prodigious work habits. These men were not only twice as smart as their colleagues, but they also worked twice as hard, and I know that they enjoyed their hard work. That is undoubtedly what Dr. Jenks was referring to in his 1962 letter when he said that the "strain of every day preparation" kept him from "look[ing] at the mountains around Lexington." These men taught by example and they taught you to strive for excellence. They made you believe that anything less than your best was unacceptable. I was fortunate to have learned that at W&L and to have had the lesson reinforced many times over.

I am happy now to be reconnected with Washington and Lee in several ways. I serve on the Board of Trustees, a labor of love, and an eye-opening experience as one gets a good look at what it takes to run a University. I also have as a second home in Hot Springs, Virginia, the house where Letitia Pate Evans, one of W&L's largest benefactors, lived for many years and where, legend has it, Dr. Gaines traveled to enlist her support for the school. The Evans Dining Hall was built while I was at W&L,

but I refer to the dining room at my house in Hot Springs as the "original" Evans Dining Hall.

When I come back to Lexington for meetings and approach the campus from Red Square, it looks no different than it did when I entered in 1958 and probably no different than when Dr. Jenks was a student. But one look at the new buildings behind the Colonnade reveals that the University has not been stagnant, but has kept pace with change and moved into the future. Just as the physical campus has changed over the years, so has the student body. But what is comforting is that change and progress have not disturbed the core of the school. It is a place dedicated to academic excellence where students govern themselves and all live under a strict code of honor. And it remains a school where the administration is dedicated to the identification, recruitment, promotion and support of faculty members like Bill Jenks. Long after the specifics of a particular course have faded from our minds, we remember, and hopefully honor, the standards he set. Dr. Jenks took us, as he said in his letter to me, as "lowly freshmen" and sent us off into the world prepared for full and productive lives. For that we are forever in his debt.

December 2006

Wien IX
Hörlgaße 11 Austria
27 May 1962

Dear Jack,

My long silence did not mean that I failed to write to Virginia (with toes crossed in the hope that Harvard would be smart enough to admit you). Surely your destiny is now known (even the Honors orals must be ended), and I do hope that all went as you wanted it to go.

With only four more weeks to stay in this apartment, I suddenly realize that I have collected a lot of material, though certainly less than I expected. Cynics among my Austrian friends assure me that I can return again and again, especially in time for the big June musical and theater events, but I honestly do not enjoy this city, or any other city, when the heat waves begin. It is bad enough to go to Durham, where the stacks at least are air-conditioned, to continue collecting what I need.

Naturally I have missed those of you in the senior class whom I enjoyed teaching when you were but lowly freshmen and later, but I have also missed—pleasantly—the inevitable paper work and strain of everyday preparation. I do not feel guilty strolling leisurely through a park here, whereas I rarely even look at the mountains around Lexington. So I do think that a sabbatical is a good idea for men who are interested in research and writing, and I trust more of my colleagues will take off in the future.

I am glad to know that the house did well in rushing, and I suppose you are now collecting manes [*sic*] for the autumn. I hesitate to mention a fine young fellow from Texas Military Institute, whose father was a Sigma Nu with me and who turned down Harvard for W&L, for I feel the letter would get lost in the Finals confusion. I will write the rush chairman later, for this young man was quite a leader at TMI and probably will be one at W&L. Mr. Gilliam wrote to implore me to use my influence to get him and said that he wanted him above all others who were applying.

I hear all too much from Washington and Lee, believe me, even transatlantic telephone calls on occasion. But I suppose it is wise to stay somewhat au courant to protect one's interests, which have a way of getting lost in absentia. There is much I should like to quiz you about, but possibly I shall drop you a list of 99 questions after you graduate. I have always respected your ideas, and I think it is time to collect the opinions of some of our recent majors regarding the Honors work, curriculum within the department, and the like. Mr. Hughes will still be around when I get back in August, so we possibly will confer on this. He looks forward to his interesting year away, of course, and I really admire his pluck in taking on such assignments at such fine schools.

Give my best wishes to Mrs. Spence and to those who know me in the house. Also to the senior majors and others who were in classes with me.

Again, the best of luck on Law School.

As ever,
W. A. Jenks

Dr. Jenks at Commencement.

Falling Short on Internationalization

H. Laurent Boetsch, Class of 1969

THE OPPORTUNITY TO help "found" a liberal arts college as I have been doing over the last three years is, in many ways, the culmination of a life spent within the confines of liberal education beginning with my undergraduate days listening with rapt attention to the likes of Bill Jenks teaching us about Russian history, or learning a foreign language, or engaging in the fundamental questions posed by philosophers, or meeting the challenge of how literature articulates the human condition, or why art is necessary to our well-being. Since then I have spent a professional lifetime in the classroom and in administration taking an active role in preserving what for me remains the supreme form of education, that is, the on-going conversation that takes place between a mentor and a student. This conversation, not just for the sake of transmission of knowledge, although that is a part of it, but rather as the fundamental building block for shaping lives worth living distinguishes liberal education from training and, if it is to occur, it occurs best in small institutions dedicated to bringing together members of a community for the sole purpose of learning from each other. In a personal way and probably owing to my own experience, I am committed to the notion that this learning is most effective when the widest possible variety of points of view are represented in the discussion. This commitment, in turn, has led me to think of international education as a fundamental vehicle for expanding the scope of the conversation.

Distance has provided me the opportunity to reflect on the relationship between liberal education and the current wave of "internationalization" of small college campus and what follows is a simple articulation of that reflection.

Falling Short in Internationalization

In so many ways the aspirations for liberal learning have always assumed that educated students must be brought into contact with ideas, beliefs, systems, and habits beyond their own experience. Standard definitions of liberal arts that speak of freeing the mind or liberating the intellect through the notion of broadening one's horizons beyond the parochial are common. In the past this has often meant exposing students to the conversation among "great" minds within "great" books, or by providing an education in or toward other cultures, or by focusing on what were thought to be the "universal" ideas and issues. Invariably this liberation has been effected through the study of classical philosophy, world literatures, comparative religions, and art histories. This type of classical liberal education prevailed long before the age of obsession with outcomes and assessments and, although little attempt was made to measure the success of such learning, it was generally recognized that this form of worldly education was in contrast to scientific or technical training and occupied a legitimate domain within higher education. The realization of the objectives of this form of education was in some sense "global" and, in some important ways their modest fulfillment may have surpassed many of our contemporary efforts,

In recent years we have witnessed an explosion of activity aimed at providing for students more opportunities to adopt a global outlook as part of their undergraduate education. Much time and energy have been dedicated to finding ways to internationalize our curricula, expand study abroad programs, and attract international students to our campuses. Goals and objectives have been outlined, grant proposals submitted, admissions materials prepared to demonstrate how any college can really be the center of the world. Our measurements suggest progress in terms of numbers of students studying in foreign lands or majoring in disciplines with significant international components. Liberal arts colleges express new confidence in responding to the demands of parents and students and employers for educating toward the world. Yet as we listen to our students in their discussion, as we evaluate their work in the classroom, as we help to advise them toward their futures, and as we confront the continuing challenges of student life outside the classroom, there is among some of us a certain unease, a persistent sense that our efforts at linking the values of the liberal arts with aggressive global education have fallen well short of our expectations. Important questions emerge that demand our attention. In what ways are whatever major differences we note on our campuses over the past twenty years and the attitudes of our students today attributable to our efforts to internationalize the curriculum? Is there evidence that high percentages of our alumni are approaching their worlds beyond graduation armed with a perspective significantly shaped by our internationalization efforts? Is student thinking about the problems and values we claim to engage as the heart of liberal education in fact shaped by internationalization? Why might it be that, in the view of some at least, the impact of our efforts to date has yet to approach our anticipation for its success?

It may be that over the last generation, as liberal arts institutions have increasingly turned their attention to providing opportunities for students and faculty to broaden their international horizons, our initiatives have too often clashed with a potentially crippling tension between the pressure exerted by contemporary trends in liberal arts education and our own missions. Although all colleges speak convincingly about the breadth and depth that four years of liberal arts provides for students, that which has traditionally distinguished a liberal education has been the quality of the *breadth*. That quality is best defined and achieved only to the degree that the general education components of our curricula are coherent, comprehensive, and fully integrated into the whole four-year undergraduate experience. For a variety of all too familiar reasons, however, many colleges are seeing their general education programs—the "breadth" part of the equation—erode against the onslaught of the perceived need for utility and training, for more focused disciplinary work, for more research time for teachers and even undergraduate students, for more internships and practical experience that will help build our students' resumes. How often do our students ask us about how best to get their general education requirements "out of the way", and how willingly do we tell them? How readily do we facilitate their access to a major by waivers and advanced placements, thus allowing them to sidestep what should be their most challenging and rewarding courses in a liberal arts curriculum? These questions are important because the fact is that in too many cases, the commitment to internationalize a curriculum has responded more to a similarly perceived need to succumb to the demands of utility and specialization than to a desire to strengthen the goals and objectives for the kind of coherent general education that is possible only within the small liberal arts environment. Perhaps even more subversive has been the attempt to provide discrete, unconnected foreign "experiences" for our students rather than marvelously new, directed opportunities for reflection on the very problems and values we claim to address as our liberal arts missions. Our efforts to internationalize our schools ought to derive from our desire to deepen the value of what we do best, that is provide our students with the kind of education that prepares them to lead good lives. Instead, we ask departments to develop courses designated as "international", not according to institutional goals for our general education mission but to the more narrow objectives of a disciplinary major. We send our students off to foreign study semesters knowing that for most of them just being there is likely to be positive but with very little preparation about the kinds of questions they should be posing, how to examine contrasting sets of values and customs, how to take maximum advantage of being abroad by engaging in all that *cannot* be done on the home campus. When they return, rather than trying to integrate that experience into an enrichment of our campuses and classrooms by consciously channeling their energy and enthusiasm back into academic and student life in the meaningful ways that our general education objectives suggest, we tend to give passing recognition to their time away and ask them to plunge back into fulfilling the requirements for graduation. As a consequence, our efforts at internationalization are too often fragmented and dispersed rather than a coherent and comprehensive. Rarely does "internationalization" represent a central manifestation of our general education core.

Finally, we have tended to confuse "international" studies with "area" studies. For too long we have been satisfied that a student's engagement with another culture, its language, history, and customs, suffices to broaden adequately that student's point of view and serves as a life-changing lesson in learning about others. Yet no matter how immersed even the most serious student in the most demanding program abroad, that experience will not necessarily translate into a productive "international" experience. The best international schools are integrating students from many countries, native languages, and experiences in a common intellectual labor that will truly educate them in viewing the world that they are about to lead from an international perspective. These students are not tucked away in "international houses" on their campuses. They are most often having to work and use their second language, English, even though the school may be located in Germany or Slovakia; and the schools are not content with a quantitative measure that predicts that every student on campus will share a class with at least one international student and therefore be exposed to a diverse viewpoint. International schools and serious international programs are building for the future but understand the vast complexity of globalization and the importance of an essential integration of internationalization in every aspect of their curricula.

If we are dissatisfied with our own efforts, it may well be because we have failed to understand that, in order to bring about a transformation of our campuses through internationalization, we need to make a commitment of a magnitude greater than we have been willing to assume. Rather than serve as a source from which we might re-define a liberal arts education for the twenty-first century, internationalization has too often become another adornment like our fitness centers or the new student union, a competitive necessity but not truly at the heart of our purpose. Often internationalization is posed as a means to "transform" a curriculum, but if it is to succeed to such a lofty goal, it is time that we fully recognize both the enormous, untapped potential in our campus communities and the full range of consequences that such a transformation might realize.

Reflections on Robert E. Lee

A. Cash Koeniger, Class of 1971

IN THE SPRING of 1870, Robert E. Lee made an extended tour of the South. The purpose was to rest up from administrative chores as president of Washington College and to restore in some measure his rapidly failing health. From that standpoint, the trip was a failure. Lee found little rest, and he would not live out the year. But from another standpoint, the trip was a triumph. From Virginia to Florida, he was met by huge, enthusiastic, adulatory crowds. Clearly Lee had emerged from the war as a hero second to none in southern hearts; and if the trip did his worn-out constitution more harm than good, as it probably did, it must have gratified the aging general to learn of the esteem and indeed the love in which he was held by so many. Years later, one who had been a young girl at the time of Lee's visit remembered his appearance as the highlight of her life. "We had heard of God," she said, "but here was General Lee!"

For a little over a hundred years following his death, Lee held an enviable position in American historical literature and in the American mind. He <u>was</u> almost a deity. He had been the only Confederate commander to win battles consistently. Almost invariably, he had won against long odds, in the face of a foe not only significantly more numerous but also better fed, better equipped, and better supported by artillery. On the rare occasions when he didn't win, he was either let down by sub-ordinate commanders or overwhelmed by impossible numbers. Tactically he was audacity personified, attacking when according to the book he should have retreated, dividing his smaller force to surprise and defeat the enemy and dazzle historians. And he made it work. With Jackson at his side, Lee had been invincible; even without Jackson, he was the Civil War's best general. To be sure, a handful of critics, such as the British military historian J. F. C. Fuller, dissented, but their views were all but engulfed by the near consensus of writers favorable to Lee—foremost among them, by the 1930s, the masterful Douglas Southall Freeman.

Even better, Lee was a class act. He was character personified; he was the essence of character; "Lee" and "character" were prac-tically redundant words. Only the great and magnanimous Lin-coln rivalled—perhaps transcended—Lee as the war's ultimate hero. As noted, his status approached that of a saint, or even something higher, in the South; more surprisingly, he was widely acclaimed in the world as well. He was an American hero.

Given the fact that among historians one well trod path to success and renown is to turn conventional wisdom upside down, it is perhaps surprising that the Lee consensus lasted as long as it did. In fact, it lasted until the late 1970s and the publication of Thomas L. Connelly's *The Marble Man*. According to Connelly,

> Lee's greatness, while real to some extent, had been much exaggerated in the late nineteenth century and into the twentieth by a "Lee cult" of manipulative Virginia writers, who had made the Confederate chieftain larger than life to further their own agenda—including the advancement of Washington and Lee University.

Connelly was a native Tennessean and a well-established his-torian of the war in the West. Manifestly he found it unfortunate that Lee and his home state had exercised the influence they had, both within the Confederacy and in the postwar literature.

Connelly also criticized what he called Lee's "repressed personality." He deplored the fact that Lee had spent much time and conscious thought nursing an "obsession" (a word which appears in *The Marble Man* frequently) with God, duty, and a better life to come in the hereafter—when he could have been, shall we say, having fun. Thus did Lee fall victim in the swinging 1970s to what might be called a Freudian interpretation, in which his very virtues were viewed as defects. Connelly opened a floodgate. In the past three decades, it has become the height of fashion among Civil War historians to bash Bobby Lee. Perhaps the pinnacle to date of this iconoclastic literature is *Lee Considered*, by Indianapolis attorney Alan T. Nolan. Appearing in the early 1990s, this book amplified another of Connelly's themes, and before that one of Fuller's: the notion that, as a general, Lee bled the South to death with a purposeless offensive strategy—what Nolan called "the grand strategy of attack"—when it should have been obvious to Lee, as it is to Nolan, that the "strategic defensive," conserving irreplaceable human resources, was the Confederacy's only hope of winning.

Nolan did not stop there. He criticized the pre-war Lee for endorsing "the common property theory" regarding slavery in the territories—the idea that the territories belonged to all the states, and that every citizen of every state had the same rights in every territory as in his home state. "This superficially plausible concept meant that slavery was exempt from majority rule and the will of Congress. It would spread regardless of the views of a majority of the people of the United States." Nolan failed to add that this "superficially plausible concept" was not Lee's pet theory but the judgment of the United States Supreme Court as declared in the Dred Scott decision. As such, it did trump "majority rule and the will of Congress"; but Supreme Court decisions work that way. To saddle Lee with blame on this point seems ahistorical—he is apparently culpable because he did not share the point of view of the Republican Party on slavery in the territories, but what Southerner did?—and is symptomatic of how Nolan interpreted a variety of other things.

Elsewhere *Lee Considered* argued that if Lee was truly opposed to secession, as he consistently stated in prewar correspondence, he should have spoken out during the secession crisis in the arena of Virginia politics (an arena in which he never spoke in any capacity in his life) in order to use his allegedly significant political influence to prevent Virginia from seceding; that a shady deal had already been made between Lee and Virginia authorities for high command when Lee resigned his U.S. colonelcy in April 1861; that Lee was as capable of shady deals as the next fellow, because honor was merely "Lee's word for what he wanted to do and what he had in fact done"; that because Lee fought on after he doubted seriously the chance for Confederate victory, he bears "personal responsibility" for the physical wreckage of the South and the lives lost on both sides in the closing months of the war. Finally, Lee's image as a postwar model of reconciliation and nationalism needs to be revised because, unlike Saul, he did not suddenly see the light. He failed to realize that the North had been right about the Civil War all along, and he failed to become an advocate of black voting rights and other forms of racial equality, which by Nolan's standard equates to "racist animosity" which Lee "shared" with such organizations as the Ku Klux Klan "whether or not he approved of their tactics." Apparently for Lee to become a legitimate advocate of reconciliation he needed to become a Republican, and preferably a Radical.

Regarding Lee's military acumen, my own suspicion is that if the Virginian had commanded anything approaching the amounts of men and resources the Federals possessed, there would be customs houses on the Potomac today. I find much cogency in the views expressed by William Tecumseh Sherman before the shooting even started: that the North by all logic <u>should</u> prevail in a long war of attrition (the very war that Lee sought to avoid with a victory that would smash the enemy totally), given enormous northern advantages in manpower, industry, natural resources, financial and monetary resources, and anything else that can be enumerated—except cotton, sugar, rice, and slaves. I will omit the boring statistics that demonstrate these northern advantages, but they are fairly amazing, and their significance is clear. To take merely one example, the northern population added about as many immigrants from 1861 to 1865 as the number of Confederates who wore a uniform over the course of the war! As for the much-ballyhooed "strategic defensive," it <u>might</u> have worked—had all Federal commanders been as obtuse as Ambrose Burnside and accommodated the Confederates by performing according to Burnside's script at Rohrbach's Bridge over Antietam Creek and later at Fredericksburg.

One suspects real history would have developed differently: that the North would have quickly wised up and played the game with a defense-minded Confederacy to its own advantage, that the Federals were capable of patiently and successfully countering undermanned Confederate defensive efforts. In fact they did just that in the North Georgia Campaign—conducted by the Confederacy's most expert defensive strategist, Joseph E. Johnston—and at places like Fort Donelson, Island No. Ten, Vicksburg, Port Hudson, and Petersburg. And of course one should not forget the Blockade. Whenever the Confederates circled the wagons, they lost. Fighting on the defensive with fewer men, lesser firepower, and meager supplies didn't work very well at Sevastopol, Bataan, Corregidor, Okinawa, Dien Bien Phu, or the Alamo, either. Maybe the "retreat to victory" writers, as Robert G. Tanner has aptly called them, aren't familiar with these defensive setbacks. Or perhaps they just prefer not to think about them.

And what about Lee's character? Here again, I find myself un-persuaded by the revisionists. Robert E. Lee was very much his mother's son, more a Carter than a Lee. He hardly knew his father, but his life was molded, very early and in a lasting way, by the shadow of family scandal on his father's side. "Lighthorse" Harry Lee had been a military hero of the Revolution, member of the Continental Congress, governor of Virginia, and United States Representative. He was also an incurable dreamer, gambler, and speculator. He habitually lost not only his own money but any he could beg or borrow from relatives and friends. When

Robert was a baby, his father served time in debtors' prison; he never returned to the family for any extended period afterwards, drifting from one scrape to another and eventually dying a pauper at Cumberland Island, Georgia. Integrity and self-control were not his strong suits.

Nor were they especially evident in the character of his oldest son and namesake, Robert E. Lee's half-brother, sometimes remembered dubiously as "Blackhorse Harry." After the tragic death of their two-year-old child, who fell down the story-high brick steps of Stratford Hall (the property of Lighthorse Harry's first wife, a Lee cousin, which she left in trust to her son rather than husband lest he squander the plantation lands further), this second Harry's wife became a tragedy in her own right, a recluse whose anguish was eased only by refuge in morphine. Grief-stricken himself by the death, and lonely in the face of his spouse's addiction and withdrawal from reality, Blackhorse Harry drifted into an illicit and notorious relationship with his wife's sister, who was not only a minor but also his legal ward.

In the wake of these Lee family misadventures, which seem almost the stuff of soap opera, Anne Hill Carter Lee, the loyal, long-suffering second wife of Lighthorse Harry and the mother of Robert, dedicated her life to teaching her children right from wrong. She must have been a good teacher.

Four themes, it seems to me, define Robert E. Lee's character as revealed in his words and deeds. First is absolute, unquestioning faith in God and resignation to His will. Lee suffered setbacks and tragedies over the course of his life; he bore them stoically because to do otherwise would be to question the judgment of God. When Federal troops occupied Arlington, the family home, he wrote his wife: "I fear we have not been grateful enough for the happiness there within our reach, and our heavenly father has found it necessary to deprive us of what He has given us. I acknowledge my ingratitude, my transgressions, and my unworthiness, and submit with resignation to what he thinks proper ...We must trust all then to him." Nine days after Gettysburg, a rain-swollen Potomac blocked Lee's line of retreat: "Had the river not unexpectedly risen, all would have been well...; but God, in His all-wise providence, willed otherwise, and our communications have been interrupted and almost cut off. The waters have subsided..., and if they continue, by tomorrow, I hope, our communications will be open. I trust that a merciful God, our only hope and refuge, will not desert us in this hour of need, and will deliver us... We must, however, submit to His almighty will, whatever that may be." When the general's wounded son Fitzhugh, a casualty of the Battle of Brandy Station, was captured by a Federal raiding party: "Had not expected that he would be taken from his bed and carried off, but we must bear this additional affliction with fortitude and resignation, and not repine at the will of God." "In His own good time He will relieve us and make all things work together for our good, if we give Him our love and place in Him our trust." And even at the loss of a daughter: "I cannot express the anguish I feel at the death of our sweet Annie. To know that I shall never see her again on earth, that her place in our circle... is forever vacant, is agonizing... But God in this, as in all things, has mingled mercy with the blow, in selecting that one best prepared to leave us... His will be done!'" To be sure, Lee suffered—"in the lone hours of the night I groan in sorrow"—but the equanimity with which he accepted tragedy and adversity seems amazing, and is comprehensible only when one begins to understand the depth of his faith.

The second theme is kindness. Lee was a caring, sensitive, gentle person, filled with compassion, charity, and love. He cherished animals; his letters over the years mention fondly the long line of pets, canine and feline, that became his loved and loving companions. While on duty at New York City's Fort Hamilton in the 1840s, he took a favorite dog, a stray which he had adopted after saving the animal from a near-death experience in the Hudson River, to church, regularly, to the delight of his children; the delight this brought other parishioners and the minister can only be surmised. He had a weakness for horses as well, and one horse above all; near the end of his life he wrote with poignant eloquence: "If I were an artist... I would draw a true picture of Traveller—representing his fine proportions... Such a picture would inspire a poet, whose genius could then depict his worth and describe his endurance of toil, hunger, thirst, heat, cold, and the dangers and sufferings through which he passed. He could then dilate upon his sagacity and affection, and his invariable response to every wish of his rider. He might even imagine his thoughts, through the long night marches and days of battle through which he has passed. But I am no artist; I can only say he is a Confederate gray."

Far more than animals, Lee cherished people. "The great duty of life," he wrote in his diary, is "the promotion of the happiness & welfare of our fellow men." His would be a lifetime of Christian service to others. At only thirteen, he became the man of the family in the absence of his father and older brothers, becoming chief nurse to a mother gradually wasting away, probably from tuberculosis. "How can I live without Robert?" she wondered as he left for West Point. As fate would have it, his wife Mary Custis Lee also became an invalid, and he looked after her with similar devotion and tenderness throughout years of crippling arthritis.

This compassionate, sensitive warrior disliked conflict and prized peace. Describing the 1847 bombardment of Vera Cruz, Lee marvelled at shells "so beautiful in their flight and so destructive in their fall. It was awful! My heart bled for the inhabitants." "You have no idea what a horrible sight a battlefield is," he wrote his son Custis a week after Cerro Gordo. He told of a small Mexican girl standing over an injured boy pinned beneath a dying soldier. "Her large black eyes were streaming with tears, her hands crossed over her breast... Her plaintive tone of 'Millie gracias, Signor,' as I had the dying man lifted off the boy and both carried to the hospital still lingers in my ear." On Christmas day, 1862, Lee was reluctantly embroiled in another national conflict. "What a cruel thing is war," he wrote his wife. "To separate and destroy families and friends, and mar the purest joys and happiness God has granted us in this world; to fill our hearts with hatred instead of love for our neighbors, and to devastate the fair face of this beautiful world!"

Lee's gentleness and love of peace extended to personal relations. He avoided rancor when possible, within his family and among his acquaintances. He spent much time in the Civil War attempting to restore harmony between feuding Confederate generals, who seemed almost as prone to fight among themselves as with the enemy. In fact, Lee is often criticized as a commander for being too <u>nice</u>. Even in battle he rarely <u>ordered</u> subordinate generals about, preferring to make suggestions, "if practicable," leaving final discretion to their judgment--a gentle and genteel approach which worked well with some of his lieutenants but less well with others.

This foremost Confederate had in fact hoped to avoid Civil War altogether. In an 1860 letter, he expressed disgust for both "the aggressions of the North" and the "selfish, dictatorial bearing... [and] threats [of the] 'Cotton States,' as they term themselves." Secession was "anarchy," he said in a January 1861, letter; it was without constitutional basis; it was "revolution." "I can anticipate no greater calamity for the country than a dissolution of the Union." Yet he concluded this revealing missive with words he would reiterate and act upon three months later when Virginia seceded: "If the Union is dissolved and the Government disrupted, I shall return to my native state and share the miseries of my people, and save in defense will draw my sword on none." To his sister Ann, now a Baltimore Unionist, he explained his determination to cast his lot with Virginia even as the Commonwealth chose the misguided course of secession: "With all my devotion to the Union and the feeling of loyalty and duty of an American citizen, I have not been able to make up my mind to raise my hand against my relatives, my children, my home."

It cannot be said that Lee's sensitivity to others was color-blind. Like all of us, he was a product of his place and time. He had owned slaves; he was no racial egalitarian. Yet in some measure his essential humanity, goodness, and love of harmony did transcend racial barriers. In the late 1850s his son William

Henry Fitzhugh Lee took up farming with slave labor at White House, a plantation inherited from his maternal grandfather on the Pamunkey River. "Attend to them & give them every aid & comfort in your power & they will be the happier," Lee advised "Rooney" concerning his slaves. "I trust you will so gain the affection of your people, that they will not wish to do you any harm." To members of his family he criticized the existence of slavery itself—"a moral & political evil"—in the 1850s.

In fact Lee was a Southerner of the pre-1830s, "necessary evil" persuasion who never made the transition to the "positive good" school of thought. Ever the moderate, he deplored the strident voices of northern abolitionists as well as those of Deep South pro-slavery advocates; slavery as an institution should and would end, he maintained, but through natural evolution, in God's own time.

In the last months of the Civil War, he concluded that the time had come, supporting a legislative effort to enlist the South's remaining slaves in the Confederate army and urging passage (unsuccessfully) of the controversial incentive of emancipation immediately upon enlistment, with a guarantee of freedom also for the soldier's family at war's end after satisfactory military service (whether or not the volunteer should survive). "In my opinion the best means of securing the efficiency and fidelity of this auxiliary force would be to accompany the measure with a well-digested plan of gradual and general emancipation," he wrote in January 1865.

Perhaps the most vivid and unambiguously selfless example of Lee's nobler nature bridging racial chasms allegedly occurred just after the war. According to a recollection published in the _Confederate Veteran_ in the 1890s, Lee was attending a Sunday service at St. Paul's Episcopal Church in Richmond. When communion began, the first person to approach the altar was a black man. For slave parishioners to attend white services had been common in the Old South, but for a black communicant to precede whites to the alter was a breach of racial etiquette. A stunned silence enveloped the crowd. But Lee, doubtless as shocked as anyone, rose from his pew, walked down the aisle, and knelt beside the black man. He had led an army of thousands; now he followed a man of color. The rest of the congregation followed the general.

Five years later, Lee was in another church, still trying to do the right thing, still demonstrating humanity and charity, still serving as peacemaker. It was September 28, 1870. The visibly worn and rapidly aging college president attended a 4:00 vestry meeting at Lexington's Grace Episcopal Church, just down the hill from the new president's house. The meeting dragged on past seven as vestrymen worried over what source could be found for 55 additional dollars to raise the rector's salary. Lee grew weary of the bickering. "I will give that sum," he said simply. The meeting ended, and after that typical gesture of goodness, having rendered his last full measure on this earth, Lee walked home, in the rain—not to the supper he expected, but into immortality.

A third key to Lee's character, and very much intertwined with faith in God and kindness toward others, was selflessness. The indulgent misdeeds of his kinsmen had left an indelible mark. Lee would live his life demonstrating an extraordinary measure of selflessness: self-control, self-denial, even self-effacement. While doing so became so habitual as to become his nature, it is clear that he consciously and constantly strived to ingrain the habit in himself and his children. "The necessity and advantage of self-denial and self-control, can be forcibly exemplified and their exercise confirmed into habit," he wrote his wife. "This exercise, this habit, is the true means of establishing a virtuous character."

Self-denial became a personal test he would always pass. He avoided alcohol and tobacco. Notwithstanding his renowned good looks and a wide circle of female friends, before and after his marriage, there was never a hint of sexual transgression. He graduated from West Point with no demerits and a positive balance in his academy account book, in which cadet expenses were charged against a monthly government allowance; each of these demonstrations of self-control and self-denial was as exceptional among cadets as the other. Indeed Lee avoided indebtedness from youth until death. "You know my objection to incurring debt," he wrote a son. "I cannot overcome it."

One of his fondest dreams, expressed throughout his life, was to retire to the country and spend his days in blissful oblivion on a farm of his own. In 1857 his father-in-law died, leaving Arlington to Mrs. Lee and a plantation or interest therein to each of Robert E. Lee's three sons; to the general (who was then the lieutenant colonel) he left only the onerous job of executing the estate. Lee's oldest son Custis perceived the injustice and attempted to transfer his titled interest in Arlington to his father; R. E. Lee was touched but returned the deed. "Your dear grandfather distributed his property as he thought best," he wrote, "and it is proper that it should remain as he bestowed it."

Lee would never own the farm of his dreams. Many of the assets he did possess he lost in the war. "I have no time to think of my private affairs," he wrote his wife at the end of 1862. "I expect to die a pauper, & I see no way of preventing it." As president of Washington College, he would not permit the trustees to raise his salary, though the size of the student body increased eightfold during his tenure and his own fund-raising efforts eased the school's financial crisis. Most of the gifts he was tendered during the war and afterward from his many admirers he directed to others whom he thought in greater need. The City of Richmond sought to give him a house; Lee thanked city fathers profusely but respectfully requested "that whatever means the City Council may have to spare for this purpose may be devoted to the relief of the families of our soldiers in the field, who are more in want of assistance, and more deserving it, than myself." From the day he was born to the day he died, Robert E. Lee never lived in a home he owned.

Notwithstanding his prominence and achievements, Lee remained a modest man. Thomas Connelly and other recent writers have reminded us that Lee was human and imperfect; these critics would not have needed to tell the general. When he learned in 1860 that Rooney had named a child in his honor, he wrote the proud father: "I wish I could offer him a more worthy name and a better example. He must elevate the first and make use of the latter to avoid the errors I have committed." Such words of humility echo in Lee's letters like a leitmotif.

His modesty was exemplified by deeds as well as words. Most Civil War commanders established field headquarters in the best house available; Lee normally lived in a tent, sharing in some measure the hardships of his soldiers and declining offers of private hospitality lest his presence and the attendant comings and goings of others "turn the dwellings of my kind hosts into a barrack." His youngest son Rob joined the Confederate army as a private and served a cannon in the Rockbridge Artillery for most of a year before promotion; his father easily could have secured higher rank and safer, softer duty for R. E. Lee, Jr., but to the general it was "wrong in principle" to decide such things on the basis of "private and social relations, rather than for the public good." "I should prefer Rob's being in the line, in an independent position, where he could ride by his own merit, and not through the recommendation of his relatives." When they met on the field at Sharpsburg, the general at first did not recognize the powder-blackened face of his boy, whose battery was in process of retiring from the front line with three of its four guns disabled. After exchanging pleasantries, Robert, Sr., promptly ordered Robert, Jr., and his unit, with their one remaining serviceable cannon, back into action.

The Civil War and its aftermath are replete with generals seeking to "set the record straight," correcting inaccuracies about matters in which they were involved and typically seeking to enhance their own image at the expense of someone else. To paint oneself in favorable colors for posterity was natural and human—doubtless in most cases done in good conscience and in some with good reason. But how refreshing, courageous, classy, and rare was the example set by Lee. When Gettysburg had been decided, General Cadmus Wilcox approached his commander with apologies for the conduct of his brigade. "Never mind, General," Lee responded. "All this has been MY fault. It is I that have lost this fight, and you must help me out of it in the best way you can." Again in his written report to Jefferson Davis, with reference to Gettysburg: "I am alone to blame."

And on the subject of Davis, and bravely assuming responsibility: after the war, Federal prosecutors subpoenaed Lee to testify in legal proceedings against the former Confederate president. Their hope was that he would strengthen their case that Davis was the arch-villain of the Confederate cause, the master-mind of the rebellion and more than anyone subject to prosecution for treason. Clearly they had underestimated Lee's character and courage; he was uninterested in trying to pin the blame on someone else. "I am responsible for what I did," he stated under oath, "and I cannot now recall any important movement I made which I would not have made had I acted entirely on my own responsibility." His questioners quickly sent him home.

A final key to Lee's character, and closely intertwined with and complementing the others once again, was commitment to duty, which time and again he would perform, as he understood it, unflinchingly, even in the face of overwhelming adversity. Whether he actually wrote that "duty is the sublimest word in the English language" is disputed; that he lived his life according to the principle is clear.

In the Mexican War, Lee's perseverance in the line of duty won the lasting admiration of his commanding officer, Winfield Scott, who proclaimed the younger Virginian's work as scout, messenger, and guide in some of Mexico's most difficult terrain, at night, "the greatest feat of physical and mental courage performed by any individual, in my knowledge, pending the campaign." In 1865, Lee was personally directing troops during the retreat from Farmville in a hail of shells and bullets when a courier rode up with a dispatch. Lee reprimanded the young man for approaching under open fire when he might have taken a safer route sheltered by a hill. The courier replied that he would be ashamed to seek protection when the general himself was standing in the open. "It is my duty to be here," Lee returned. "Go back the way I told you, sir."

Lee would act upon what he regarded as his duty in the sometimes more difficult arena of noncombat decisions as well. As
noted already, he followed his conception of duty in the secession crisis, notwithstanding his lack of sympathy for Virginia's
course of action. War, he understood better than most, would
bring suffering to the South, himself, and his family. Unlike naive optimists in the early conflict, Lee had no unrealistic notions
of a short war and easy victory. "The war may last ten years," he
wrote his wife in April, 1861. Yet he did not flinch from what had
to be done. He gently told Mary that Arlington must now be
abandoned to the Federals. "It is sad to think of the devastation,
if not ruin, it may bring upon a spot so endeared to us," he wrote.
"But God's will be done. We must be resigned." Four years later
he had to resign himself to a far more painful manifestation of
God's will: the war was lost, and all his sacrifices, and those of
the young men he had led, living and dead, were in vain. Duty
again was clear. A few diehards spoke of fighting to the last man,
of taking to the hills for guerilla warfare. To Lee such "useless ef-
fusion of blood" made no sense; his was a nobler vision of the future. The South would need her remaining sons and other meager resources for the long and difficult recovery ahead. He was
unwilling for the remaining handful of brave troops to become
thieves and marauders, and equally distressed to contemplate the
harsh retaliation such partisan tactics would provoke. The nation
was too demoralized by war already. "There is nothing left me
but to go and see General Grant," he concluded, "and I would
rather die a thousand deaths."

The story of Lee's greatness might have ended there; it did
not, as those familiar with his life or with Washington and Lee
University know well. Duty would never allow Lee to stop acting
constructively. He urged disgruntled veterans to take the hated
Amnesty Oath and reinstate their U. S. citizenship. "Do not leave
Virginia," he counseled one considering a move abroad.

"Our country needs her young men now." His own duty to
serve led him in the twilight of his life not to the quiet farm he

still craved but to the presidency of Washington College—a call he accepted only after asking the trustees (with typical modesty and self-doubt) to reconsider their offer in light of his weakened health and the probability that his leadership would "draw upon the college a feeling of hostility" in the North.

Above all postwar obligations, Lee steadfastly shouldered the duty to be a loyal American once again, setting an example of sectional reconciliation equalled by few in those troubled times. He did not defend himself against accusations, some outrageous, which appeared in public discourse: "I have thought, from the time of the cessation of hostilities, that silence and patience on the part of the South was the true course... Controversy of all kinds will, in my opinion, only serve to continue excitement and passion." In the same letter in which he tentatively accepted the college presidency, he told the trustees: "I think it the duty of every citizen, in the present condition of the country, to do all in his power to aid in the restoration of peace and harmony, and in no way to oppose the policy of the State or general government directed to that object. It is particularly incumbent on those charged with the instruction of the young to set them an example of submission to authority." When he wrote those words, Lee had applied for his own pardon already, in June 1865. Not all Americans were so reconciliation-minded; the request was pigeonholed by Secretary of State William H. Seward, and the pardon was granted by Congress—and President Gerald R. Ford—105 years after Lee's death.

The Last Carrier

Andrew H. Farmer, Class of 1975

THE FOLLOWING ARTICLE was drawn from the book *Finding the Way: The Story of a Combat Navigator in World War II* by Andrew H. Farmer published in 2006.

There was an atmosphere of added tension and excitement as a special predawn briefing got underway at Yontan airstrip on Okinawa on August 8, 1945, for the B-25 crews of the 38th Bombardment Group (Medium). The mission objective had changed overnight and now the six-man crews from twenty-four bombers were told they were going to finish off what was believed by American intelligence to be the last operational aircraft carrier in the Imperial Japanese Navy. The U.S. Fifth Air Force ordered the group late on August 7, 1945, to prepare plans to sink the *Kaiyo*, an escort carrier that was spotted in Beppu Bay near the town of Higi on the northeast coast of Kyushu, the southernmost home island of Japan. Anchored close to the shore of the bay, the *Kaiyo* was covered with camouflage netting and fake trees so that it appeared to be an extension of the forested coastline. On July 24, airplanes from British Royal Navy aircraft carriers had attacked the *Kaiyo* in Beppu Bay and reported that the ship was heavily damaged. Allied air reconnaissance units then lost sight of the carrier until a sharp-eyed analyst discovered the outline of the ship under the camouflage in recent aerial photographs of Beppu Bay. Intelligence officers were worried the Japanese might be repairing the ship and preparing it for combat.

The four squadrons of the 38th Bombardment Group were seasoned outfits in the Pacific war that flew the versatile and formidable North American 8-25 Mitchell. Nicknamed the "Sun Setters" whose calling was to "smash the rising sun so it would rise no more," the group was renowned for its precision raids on Japanese targets. The Mitchells of the 38th Bombardment Group were known as "commerce destroyers." Since the group's early combat missions in New Guinea in 1942, the Sun Setters had refined the tactics of attacking Japanese shipping, airfields, factories, and other targets in daring low-level raids, often executed from less than seventy-five feet above the ground. Flying in the most heavily armed versions of the B-25, the Sun Setters would sweep in low over the sea or land, strafing targets with the concentrated fire of eight .50 caliber machine guns in the nose of each airplane and precisely drop bombs with delay fuses or parachutes. The experienced crews in the group had destroyed hundreds of enemy ships over the last three years including 55,000 tons of shipping in one day at Ormoc Bay in the Philippines in November 1944. But it was the medium bomber group's chief ambition to sink a major Japanese naval ship such as an aircraft carrier.

An all out effort by twenty-four B-25s from the 38th, six from each squadron, was scheduled to attack the *Kaiyo* on August 8. But poor weather prevented the bombers from contacting their fighter cover before they approached Beppu Bay, and the group leader decided the weather conditions would make the attack on the carrier very hazardous. He led the Sun Setters to the secondary target at Takanabe where they bombed and strafed railway and highway bridges instead. The chance to sink Japan's last aircraft carrier would have to wait for the next day.

The fact that they were going after an aircraft carrier only intensified the anxiety of the men of the 38th Bombardment Group as the Allied forces prepared to conduct the final operations of World War II. There were more than the usual number of lights shining in the Sun Setters' tents at Yontan airstrip on the evening of August 8. Tents that boasted radios were natural gathering spots for men eager to hear the latest shortwave news broadcasts from the Armed Forces radio station KGEI in San Francisco or the BBC in London on whether the Japanese had accepted the Allied demands for an unconditional surrender. The day before, during the noon news broadcast on KGEI, the men received the electrifying news of the destruction caused by the detonation of the first atomic bomb over the Japanese city of Hiroshima. President Harry S. Truman and other Allied leaders had issued an ultimatum to Japan on July 26 at the Potsdam Conference near Berlin, calling on her to surrender immediately or suffer the consequences of new and terrible weapons. One of those terrible weapons, a uranium bomb called "Little Boy," was dropped from 31,000 feet by a B-29 Superfortress named *Enola Gay* and exploded above the center of Hiroshima at 9:15 in the morning on August 6. Four square miles of the city vanished in a second and as many as 118,661 people died instantly.

The anonymous author of the 386 Bombardment Group's August 1945 summary of action said there was growing hopefulness among the 1,900 men in the unit that the war would end soon. "Men who had been confirmed cynics about Japan's fight to the bitter end had something new and unexpected to think about, something that might end this war over night." The August 1945 combat narrative for the 71st Bombardment Squadron, one of the four squadrons assigned to the group, described the atmosphere at Yontan as a nerve-shattering mixture of moods for the men. " 'Will they quit or fight and die?' was the ubiquitous question," according to the narrative.

Some elements of the group had been among the first Army Air Forces units sent to the southwest Pacific in early 1942 to stop Japanese advances. The Sun Setters had seen heavy action flying over 2,700 combat missions in three years in New Guinea, the Bismarck archipelago, the Philippines, and Formosa. Yet on the afternoon of August 8, the atmosphere at Yontan was described as almost festive in a unit history. About half of the troops in the group that made up the ground echelon of the group had just pulled into camp after a two-week voyage in large landing craft to bring mess equipment, jeeps, trucks, and heavy gear from Luzon in the Philippines and Okinawa.

The air echelon of the group made up of the bomber crews, the operations staff, and essential mechanics had moved to Okinawa from Luzon in the third week of July as part of the huge buildup of American air power that was conducting a pre-invasion aerial offensive against Japan. The bombers were flown to Okinawa on July 25 and were ready for combat by the next day. The air echelon was ordered to bring only limited personal gear and the necessary equipment to keep the airplanes flying and fighting. They were living in primitive pyramidal tents on rough ground a few miles from their airplanes at Yontan, depending on other Army Air Forces units and Navy "Seabees" (Construction Battalions) for mess halls and other necessities. The support troops from the ground echelon and all of their supplies were a welcome sight, made even more celebratory when news was announced that the Soviet Union had entered the war. "It was worse than an old lady's sewing circle," exclaimed the author of the group's combat history.

But there was little time for the Sun Setters to enjoy themselves. They had to prepare forty one B-25s for missions scheduled for August 9. Almost all of the operational aircraft and combat crews in the group were scheduled to fly that day, including twelve B-25s slated to attack the *Kaiyo*. With the possibility of the war ending soon, the August 9 mission might be the last chance for the Sun Setters to realize their goal of sinking a major Japanese naval vessel.

Captain John Warren Long, Jr., the senior navigator in the 38th Bombardment Group, most likely had little time to listen to the news broadcasts on the night of August 8. He was working with the group operations and intelligence staffs to prepare the plans for the next day's missions. The day before, he had a sleepless night getting plans ready for the first mission against the *Kaiyo*. A revised strategy for attacking the *Kaiyo* was being prepared for August 9, and the twelve bombers were scheduled to take off at six in the morning. Later in the day, twenty-five bombers from the group were heading for Oita on Kyushu to hit railroad and highway bridges. Several single-airplane armed reconnaissance and cover missions also were scheduled for August 9. Besides preparing the plans for the primary targets, information was collected on several secondary targets in case poor weather once again prevented the Sun Setters from reaching Beppu Bay.

The missions had to be coordinated with other Army Air Forces units and airplanes from American and British aircraft carriers scheduled to attack Japan's home islands. Hundreds of Allied aircraft were now flying missions over the Japanese home islands on a daily basis from the carriers and airfields on Okinawa, Iwo Jima, and the Marianas islands, including devastating firebombing raids on Japanese cities conducted by waves of B-29s. Allied battleships and cruisers were shelling Japanese coastal cities at will. Now the Americans had demonstrated to the world that one bomb could inflict as much or more destruction as the massive aerial attacks against Japan and Germany using conventional bombs.

Only a select few Allied aerial mission planners were aware that President Truman had authorized the use of a second atomic bomb and August 9 was the date selected for the mission. Under heavy guard on an isolated section of an air base on Tinian in the Marianas, a 13-29 Superfortress named *Bock's Car* was being loaded with a plutonium bomb known as "Fat Man" on the night of August 8 for a predawn flight to Kyushu where several cities were selected as potential targets, including the port city of Nagasaki.

Captain Long certainly would have given extra attention to planning the mission to strike the *Kaiyo* in Beppu Bay, thoroughly studying the reconnaissance photos, reviewing the available air navigation charts and maps, and collecting the latest weather forecasts. He was going to be the lead navigator for that mission, flying with the 38th Bombardment Group's commanding officer, Col. Edwin H. Hawes. As the lead navigator, Long was the "pathfinder" for the bombers and was responsible for plotting the course to the primary target as well as secondary targets and any rendezvous points with fighter escorts and air/sea rescue units. All of these targets were protected by numerous antiaircraft batteries, and the low-flying B-25s of the Sun Setters were vulnerable to ground fire. Only three days earlier, a bomber from the group was hit by antiaircraft fire during a raid near Nagasaki, knocking out one engine. The pilot coaxed the damaged plane to a point about ten miles off the coast of Kyushu and was forced to ditch. The crew made it into a life raft and fortunately was picked up by an American submarine on lifeguard duty.

It was no surprise that the twenty-five-year-old Long was going on the *Kaiyo* strike. He was the most skilled navigator in the group and volunteered to join his commander for the attack on the enemy carrier in a remote bay on Kyushu in marginal weather conditions. Long had been overseas for only nine months and had been serving with the Sun Setters since mid January 1945. He was promoted from combat navigator to squadron navigator after his first month with the group. In late May, he was promoted to the position of assistant group navigator on the headquarters staff, and a month later he was picked as the group navigator. In addition to helping plan the missions for the approximately sixty 13-25s assigned to the Sun Setters, Long oversaw the certifications for combat duty and ongoing training for all of the navigators in the group's four squadrons. An accomplished teacher, Long was a navigation instructor for two years at Army Air Forces bases in Texas before coming to the Pacific in late 1944.

Although he excelled at the staff duties and administrative work of a group navigator, Long took every opportunity to get into the air. He still enjoyed flying after four years in the Army Air Forces and took all of the stresses associated with combat missions in stride. In a letter written to his parents in June 1945, he described the extended flights over water in the Pacific. "Nothing was more beautiful on the way across than to see that streak of white on the horizon which you knew was the island you were trying to hit. You see, you can observe the surf even before you see the land because of the marked contrast in color. Also, the north shores of Luzon look mighty inviting returning from Formosa. There is something enchanting about flying over the sea that you don't get over land, something soothing."

There also was a practical side to Long. He knew that each combat mission would add rotation points to the total every soldier needed to get home from a combat zone. It was a complicated and ever-changing formula that took into account the number of combat missions he had flown, the number of combat hours he accumulated (the Sun Setters routinely flew 1,000-1,200-mile missions that lasted up to ten hours), any decorations that he had received, and other factors. The strike against the *Kaiyo* would be Long's thirty-eighth combat mission and he estimated that he had logged approximately 360 combat hours by August 1945. At the time, airmen in the Pacific theater needed at least 100 points before they could go home. Long calculated that he had between seventy-five and eighty rotation points and thought he might be able to return to the United States in late 1945.

On July 29 Captain Long received the belated news of the birth of his second daughter, Louise, on July 15. A telegram announcing the birth had been delayed because of the 38th's movement from the Philippines to Okinawa. He very much wanted to get home to Lancaster County in southeastern Pennsylvania as soon as possible and pick up his life with his wife Mary Louise and his young daughters Judy and Louise. He also was eager to see his parents, three sisters, and brother after nine months of being overseas. He admitted to them in his letters that during occasional lulls in air operations, he grew restless and experienced bouts of homesickness. In letters to his wife, he tried to lift both of their spirits, "Each night brings me closer to that final day when we will enjoy our lives together and look back upon these months as beautiful, not because they existed but because they are past and gone. These days will become remote and a happy heart will reflect the lonely one that tears at my soul each day."

Long's morale had picked up considerably over that last month with the news of Louise's birth and the movement of the group to Okinawa. He was extremely busy with challenging work, and he noted that the attitude of all the men around him had greatly improved since the transfer. The Sun Setters were in new surroundings and in the thick of the action with a possible end of the war in sight. In several letters, Long had reflected that he never imagined his life would take so many twists and turns since he graduated from college in June 1941 and headed off to the Army Air Forces as a draftee. He had started out as an enlisted man working on the technical supply line at a base in Texas, then graduated from the aviation cadet program at the beginning of the war. He received an officer's commission and spent two years as a navigation instructor. Along the way he had gotten married and started a family. Now he was a senior combat navigator taking part in the decisive air battles that would bring the end to a global war. The group commander was going to lead the attack on the last Japanese aircraft carrier tomorrow, but he was depending on Long to find the way.

The *Kaiyo* was originally built as a civilian passenger liner. Completed in late 1938 in Nagasaki, she was taken over by the Imperial Japanese Navy in 1941 for use as a troop transport, serving under her original name, *Argentina Marts*. With the huge losses of aircraft carriers during the Battle of Midway in 1942, the Japanese navy was in desperate need of replacements. The *Kaiyo* was an experiment at converting a passenger ship into an escort carrier by removing most of the superstructure and building a flight deck. The conversion began in December 1942, and the ship was renamed. Beginning in November 1943, she served as an escort carrier, aircraft transport, and training carrier. With a relatively short flight deck and small hangars, the *Kaiyo* could carry only twenty-four aircraft. The overall length of the ship was 546 feet with the flight deck length of 492 feet and width of seventy-two feet. It was a true "flattop" with no island for the bridge on the flight deck. The bridge was placed at the forward end of the ship, below the flight deck. Fully loaded, the ship displaced 17,500 tons and had a crew of up to 829 men. (Some records list the displacement of the ship at 21,250 tons.)

Colonel Hawes thought an attack on the carrier by a smaller number of airplanes and slightly different tactics than the Sun Setters planned for their mission on August 8 would provide an element of surprise. According to a group summary report on the August 9 mission, Hawes was convinced the carrier could be destroyed with twelve bombers, each carrying two 1,000-pound armor-piercing bombs with eight- to eleven-second delay fuses. The bombers would attack on a heading of 180 degrees in tight formations of three-airplane elements flying "on the deck" to ensure that every airplane in each flight passed over the carrier. The attack was synchronized so that each flight was twenty seconds apart, allowing time for the bombs to penetrate the carrier hull, explode, and any debris to settle before the next wave of airplanes came over the ship. The distance between the flights would be about one mile. The bombers would approach the carrier over land flying from the north to south. The cloud cover in the area and land approach would serve as protection from concentrated antiaircraft fire and permit the Americans to attain a degree of surprise. The plan called for the bombers to take off from Okinawa at 0600 in hopes of reaching the target area before the normal midday buildup of clouds over Kyushu. Hawes directed that radio silence would be in effect for the mission.

Each squadron would contribute three B-25s for the mission. The airplanes in the lead and last flights were each fitted to carry eight high-velocity five-inch rockets on under-wing mounts, the first combat use of rockets by the group. The rockets would be fired approximately 2,000 yards from the target along with the forward-firing machine guns to suppress any enemy antiaircraft fire. The *Kaiyo* was heavily covered with camouflage netting and artificial foliage, but American photo interpreters believed there were three antiaircraft sponsons on each side of the ship that were equipped with twin 25 mm automatic antiaircraft guns. Antiaircraft guns also were expected in the town of Hiji and along the shoreline of the bay. The bomber crews were instructed to drop propaganda leaflets over inhabited areas on the approach to the target.

Photos taken by reconnaissance aircraft showed the bomber crews that they could expect the *Kaiyo* to be anchored approximately 100 feet from the shore of the bay alongside a clump of trees and near a four-story building. Because the planes were approaching from the north, the trees and buildings on the shore would hide the carrier. The cloud cover also would be a handicap. No fighter escort was provided for the strike, although eight P-51 Mustang fighters would be operating in the area on ground attack sweeps and could cover the bombers in case enemy fighters were spotted. A rescue flying boat would be circling nearby at the mouth of Beppu Bay. According to the combat narrative for the 822nd Squadron, "Preparations for the strike were very thorough but everyone was more excited than usual because this was the carrier that we had never gone after."

Hawes was extremely enthused about the mission according to a unit history of the Sun Setters written in 1945. He was a highly skilled pilot with over 1,000 combat hours including hundreds of hours of instrument flying in the Caribbean where he commanded the 35th Bombardment Squadron on antisubmarine patrols early in the war. Since taking command of the group in March, Hawes insisted on leading his men on difficult missions or flights over new targets. According to the 38th's unit history, Hawes would not ask his men to do something that he would not do. However, officers from higher commands realized that an attack on the heavily armed carrier would be particularly risky and urged Hawes to stay on the ground. He would not change his ritual of being in the lead of the group on a dangerous mission. If Hawes' name was on the alert list to fly, Long's name would be right below his. Several other senior officers in the group added their names to the roster for the mission. Major

Dorence L. Van Fleet, the commander of the 405th, would be leading the flight from his squadron and second in command for the mission. Major J. C. O'Donnell of the group staff would be leading the flight from the 71st, and Capt. J. D. Johnson would be leading the flight from the 823rd.

Hawes would be piloting a B-25J (aircraft number 44-31054) for the mission from the 822nd Bombardment Squadron. Long would serve as the lead navigator for the twelve bombers. Rounding out the six-man crew on the lead plane was twenty-one-year-old copilot 2d Lt. Paul F. Kringel, Jr., originally from Iowa although his family had moved to Arlington, Virginia. The engineer/turret gunner was T. Sgt. Frank L. D'Arcy from Newark, New Jersey. He was nine days short of his twenty-seventh birthday. The radio operator/waist gunner was twenty-two-year-old S. Sgt. Edward C. Mitchell from Wilkes-Barre, Pennsylvania. The tail gunner was Sgt. Morris Zissman from Chicago, Illinois. His age was not available from existing records and his enlistment record was not found in the U.S. National Archives database. Frank D'Arcy had flown with Long on his first combat mission with the Sun Setters on January 20, 1945.

Ground crews were up well before dawn on August 9 at Yontan airstrip to load fuel, bombs, rockets, and ammunition on the Mitchells that were going on mission number FFo 221-A-13. Mechanics and communications technicians checked the engines and all other systems on the airplanes while the combat crews attended a final briefing on the mission before picking up their flight gear and driving the two miles to the hardstands along the runway. Shortly before 0600, the Wright Cyclone engines on the B-25s roared to life for a preflight warm-up that usually lasted ten to fifteen minutes. One of the airplanes from the 823rd experienced a failure of the plugs in the left engine as it warmed up and had to be scratched from the mission. As the remaining eleven bombers began taxiing to the runway, one airplane from the 71st suffered a flat tire and wheel damage, meaning that a second bomber was scrubbed from the mission. No standby airplanes were available that morning in the group because of the other major missions planned later in the day. In fact, the 822nd had to borrow a B-25 from the 405th for the *Kaiyo* strike because of a shortage of serviceable airplanes in the squadron.

With the usual rapid takeoff sequence of the Sun Setters, the ten remaining airplanes were in the air shortly after 0600 and circled the airfield as they took up their formation for the three-hour flight to the northeast to Beppu Bay. The three B-25s from the 822nd took up the lead position followed by the airplanes from the 405th, 823rd, and 71st. Flying at 5,000 feet, the crews encountered good weather for most of the flight over the water. As they approached the Japanese coast, the land was covered with stratocumulus clouds with bases at 1,500 feet and extending up to 2,000 feet. Visibility decreased to only a mile-and-a-half over land, and the formation encountered thick haze as it flew over the Inland Sea. Due to the haze, Hawes decided to turn the bombers west over land south of the planned approach and work their way to a point about twenty miles northeast of Beppu Bay to begin the final run towards the *Kaiyo*. The first two flights formed tight "fingertip" formations with the middle bomber slightly ahead of the two wingmen. The third and fourth flights would fly in tight pairs. As the airplanes turned to the southwest and began to descend through the overcast to an altitude of between 300 and 500 feet, some of the flights lost sight of each other. The first and second flights stayed together on the right approach to the aircraft carrier. The third and fourth flights became separated but continued flying in what they thought was the correct heading and did not break radio silence.

The six B-25s in the first and second flights soon drew near the outskirts of the town of Hiji, skimming over the treetops and buildings only a few feet below. White tracers from enemy machine guns were spotted but no hits were reported. At this point, visibility was restricted to a distance ranging from one to three miles. As the bombers began the attack run, the slope of the ground was descending and the bombers dropped to about 30 to 50 feet above the trees. The pilots found that fog and low clouds still obscured the carrier. When the ship finally came into view about a mile away, the Mitchells in the lead flight fired their rockets and machine guns. Long's airplane was in the middle position of the first flight slightly ahead of the two wingmen and the time was 0928.

Accounts of exactly what happened during the next minute differ significantly. First, there is the description found in the official narrative report of the mission from the 822nd Bombardment Squadron submitted to the U.S. Far East Air Forces on August 10, 1945, by Capt. Karl D. Henze, the squadron intelligence officer. In that report, Henze stated that Hawes apparently realized his bomber was too far to the left of the carrier to effectively drop the bombs amidships and only had a few seconds to adjust the flight path. Hawes banked the plane sharply to the right in an effort to fly directly over the carrier at mast height through scattered antiaircraft fire from guns along the shore. But the right wing of the B-25 struck the treetops below, shearing off five feet of the airplane's wing. Hawes righted the aircraft enough for his copilot Kringel to release the two 1,000-pound bombs into the port side of the *Kaiyo*. As the B-25 roared over the ship, the airplane rolled back to the left. The other wing caught the camouflage netting that was draped over the ship superstructure and hit the carrier deck. The airplane veered to the right, cart wheeled end over end into the bay and exploded 100 to 150 feet past the carrier.

The wingmen in the lead flight managed to pass over the carrier despite the leader's violent maneuvers and dropped their bombs on it. Badly shaken by the crash, the wingmen peeled out through Beppu Bay. A tail gunner reported one bomb blew debris from the bow of the carrier. Heavy black smoke was seen coming from the ship.

One eyewitness to the crash was T. Sgt. Harold M. Shroy, a radio operator/gunner from the 822nd Bombardment Squadron who was a crew member of one of the B-25s to the left or right of Long's airplane. His position was in the radio compartment behind the bomb bay. Shroy had flown with Long several times and must have been mentioned in some of Long's letters to his wife Mary Louise. She had written to Shroy after the crash to find out more information on the mission. In his response written on October 19, 1945, Shroy referred to Long as "Johnny" and said he was flying with the best pilot in the group, Colonel Hawes. Shroy briefly described the approach to the carrier, and then wrote: "When we were almost to the carrier but still over land, it looked to me like Col. Hawes got a little to [sic] low and dug one wing into the ground. He pulled up, righted the plane, and in that fraction of a second they were over the carrier, dropped their bombs, then the plane flipped over on its back and went in."

Shroy said there was some speculation among the men that Long's aircraft was hit by antiaircraft fire as it approached the carrier. "No one knows exactly, but the pilot might have been hit and before the copilot could take over, the wing dug in the ground. There was a little bit of light ack-ack but not much. When the plane hit the water, it broke all to pieces and sunk. No one had a chance of getting out." Shroy said that he would be happy to answer additional questions. Because he was to be released from the Army shortly, he said Mary Louise could write to him at his home in Craig, Alaska.

Another eyewitness to the crash of Long's airplane says the official record and Shroy's account are incorrect. Second Lieutenant Charles M. "Chuck" Crawford of the 405th Bombardment Squadron was the copilot for Major Van Fleet in the B-25 flying immediately behind the group leader's B-25 and was carefully watching the airplane ahead of him to verify that bombs had hit the target. That was what he was instructed to do during the preflight briefing. Crawford stated that as the first flight approached the carrier, the group leader's airplane was on a heading that would take it almost directly over the middle of the ship, and he saw two bombs drop from the B-25. "I did not see Col. Hawes make any abrupt changes in his flight path by going too far east over the carrier mid-section, and neither did we," Crawford wrote in a letter to the author in July 2005. "I believe his [Captain Henze] description of what happened to that airplane was wrong!" Crawford, a retired U. S. Air Force lieutenant colonel living in California, had written an article on the mission for the September 2003 edition of the 38th Bombardment Group Association newsletter, hoping to set the record straight.

According to Crawford, as the group commander's airplane reached the carrier it appeared as if it took a direct hit from antiaircraft fire in the right engine after the bombs fell away. "Our bomb runs were always made with throttles to the firewall to go as fast as you could. With high torque from the left engine and the drag from the loss of the right engine, his [Hawes] B-25 did a rapid snap roll to the right, one and a half times around and dove into the water at about a 20- or 30- degree angle, upside down, several hundred yards past the ship. With its speed, angle of impact, and being inverted, there was no chance for survivors from that crash," Crawford wrote.

Crawford said the airplane did not appear to yaw to the left as described in the official narrative report. And the airplane did not cartwheel according to Crawford. A photo sequence of the bombing run taken by an automatic camera on one of the other bombers in the first flight does not show multiple splashes that would have come from a cartwheeling airplane. There was only one large splash from the crash of Long's B-25 and smaller splashes that might have been made by bombs going over the ship and machine gun fire. Crawford maintains that Van Fleet and he were the only two men participating in the mission who had a good, straight-ahead look at what happened.

The flight of bombers from the 405th attacked immediately after the first wave. Crawford's bomber made a run almost directly over the middle of the carrier and the wingmen went over the bow and stem. Crawford believed his bombs went into the side of the ship, but the wingmen scored no hits. Photos showed their bombs skipping away on the water.

The third flight of bombers from the 823rd was completely out of position to attack the target and passed two miles west of the carrier. The airplanes from the 71st also passed wide of the carrier. One of the bombers from the fourth flight attacked several small boats in the harbor with machine gun fire. The four air-planes from the third and fourth flights flew on to the secondary target at Noma and hit a radio station.

Van Fleet was now the senior officer for the group on the mission, and as his plane climbed away from Beppu Bay, the remaining four bombers from the first and second flights as-sembled with him for the journey back to Okinawa. Van Fleet radioed the strike report to headquarters, although it was printed under Hawes' name. After bombing Noma, the four bombers from the third and fourth flights also headed to Yontan airfield. All of the crews were in a state of stunned silence according to the squadron combat narratives. About 100 miles from the Sun Setters base at Yontan, four Marine F4U Corsair fighters made a pass extremely close to some of the bombers. A tail gunner in one of the B-25s alarmed by the risky maneuver fired a warning burst from the two .50 caliber machine guns in the general direc-tion of the fighters.

A report by the 822nd Bombardment Squadron's air-sea rescue officer on August 10, 1945, stated there were no possible survivors from Long's aircraft. The rescue flying boat could not enter the bay to conduct a search because of enemy antiaircraft fire and small boats spotted in the water near the carrier. The crews of the other aircraft from the 38th Bombardment Group reported see-ing only an empty life raft, a nose wheel and small debris floating in the water at the crash site.

After the return of the crews to Okinawa, it could not be de-termined with certainty what damage had been inflicted on the *Kaiyo*. A few days later, a follow-up photo-reconnaissance flight showed the bombs from the two flights apparently caused seri-ous damage. The ship was listing heavily to the starboard side and the bow settled onto the bottom of the shallow bay. The carrier was classified as sunk by the Army Air Forces and had to be cut up for scrap in the bay a year later. Long's mission to sink the last Japanese aircraft carrier took place five days before the end of hostilities against Japan and eight days before his twenty-sixth birthday. He and his crew were the last six of the over 500 men of the 38th Bombardment Group to be killed in action during the war.

Inaugural Address
Washington and Lee University
October 21, 2006

Kenneth P. Ruscio, Class of 1976

MEMBERS OF THE Board of Trustees; colleagues on the faculty; fellow alumni represented here by the delegates of more than 50 alumni chapters from across the country; the hard-working staff from facilities management; the anxious dining services crew awaiting the conclusion of these remarks and mobilized for the lunch of a lifetime; friends from the community, from Richmond and the Jepson School and from Omicron Delta Kappa; new and future friends among the students, …my thanks to all of you for joining us today… as we celebrate Washington and Lee University, for although a presidential inauguration is about a transition in one office, it is far more importantly about our community, a time to reflect on its values, to take stock of where we are and where we have been, and prepare for what lies ahead.

That is why we are here today, and it is why I am privileged and honored to be joined by my predecessors, Bob Huntley, John. Wilson, Tom Burish, and of course Harlan Beckley and Larry Boetsch who played critical roles at important times.

Their presence and our fond memories of John Elrod send the unmistakable message that I need not go back to the presidencies of Francis Pendleton Gaines or Robert E. Lee to realize that

I have big shoes to fill. It is humbling to consider their legacies with thoughts of adding to it in the years to come.

A special thanks to my presidential colleagues who have joined us today from other colleges and universities—and to the delegates representing some of the finest institutions and societies in higher education. Thanks also to yesterday's panelists, including our own Roger Mudd for helping us shape the conversations we will have on campus this year. You honor all of us at Washington and Lee by your presence this weekend, and you have our gratitude.

To the greeters for their kind and eloquent remarks, thank you. And of course, thanks to Mike Luttig and June Aprille. Mike, fellow member of the Class of '76 and longtime friend, is now senior vice-president and general counsel of Boeing; he suffered the ultimate indignity of having to fly commercial to be with us today.

June's presence, I'm sure, was motivated by the need for assurance that the deal is closed—that her troublesome dean of the past four years is in fact safely installed, no longer a threat. As provost of the University of Richmond, she can now safely report back that all is well. Seeing is finally believing.

They are true friends, the best that anyone could hope for, and they have made this very meaningful day even more so.

And last, but certainly not least, my family… my father who almost exactly thirty-five years ago to the day stood with me by the tree over to your right and took a picture we would later show my mother… a picture of me as a high school senior on the front lawn of a college we knew almost nothing about. The expression on my face is typical of a young man visiting a college with a parent—an expression that says at one and the same time I wish my father would disappear and I hope desperately he does not. Our prayers that day were focused entirely on the prospects for admission. This particular moment was far, far beyond the realm of our imaginations.

And of course, Kim and Matthew. Matthew, our son, born and raised in the shadows of Washington and Lee, not quite knowing what all this means today but knowing that it means a lot to his parents. He sacrificed a session with the PSAT's this morning—perhaps the only alternative that could make him thankful he is here rather than somewhere else.

Kim, by no means a native of Lexington, who returns now for her third time—the first time having sacrificed a promising position in the center of New York's fashion world, the second having sacrificed yet another position back at the center of women's fashion, and this time sacrificing life as we knew it. For those and so many other reasons, I wouldn't be here without her. We are a package deal. And we both now realize, this is home, and we are glad to be back.

As president of Washington and Lee I can't help but feel even more acutely than I did before the power of the history of this place. There are the standard stories we all know so well, such as the saga of George Washington's gift of James River Canal stock, given to him in gratitude for his service to the country. For someone like Washington, who had a noble vision of public service, the prospect of personal gain from doing his duty presented a true dilemma.

Too much of a gentleman to insult his well-intentioned benefactors by refusing the gift, but too much a man of integrity to accept it, he consulted widely with friends about what to do. Augusta Academy, the precursor of what would become Washington College, was the solution and the ultimate beneficiary. The funds would support the education of our nation's youth. Washington never slept here, but his legacy is direct and real. From that point on, a sense of duty and integrity became part of our fabric.

Then of course, there is Robert E. Lee, assuming the leadership of Washington College after the Civil War. Offered numerous other opportunities, Lee chose a college presidency because it was the only option that allowed him to help bind the wounds of a divided nation. If the United States was to recover from the devastation and moral wounds of the Civil War, the healing had to begin with education. We build upon the legacy of Lee, the educator, with an ongoing commitment to educating citizens and leaders for a complex world.

Or the story of how Doremus Gymnasium came to be. It was a gift from a couple with no prior connection to the University, but with a clear impression of a welcoming and friendly place, which they experienced early in the 1900's during an unplanned stopover in Lexington on their way back home from Charlottesville. That "other" University of Virginia was originally to be the recipient of their largesse, but their minds were changed by the uncommon civility of this campus. Though the Doremus gift was the consequence of the speaking tradition and not its beginning, it serves as a tangible reminder why respect for others, whether friends or strangers, is a defining quality of our culture.

But there are also the lesser known stories, hidden away in the corners of our history, hidden away even further in the literature that this place has spawned. They evoke the spirit of our University. In 1839, Henry Ruffner, an alumnus of Washington College then serving as its sixth president, published a novel—a feat almost certainly not to be replicated by the twenty-sixth president.

Judith Bensaddi was its title. It contains a passage about how groups of college men would go hiking and gaze down on the vista from high atop House Mountain—a mountain that, in Ruffner's words, "hides the setting sun and not infrequently turns the summers showers that come from the west wind... It stands like an island of the air, with its huge body and sharp angles to cut the current of the winds asunder." And here is how the student described the experience:

"The little homesteads that spotted the hills and valleys under the mountain, the large farms and country seats farther away, and the bright group of buildings in the village of Lexington relieved the mind from the painful sublimity of the distant prospect and prepared us, after hours of delightful contemplation, to descend from our aerial height and return with gratified feelings to our college and our studies again."

Or from a more recent time, *The Foreign Student,* written by another alumnus, the famed French broadcaster Phillipe Labro, who spent a year in Lexington as an exchange student in the late 1950's. His fictional account of that year became a bestseller in France, winning several awards. It later became an atrocious American movie that won absolutely no awards. Though Washington and Lee is never identified by name in the book, in Labro's eloquent reminiscing there's no mistaking where we are.

> They come back to haunt me like a piece of music that enfolds me, catapulting me back in time to where the present slips away and memory calls the tune: whiffs of green lawns; the bubbles of Pabst Blue Ribbon beer over the metallic taste of the chilled can; the scent of the bay rum the boys sprinkled on themselves on Saturday night when an entire male community primped and powdered for the great stampede to any girls' school within a sixty mile radius. Like an overdose streaming into my body the memories come; the trombones in Stan Kenton's band during the big spring concerts, with all the young people sitting on the lawn; the red mud on the long cement footbridge that crossed a straggling train track and linked the football field to the gym, comings and goings under the colonnade on a sparkling fall morning with the sun sliding across the grass from behind Lee Chapel. I hear the silence of the campus during classes when, through open windows, a tardy student's anxious steps echoed on the flagstones as he ran.

From across the centuries come stories that reveal our principles and values; from literature comes the intangible sense of place, in words that resonate with members of the Class of 2010 as easily as they do with those of an earlier vintage. Washington and Lee thankfully has changed over the years. But even as we change, and acknowledge we are a better institution with each passing year, we embrace the imperfect perfection of the past.

∞

We honor that past by building upon it, and so for at least a few moments this morning, let us be not unmindful of the future, of the opportunity we face in the coming years. For I truly believe that Washington and Lee University offers not just an exceptional liberal arts education, but a particular version of the liberal arts appropriate for this day and age, appropriate in ways that few other universities can match. Those qualities spring from our past. But unless we aggressively adapt them to the demands of the future, we risk squandering the precious legacy given to us.

Earlier this month, I was visiting alumni in Birmingham and met with the CEO of a highly successful publishing company. A graduate from the mid 70's, he told me that he sort of majored in history and philosophy, or more specifically intellectual history of the eighteenth century, or to be even more accurate, he said, he majored in Jenks and Jarrett.

I knew the feeling. When I was a student, you could describe my major as Politics with a heavy dose of American Government and political philosophy, but the reality was that I majored in Hughes with a minor in Buchanan. And I suspect that there are others like us. For students at Washington and Lee University, the subject comes alive through professors. And just as Jenks and Jarrett, Hughes and Buchanan infused a passion for learning among an earlier generation, so too will Simpson in Art, Brown in Religion, Connor and Keene in English, Morel and Dickovik in Politics, Greer in Geology, Murchison and Johnson in Law, and Goldsmith and Hooks in Economics do the same for this generation.

But there is more at work here than dynamic, charismatic personalities, a certain flare or style. Faculty know that they are helpless without their own knowledge; it's not about them. And the ultimate accomplishment of teaching is when students venture out on their own.

The words of John Henry Cardinal Newman, the famed Irish educator, come down to us from the 1850's, describing the idea of a university. "An assemblage of learned men"—we can add women—"are brought together... They learn to respect, to consult, to aid each other. Thus is created a pure and clear atmosphere which the student also breathes... A habit of mind is formed which lasts through life, of which the attributes are freedom, equitableness, calmness, moderation, and wisdom." Newman concludes, "This is the main purpose of a University in its treatment of its students."

True, but somehow too quaint in this day and age, or at least too simplistic. Our faculty today, while holding fast to this ideal, face difficult challenges of rapidly changing fields of knowledge. Standard disciplines dissolve before our very eyes. Psychology bleeds into biology and chemistry through the new field of neuroscience. Politics and economics cross their divide through the bridges of game theory and rational choice. And the list goes on.

There are also different patterns of student learning, some brought on by the technology which shapes our lives, some by the culture in which we live. Students don't read anymore; they search. They assemble data with great facility but struggle with complex arguments. Attention spans collapse under the weight of instantaneous and multiple forms of communication. We tend to forget that information is not knowledge and knowledge is not wisdom.

Our faculty are in a constant state of learning themselves, in order to be better teachers. But how not to lose sight of the students as they engage in their own learning?

For liberal arts colleges everywhere, but especially so for Washington and Lee, we need to develop a distinctive model of scholarship, one especially suited to a college where the ultimate prize is the passion for learning we see among our graduates.

Teaching introductory courses—and I mean really teaching them—conversing with colleagues outside your field on a regular basis, attending public lectures and meeting with visitors in different disciplines, all of that is bound to result scholarship that is original and creative, genuinely interesting and imaginative. The teacher-scholar model in a liberal arts college is not an adaptation of the research university approach to a constrained organizational setting. It is not Berkeley-lite. Instead it is a model with virtues all its own pursued in a setting that affords advantages not available elsewhere.

Cultivating, nurturing, and defining that distinctive model, remembering as we do that the true measure of its success will be its benefit to students, is one of our greatest challenges and opportunities.

But let me move on to another. We need to be more thoughtful in helping students draw the connection between their education and the world around them. We already do that in a few ways. Our interdisciplinary programs in poverty, women's studies, the environment, ethics, and African-American studies, among others, are good examples. But let me focus for a minute on the professional programs in business, law and journalism.

Step back for a moment and ask the broader question why professional programs even exist in higher education. Why not leave the training required by each profession to the profession itself, to the apprentice model of learning?

The answer requires too long a departure into the history of higher education, but in nutshell, the answer is this. A profession should serve the public good; it has a responsibility to hold itself accountable to an ethic of service. That higher calling can best be understood, perhaps can only be understood, through an educational process that cultivates a philosophical habit of mind.

Too quickly we assume that the practicality and applied nature of professional education collides with the fundamental, philosophical, and timeless nature of the liberal arts. Under some conditions, yes, especially when we define professional education and the liberal arts in those too simplistic ways.

But under other conditions, such as what we strive for at Washington and Lee, they complement each other. When the law school looks at fundamental questions of justice and equity, or when the Williams School looks at the economic and political factors affecting inequality, or when our journalists look at the impact of modern communications on democratic processes, professional education and the liberal arts come together in the best possible way.

The professional programs at Washington and Lee are better because they exist in a liberal arts setting. But the liberal arts are better because of the hard questions asked by the professions, the problems of the world they bring to our attention, and the context they offer for interpreting the economic, political, legal and cultural settings in which we live.

The University needs to leverage this distinctive quality. I'm convinced it will cause others to look to us for guidance in the coming years.

One final challenge for Washington and Lee. How do we prepare students for a world in which most problems require ethical insight and moral reasoning, as well as technical and analytical skills?

If we look beyond the borders of our ivory towers to the public world our students will enter, the picture is both daunting and depressing. Daunting because of the magnitude and complexity of the problems. And depressing because at precisely the time we need mutual understanding, we are descending inexorably into a public discourse of incivility and mistrust.

I am not an alarmist about the state of democracy, but no one can be happy nowadays with the harshness and anger of the public sphere, or with the obsession over trivial matters to the exclusion of the consequential.

The opportunity for higher education—indeed our obligation—is to model a democratic culture of mutual respect and trust. Graduates of Washington and Lee should be critical and skeptical without being dismissive and cynical. They should not mistake tolerance and open-mindedness for relativism. Certitude should give way to humility and a willingness to learn from others. A Washington and Lee education should convey this compelling message: a strong community is one where we learn in common that which we cannot learn alone.

When we claim to be developing character, that is what we

mean. Our alumni, many of whom have taken center stage in public life, have been models of independence, integrity, and intelligence. Quite rightly, we point to our honor system as the cornerstone of that mission and our most successful feature. No alumnus can look back on his or her four years unmindful of why trust matters in a community.

But because of the honor system's durability, and because we take it as self-evident that learning for leadership occurs outside the classroom, we pay less attention to other ways of exploring complex ethical and moral questions. Especially in modern times, developing habits of the heart requires developing habits of the mind. The way to one's heart should be through the head. If we wish to shape character, we need to shape the philosophical habit. Students will do well if they reason well.

That is why, in the end, the signature strengths of Washington and Lee—our academic excellence and the development of the character of our students—are so intertwined. We take pride in educating students who will make a difference, and we should never underestimate the academic challenges that presents, especially as the world changes in profound ways.

I close this morning with a request.

Take a second to appreciate where we gather this morning: one of the most graceful and beautiful settings in higher education, embraced on one end by Washington Hall and on the other by Lee Chapel. Think not only of the architectural symmetry but the visual reminder of the incredible legacy that has been given to us, in a straight line from Washington to Lee to us today. Consider the obligation it places on us to build a future worthy of our past.

We have much to do. Restore the colonnade for future generations… attend to other building projects with a constant awareness that the civility found on our campus flows in part from the gracefulness of our physical surroundings… keep our curriculum vibrant and enriching… bring the best faculty and staff we can to this campus and enable them to develop their talents throughout their careers… and do everything we possibly can to attract students who possess exceptional academic and personal qualities no matter their origins, backgrounds, or financial capacity.

And let us achieve those goals by embracing the spirit that has always defined Washington and Lee. It is a difficult quality to articulate, but Abraham Lincoln, one of my favorite historical figures, provides a start. I have long admired how Lincoln, despite having every reason to dwell upon the worst features of humankind, always focused on the best. That uncommon sentiment received its most eloquent expression at a time when it was needed most, at the end of his first inaugural address:

> We are not enemies, but friends. We must not be enemies. Though passion may have strained it must not break the bonds of affection. The mystic chords of memory, stretching from every battlefield and patriot grave to every living heart and hearthstone all over this broad land, yet will swell the chorus of this Union, when again touched, as surely they will be, by the better angels of our nature.

As all of us—alumni, students, faculty, staff, friends, and supporters—embark on our journey together, I hope we create an educational institution that calls upon the best qualities of humanity. I hope we foster conversations in which the objective is to understand rather than prevail. I hope we develop within our students a commitment to something greater than the self. And I hope that we will always offer an education that cultivates those better angels of our nature.

With gratitude for all that you have done so far, I look forward to working *with* you and *for* you... I pledge my firm commitment to each of you as individuals... and to a University made good by our predecessors, now entrusted to us to make even better for those who will follow.

Biographies of the Contributors

H. Laurent Boetsch, Jr

H. Laurent Boetsch, Jr, has been closely tied to Washington and Lee University for the greater part of his adult life. He graduated from W&L in 1969 with a B.A. degree in Romance Languages, and from Middlebury College in 1976 with a D. M. L. degree, also in Romance Languages. He returned to W&L in 1976 as a member of the faculty, taught Spanish, moved rapidly through the ranks, serving as chair of the Department of Romance Languages, Associate Dean of the College, Dean of the College, and Vice President for Academic Affairs. Following the death of John Elrod in 2001, he became Acting President of the University. During his term as Acting President, he launched the highly successful Campaign for the Rising Generation that raised $242.6 million.

In 2002, he became the first Provost in the history of the University. Since 2004, Boetsch has been the Head of the European College of Liberal Arts in Berlin, Germany. In 2006, to express its "deep and profound respect for the work of both Larry and his wife Elizabeth," the Board of Trustees established an academic scholarship in their honor. A year later, the Class of 1978 established a need-based scholarship to recognize their contributions to the University for more than three decades.

Thomas Carl Damewood

Thomas Carl Damewood was born in 1929 at Ronceverte, Greenbrier County, West Virginia, and educated in the public schools of the state's capital, graduating as student body president and valedictorian of the 1947 class of Charleston High School.

He received his B.A. *magna cum laude* in 1951 and his J.D. *summa cum laude* in 1953 from Washington and Lee University, where he belonged to Phi Kappa Psi social and Phi Delta Phi legal fraternities, was Editor of the W&L *Law Review*, and was elected to Phi Beta Kappa and the Order of the Coif.

After passing the Virginia and West Virginia bar examinations and through the JAG School of the Army, he served as a first lieutenant prosecuting and defending general courts-martial in Korea and Japan and received the Army Commendation Medal. Continuing in the W. Va. Army National Guard, he retired as a colonel

In law practice in Charleston through 1994, concentrating on real estate, bank trust matters, and the administration of decedents' estates, he retired as a partner in Kay, Casto & Chaney. From 1973 through 1994 that practice included being general counsel of the Charleston Urban Renewal Authority, which transformed the downtown of the capital. In 1994 he was named a Life Member of The American Law Institute.

Wed in 1961 to Betty Sims (B.A., Rhodes; M.A., WVU), they have two daughters, both married to W&L graduates, Elizabeth (B.A., Davidson) to Jamie O. Gaucher (B.A., W&L) and Carol (B.A., W&L; M.A., UGa) to Bryant J. Spann (B.A., W&L; J.D., UGa).

Betty is currently and Tom a former elder of First Presbyterian Church. Their travels have ranged from Krakow to Hong Kong and from Sydney to Copenhagen. His memberships include the Charleston Tennis Club, Rotary Club and several Masonic bodies.

Andrew H. Farmer

My memories of Dr. Jenks are indeed well-defined. It was the first semester of my freshman year, and I discovered the head of the Department of History was teaching my introductory European history class! Instead of being an intimidating experience, Dr. Jenks' lectures were fascinating and helped motivate a reserved freshman to pursue a history major at Washington and Lee.

Although my professional careers have been in television journalism and public relations for several state agencies in Virginia, I have always maintained a passion for history. In recent years, I have written a book that chronicled my father's experiences as an Army surgeon in the Pacific jungles during World War II. I am finishing a second research project that is the story of another family member killed during World War II when his bomber was shot down in Japan on August 9, 1945, the day the atomic bomb was dropped at Nagasaki.

After graduating from W&L in 1975, I worked for TV stations in Pennsylvania and Richmond. I switched to public relations in 1987, working for the Virginia Department of Health, the Virginia Department of Transportation, and now the State Corporation Commission. I briefly visited Lexington last week to attend a conference at VMI. My schedule was so full that I was only able to visit the W&L campus one rainy evening.

Robert Fishburn

Robert Fishburn graduated from W&L in 1955, having majored in history and minored in American Studies. After serving in the Navy as a meteorologist, he attended Columbia University, studying Victorian literature.

From 1961 to 1983, he worked for the *Roanoke Times as* reporter, arts and music reviewer, desk editor and editorial editor.

He is a former trustee of Roanoke College and a former member of the boards of the Roanoke Museum of Fine Arts, the Roanoke chapter of the Red Cross, the Roanoke Symphony, Opera

Roanoke, and the Virginia Center for the Book He is currently a member of the board of North Cross, a preparatory school.

He and his wife Sibyl have been married for 47 years and have three daughters.

William R. Goodman, Jr., Ph.D.

A native of Rockbridge County, Virginia he holds a B.A. in European History, Washington & Lee University, a M.Div. from Union Theological Seminary (Richmond), and a Ph.D. from Duke University. He was a Fulbright Scholar at the University of Edinburgh. He is Professor of Religious Studies Emeritus at Lynchburg College, Lynchburg, Virginia. He served as Assistant Governor of Area 4 for Rotary International District 7570, and as Vice-President and President of the Lynchburg Plus Sister City Board and helped establish the twinning between Lynchburg and Rueil Malmaison, France and Glauchau, Germany. As President of the Lynchburg Rotary Club he led a delegation to Vicenza, Italy and signed a Sister-Rotary Club document of friendship with the Rotary Club of Vicenza. His career includes pastorates in Highland and Bath Counties, Virginia; superintendency of the Durham County Youth Home (North Carolina); and teaching at Duke Divinity School; Damavand College, Tehran, Iran; and Lynchburg College. He has organized and led tours to China, Japan, Korea, Hong Kong, Taiwan, Thailand, Singapore, Malaysia, Italy, Greece, France, Germany, Netherlands, Ireland, England, Scotland and Wales. He has organized and led over a dozen tours to Egypt. He lectured on Ancient Egyptian Literature in the 2005 W&L Alumni College and led the second February 2006 W&L alumni trip to Egypt. With his wife Martha he has organized and led the Lynchburg Youth String Orchestra on their four European concert tours. Since retirement from teaching at Lynchburg College in 2001, he has continued to travel, do research on a variety of subjects including the archaeology of the ancient Near East and New Religious Movements. He is the author of two books and most recently a contributor to the *Anchor Bible Dictionary, Erdmans Dictionary of the Bible* and *Women in Scripture.*

He holds membership in the American Academy of Religion Society of Biblical Literature; Middle East Studies Association International Society for Iranian Studies; US-Egypt Friendship Society International; Association of Egyptologists; and American Research Center in Egypt.

Richard Wilson Hoover

Richard Wilson Hoover is a retired Foreign Service officer and graduate of Washington and Lee University ('61) and Indiana University. He majored in European History and in Soviet and Eastern European affairs. His foreign posts include Ulm, Bonn, Prague, Gaborone, Nicosia, Rabat, Vienna and Nairobi. He has served as President of the Warren County Heritage Society, President of the Kiwanis Club of Front Royal, Commander of Col. John S. Mosby Camp (Sons of Confederate Veterans) and Commissioner from Warren County on the Northern Shenandoah Valley Regional Commission. He is on the Board of the Mosby Heritage Area Association. Hoover and his wife, Catalina, live in Liberty Hall, near Browntown, in Warren County, Virginia. Two sons are Washington and Lee graduates, Alejandro Lopez-Duke ('87) and Richard W. Hoover Jr. ('93)

Hoover lectures on art and history and conducts a small antique arms business. He attends nearly 20 arms shows a year, from Hartford to Charleston and from Philadelphia and Northern Virginia to Atlanta and Louisville.

Thomas C. Howard

Historians tend to be packrats. This helps to explain why I still have a box containing lecture notes I took between 1956 and 1960. My history major meant mainly courses taught by William Jenks, who came to exemplify for me the profession that I hoped to pursue. There were no "career counselors" then; it was Bill Jenks who provided the insights that guided me.

He taught courses that created a love of the study of history, and he also had practical advice for those who aspired to continue at the graduate level. I completed an Honors thesis with him, and wrote the exams that helped prepare me for what was to come. Of the graduate programs where I was accepted, he urged me to accept the offer from Florida State University in my home state. Not only was it the most generous, but also he knew members of the graduate faculty of whom he spoke highly. I completed the PhD, working primarily with Earl Beck and Victor Mamatey.

After service as an army officer to fulfill my ROTC commitment, I accepted a "temporary" position in the Department of History at Virginia Tech that has stretched to forty years of teaching, writing, and far too many meetings (something Bill did not warn me about!). Postdoctoral work at the University of Wisconsin with Philip Curtin added African history to my teaching fields. In addition to Africa, my teaching and publications have been mostly in British history, with a focus on the history of imperialism. My contribution to this volume expands on ideas in my chapter of the book I co-edited in 2003, *Franklin Roosevelt and the Formation of the Modern World*. I have been fortunate to have a career doing what I love, the inspiration for which I owe so much to William Alexander Jenks.

Robert E. R. Huntley

Robert Huntley, a native of North Carolina, was graduated from Washington & Lee's undergraduate and law schools. He enrolled as a freshman in 1946. A major in English, he took history courses taught by the young Bill Jenks, a rising star on the faculty. Between undergraduate and law schools, Huntley spent three years in the U. S. Navy; he also married Evelyn Whitehurst of Virginia Beach, his life-long companion of 53 years.

After practicing law in Alexandria, Virginia, for a short while, Huntley returned to W&L as assistant professor of law. He served briefly as Dean of the Law School before he was named as President of W&L in 1968. He held that position for fifteen years. He returned briefly to teaching in the law school and in 1984 took an executive position at Best Products, Inc. When that company was bought out in 1988, he joined the Richmond law firm of Hunton & Williams as counsel. Huntley has served on the boards of several business corporations and philanthropic organizations and has performed public service on the Virginia State Board of Education as well as various commissions and study groups.

The Huntleys have three daughters and six grandchildren. The eldest, a granddaughter, was graduated from W&L in June of 2007. Another granddaughter is a rising sophomore and a third enrolled in September of 2007.

John B. Kinkead

After graduation from W&L, I moved to Charlotte, N.C. to work for one year. In 1954, I joined National Mower Co., our family firm started in 1919 producing grass cutting equipment for golf courses and highway departments in the U. S. Canada, and Europe. I started KinCo in 1968, sold it in 1989, bought Sod Master Co. in 1964, sold it in 1969. The company was bought back in 1978 and renamed Turfco Manufacturing. We manufacture top dressers, seeders, and sod cutters. You may see some on your golf course. My two sons, George Kinkead, W&L '85, and Scott Kinkead, W&L '91 run the company.

I married Judith Perkins in 1956. My daughter, Eleanor, is a partner in Collaborative Design Associates, a landscape design firm in Seattle, and my other daughter, Laura, is a consultant to medical professionals in Minnesota and elsewhere. I have three wonderful grandchildren.

My hobbies are politics, history, and especially collecting and restoring Classic Cars, four Rolls Royces in various stages of restoration and a variety of others. My favorite pastime is spending weekends with my family at our cabin on the St. Croix River.

Dr. Jenks was my favorite professor. There were lots of rumors about what he had done during WWII, and he was secretive about it. His wife also worked on a secret project at W&L during the war. He told me he was amused that even after the war, she wouldn't tell him what it was about. Perhaps he should write a book.

A. Cash Koeniger

I graduated from Washington and Lee with Honors in History in 1971. During my last year I served on the Student Advisory Committee for the History Department, a council consisting of five senior majors selected by the new department chairman, Bill Jenks. Dr. Jenks, as I recall, listened thoughtfully and graciously to our opinions whether they were cogent or not (I have lingering suspicions about that). Matriculating next at Vanderbilt, I studied the South and the Civil War with Jacque Voegeli and the South and twentieth-century America with Dewey Grantham, earning a Ph.D. in 1980. Since 1979 I have taught American history at Murray State University, Mississippi State University, the University of Southern Mississippi, Washington and Lee University, and the Virginia Military Institute. Along the way I have authored numerous articles and chapters, among them essays published in the *Journal of American History*, the *Journal of Southern History*, the *Journal of Military History*, and the *South Atlantic Quarterly*. From 1996 through 2006 I directed VMI's annual summer alumni college on the Civil War.

My love for Washington and Lee and admiration for its most distinguished president have long been intertwined, and I don't claim to be entirely unbiased in my essay.

H. F. (Gerry) Lenfest

Mr. Lenfest was born in Jacksonville, Florida, and grew up in Scarsdale, New York, and north of Lambertville, in Hunterdon County, New Jersey. He graduated from Mercersburg Academy, Washington and Lee University, and Columbia Law School. He resides in Huntingdon Valley, Pennsylvania, and is married to the former Marguerite Brooks. They have three children and four grandchildren.

Following graduation from law school, he practiced law with the New York firm of Davis, Polk & Wardwell before joining Triangle Publications, Inc., in Philadelphia as Associate Counsel in 1965. Triangle, a large privately owned communications company headed by Walter Annenberg, then owned television and radio stations, two major newspapers in Philadelphia, *TV Guide, SEVENTEEN* magazine, racing newspapers, and cable television systems. After five years, Mr. Lenfest was placed in charge of Triangle's Communications Division, consisting of *SEVENTEEN* magazine and Triangle's CATV interests where he served as Editorial Director, Publisher of *SEVENTEEN* and President of the CATV Operations. In 1974, Mr. Lenfest, with financial support of two businessmen from Lebanon, Pennsylvania, formed a new company which purchased Suburban Cable TV Company and Lebanon Valley Cable TV Company from Triangle with a total of 7,600 cable subscribers. This was the beginning of Lenfest Communications, Inc. The company grew in size to become one of the top twelve cable television companies in the United States with cable television systems in Pennsylvania, Delaware, and New Jersey, as well as interests in France and Australia. In January 2000, Mr. Lenfest and his children entered into a transaction by which their ownership in the cable television operations of Lenfest Communications was transferred to COMCAST Corporation.

Mr. Lenfest served in the United States Navy aboard destroyers and retired with the rank of Captain. He had command of a Destroyer Escort and three Destroyer reserve crews and received commendations from the Secretary of the Navy, Chief of Naval Operations, etc.

John D. Maguire

After 28 years as a university president, the final 17 at Claremont Graduate University, John D. Maguire became president emeritus in 1998 and senior fellow in the Institute for Democratic Renewal in the University's School of Politics and Economics. A senior consultant to Oakland based Project Change—with which the Institute formed a joint partnership in 2002—he is engaged full-time in a range of anti-racism, democratic community building projects and activities while serving on the boards of Union Theological Seminary, the NAACP Legal Defense & Educational Fund, the Tomás Rivera Policy Institute, and as senior consultant in poetry to California's Idyllwild School of the Arts and of counsel to the Claremont Museum of Art.

John Maguire has written and spoken widely on issues of human rights and social justice, on the arts and politics, and on issues confronting education at all levels. In more than 50 articles and contributions to books, he has focused particularly upon the college presidency, higher education, the arts, and racial and social justice.

A colleague of Dr. Martin Luther King Jr., he is a life director of the King Center and served in its initial year (1968-69) as chair of the board. He has been formally associated with the NAACP LDF since the 1980s and a board director for nearly 20 years. He was one of the founders of the Tomás Rivera Policy Institute and a charter member of the Pacific Council on International Policy. Maguire serves on the advisory councils of the Andrew Young School of Policy Studies at Georgia State University, Pacific Oaks College, the Advancement Project, and the University of Iowa's R*E*A*C*H program for students with multiple LD. He and Mrs. Maguire (Billie) serve as annual Woodrow Wilson Foundation Visiting Fellows to colleges throughout the country. He is a member of the Council on Foreign Relations.

Roy T. Matthews

Roy T. Matthews, who came to Washington and Lee to study journalism, switched to History his sophomore year and took as many "Jenks" courses as his schedule permitted. He graduated as a History major in 1954, and, following Dr. Jenks' advice, attended Duke University where he earned a MA in Modern European History. From 1955 to 1958 he was in the real estate business in Baton Rouge, where he met his wife of forty-eight years, Lee Ann Goodrich. In 1958 he began his teaching career at the Georgia State College for Women, and from 1960 to 1964 studied Modern European History at the University of North Carolina, Chapel Hill, receiving his PhD in 1966. After a year at the University of Houston, he went to Michigan State University where he taught from 1965 until his retirement in 1996. He was a member of the Department of Humanities, the Department of History and on the faculty of Justin Morrill College, a Liberal Arts residential college. He helped establish the Department of Humanities London program, which he conducted for many summers, and a program in Florence. In 1982 he co-authored *In Vanity Fair*, a study of the nineteenth-century English society magazine and its caricatures of prominent Victorians. In 1990 he co-authored *The Western Humanities*, a textbook now in its sixth edition. While at Michigan State, he was actively involved in academic governance, the American Association of University Professors, and Phi Beta Kappa. Although he seldom succeeded, he attempted to bring to his classes Dr. Jenks' celebrated standards as scholar, lecturer, and mentor.

Roger Mudd

Roger Mudd was the documentary host and correspondent for The History Channel from 1995 until he retired in 2004. He is currently writing a memoir.

Between 1961 to 1992, he was a Washington correspondent for CBS News, NBC News and the MacNeil/Lehrer Newshour on PBS. He won the George Foster Peabody award for "The Selling of the Pentagon" in 1970 and for "Teddy" in 1979 and the Barone Award for Distinguished Washington Reporting in 1990.

Between 1992 and 1996, he was a visiting professor of politics and the press at Princeton University and at W&L University.

Mudd was the editor of *Great Minds of History,* interviews with five American historians published in 1999 by John Wiley & Sons.

Mudd graduated from W&L University in 1950 and from the University of North Carolina in 1953 with a master's degree in history.

He enlisted in the US Army in 1945 and served with the 2nd Armored Division.

Mudd is on the board of the Virginia Foundation for Independent Colleges and the National Portrait Gallery, the advisory boards of the Eudora Welty Foundation and the Jepson School of Leadership at the University of Richmond.

Mudd, born in Washington, D.C. in 1928, is married to the former E. J. Spears of Richmond, Virginia. They have four children, eleven grandchildren and have lived in McLean, Virginia for 35 years.

Robert O. Paxton

Born in Lexington, Virginia, I was more or less predestined for Washington and Lee, which members of my family had attended since the early 19th century. But my parents didn't want me to be regarded as a "towny." So when I entered in fall 1950 I lived in the freshman dorm, and thereafter my social life centered on the SAE house, until I slipped up the back stairs at home late at night. I majored in history, was elected Vice-President of the Student Body and served as valedictorian of the class of 1954.

On graduation, I had the great good fortune to be chosen for a Rhodes Scholarship and spent the years 1954-1956 at Merton College, Oxford where I continued to study history.

In fall 1956, I began two years of military service. Just before I had entered W&L, in June 1950, the Korean War had broken out, and I had joined the Naval Reserve in order to be able to stay in college and do my service as an officer after graduation. The Navy had deferred me to go to Oxford. When I finally served, the Navy wanted to put my studies to use. For two years, as a very junior officer in the foreign affairs section of the staff of the Chief of Naval Operations in the Pentagon, I helped brief the brass on areas of tension around the world where the U. S. Navy might become involved.

Upon finishing my military service, I was tempted momentarily by the Foreign Service, but the appeal of college teaching won out and I entered the doctoral program in modern European history at Harvard in the fall of 1958. Luck was with me again when I chose Vichy France, the French regime that collaborated with the German occupation of 1940-1944, as the subject for my doctoral dissertation. In the way I explain in my contribution to this volume, the heated and even angry debates my books about the Vichy regime provoked in France over the years gave my professional life some extra challenge and excitement.

I started teaching at the University of California at Berkeley in the fall of 1961, and finished my doctoral dissertation there while I was learning what to do in the classroom. In 1967 I moved to the new campus of the State University of New York at Stony Brook, on Long Island, and, in 1969, I accepted a position as full professor at Columbia University. I remained at Columbia until I retired in 1997 with the title of Mellon Professor of the Social Sciences.

Over the years I published seven scholarly books and several articles, many of them translated into foreign editions. In addition to three books about Vichy France, my books included a study of fascism—*The Anatomy of Fascism* (Knopf, 2004), translated into eleven languages, —and a textbook, *Europe in the Twentieth Century* (updated 4th edition, Harcourt Brace, 2005). I dedicated my first book to three people who had set me on the road to becoming a history professor, including William A. Jenks.

Dr. John R. Pleasant, Jr.

Dr. John R. Pleasant, Jr. was born October 26, 1938, in Shreveport, Louisiana, the son of Judge John R. Pleasant and Margaret Noble Pleasant. He attended public and private schools in

Shreveport, graduating from C. E. Byrd High School in 1956. With Dr. William A. Jenks as his major professor, he graduated from Washington and Lee University in 1960 with a B.A. in history. At W&L, he was a member of Beta Theta Pi fraternity, Scabbard and Blade, and the cross country and track teams. Commissioned an infantry second lieutenant at his June graduation, Dr. Pleasant served 18 months of extended active duty and four years in the Louisiana Army National Guard, earning the rank of captain.

Dr. Pleasant received an M.A. (1965) and Ph.D. (1976) in English from Louisiana State University. He taught at Southeastern Louisiana University from 1965 - 1997, retiring as Associate Professor Emeritus. A charter member of The Thomas Wolfe Society, he wrote his M.A. thesis and Ph.D. dissertation about Wolfe. Since retirement, Dr. Pleasant has taught as an adjunct at LSU-Shreveport.

Dr. Pleasant has three children: Elizabeth Pleasant Hudson, Dunwoody, GA; Margaret Evelyn Pleasant, Denver, CO; and John Kirk Pleasant, Vancouver, B.C. He is married to Deborah Tramel Pleasant.

"My tribute to the late William B. Wisdom, Jr. in *The Thomas Wolfe Review* can also be seen as a tribute to Dr. Jenks, whom I know Bill considered a friend as well as his favorite professor. It was Bill Wisdom who advised me to major in European history, mainly because of Dr. Jenks' reputation. Bill Wisdom and William A. Jenks each epitomize, in my opinion, the Washington and Lee scholar and gentleman."

Kenneth P. Ruscio

Kenneth P. Ruscio was elected the 26th president of Washington and Lee University on March 7, 2006. W&L alumnus and distinguished scholar in the study of democratic theory and public policy, Dr. Ruscio served as the Dean of the Jepson School of Leadership Studies at the University of Richmond for four years before assuming his present position. Prior to his tenure at the

University of Richmond, he held various positions at W&L including Professor of Politics, Associate Dean of The Williams School of Commerce, Economics and Politics, and Dean of Freshmen. He was a postdoctoral research scholar at the University of California, Los Angeles from 1983 to 1985, and taught at both Worcester Polytechnic Institute and Kansas University.

Ruscio earned his B.A. in politics from Washington and Lee University in 1976 and earned an M.P.A. and Ph.D. from Syracuse University's Maxwell School of Citizenship and Public Affairs in 1978 and 1983, respectively.

Ruscio has authored numerous articles and essays and one book, *The Leadership Dilemma in Modern Democracy* (Edward Elgar Publishing, Inc. 2004). He recently completed his second term as national president of Omicron Delta Kappa, a leadership society begun at W&L in 1914 that now has chapters at over 300 campuses. He has led, and served on, dozens of academic, professional, and civic committees.

Ruscio is married to the former Kimberley O'Donnell of New York. They have a son, Matthew Christopher, age 16.

Samuel A. Syme

After a brief stint at Fort Sill, I was admitted to the Duke Graduate School in history, thanks, I am sure, to the efforts of Professors Turner, Jenks and Leyburn. I soon ran short of money and taught two years in high school (and one at Duke), while finishing my masters and doctoratal degrees.

In the early 60's, I was assistant director of the Master of Arts in Teaching program at Emory University. In 1964, I moved to Winston-Salem as a staff member of the experimental North Carolina Advancement School, with a joint appointment at Wake Forest in history and education.

Following years of frequent visits to Myrtle Beach, the chance came in the 70's to join the newly created Coastal Carolina. College as Assistant Director for Student Affairs, with a position in the History Department. My relationship with Coastal has continued to this day. I have seen it become a university with over 7,500 students and four endowed colleges offering both under-graduate and graduate degrees. (Too, spending the academic year at the beach has an appeal all its own, and I know has contrib-uted to the numerous applications which are annually received. It is probably true of faculty inquiries, as well.)

At some point, in the midst of all. of this, I've owned and operated a catering company; managed a beach house primarily for the buyers and other guests of a large tobacco company; bred and raised Welsh Corgis and travelled many times to Canada, Europe and Russia—sometimes with students and sometimes without.

Henry Turner

Born in Atlanta, I grew up in Bethesda, Maryland, attended public schools there and was the first in my family to attend college. Having edited the student newspaper in high school, I signed on as a reporter for the *Ring-Tum Phi* with the intention of pursuing a career in journalism. But exposure to European history in Dr. Jenks's courses quickly aroused what has proved to be a life-long desire to learn more. I also came to know and admire Dr. Jenks personally.

As a Junior, I wrote the following to my family: "I can't really explain why Dr. Jenks is so different from the other professors whom I know except for the important fact that he doesn't keep up the student-faculty barrier that most professors maintain. It's quite a refreshing experience to be able to go to someone and expect to be treated as another person rather than as just another pupil or student. I hope to see a good deal of Dr. Jenks from now on. By the way, he is giving me a inside view of the college teach-ing profession and there is more there than strikes the eye!"

I soon decided that was the right profession for me. On Dr. Jenks's advice, I added German to my French and applied suc-cessfully for a Fulbright scholarship to Germany, where I spent one semester at the University of Munich and one at the Free

University of Berlin. Thanks to a fellowship for which Dr. Jenks nominated me, I then continued my studies at Princeton, where I received my Ph.D. in 1960. Two years earlier, I was appointed an instructor at Yale, where I continued to teach European and German history until my retirement as the Charles Stifle Professor at the end of 2002.

Ruel W. Tyson, Jr.

Ruel W. Tyson, Jr. has been a member of the Department of Religious Studies at the University of North Carolina at Chapel Hill since 1967, three times chairman of the Department, and the Director of UNC-Chapel Hill's Institute for the Arts and Humanities. He was born in Winterville Township, North Carolina, and educated in the public schools of Greenville, North Carolina. He earned an A.B. with exceptional honors in Philosophy at Washington and Lee University in 1953, and a B.D. at Yale University in 1957. He carried out additional work at the Victoria University of Manchester, the University of Chicago, and St. Anthony's College, Oxford University. In addition to the University of North Carolina, he has taught at the University of the South and the Episcopal Theological Seminary of the South at Austin, Texas.

Tyson has taught a wide variety of courses that encompass religious ethics, the rhetoric of religion, religious ritual and practices, and theories of religion and culture. In 1987, he founded the Institute for the Arts and Humanities, and was its director until 2006. The Institute supports outstanding faculty by funding semester-long on-campus leaves, and by organizing weekly meetings at which recipients of its grants discuss ways of improving their research and teaching. In 1998, his work with the Institute earned him a Chancellors Award, recognition of his "outstanding contributions toward enhancing the quality of the work place." History professor Lloyd Kramer wrote of him, "I have never encountered a colleague who was so willing to give his time and energy and talents in the service of other professors." In 2001 the University endowed a professorship to honor Tyson and support the work of the Institute.

Tyson is married and the father of two grown sons.

Jack Vardaman

Jack Vardaman grew up in Anniston, Alabama. He entered Washington & Lee in 1958 where he majored in European History. He graduated with an AB degree in 1962. He then enrolled at the Harvard Law School where he graduated with a JD in 1965. He served as a law clerk for Justice Hugo L. Black of the United States Supreme Court for the 1965-1966 term of Court.

Mr. Vardaman entered private practice in Washington, D.C. and has been at the firm of Williams & Connolly LLP since 1970. He has appeared in the United States Supreme Court and in state and federal courts throughout the country at the trial and appellate levels and was identified as one of "Washington's Top Lawyers" by *Washingtonian* magazine (December 2004).

From 1999 to 2002, Mr. Vardaman served as General Counsel to the United States Golf Association. He is a member of the American College of Trial Lawyers.

Mr. Vardaman is also currently a member of the Board of Trustees of Washington & Lee University and Chairman of the Board of Trustees of Gonzaga College High School. He received the Washington & Lee Distinguished Alumnus Award in 2002.

He has continued his interest in golf and is a frequent participant in senior golf championships. He was ranked as one of the top ten senior amateurs in the country in 2001.

He and his wife Marianne have four children, including son Davis, who graduated from Washington & Lee in 1995, and eight grandchildren. They have as a second home in Bath County, Virginia, the former home of W&L benefactor Lettie Pate Evans, where they have hosted numerous W&L functions.

G. William Whitehurst

G. William Whitehurst was born in Norfolk, Virginia on March 12, 1925. He was educated in its public schools, graduating from

Maury High School in 1942. During World War II he served in the U.S. Navy as a radioman/machine gunner with Torpedo Squadron 88 and flew combat missions against naval and air targets in Japan in the summer of 1945.

Following his military service, he was admitted to Washington and Lee University in 1946, graduating with a B.A. in history in 1950. He earned his M.A. in history at the University of Virginia in 1951. He commenced his academic career as a history instructor at the Norfolk Division of William and Mary in 1950, taking leave in 1956 to begin residence on his Ph.D. in history at West Virginia University, receiving that degree in 1962. In the meantime, he returned to what became Old Dominion University and was appointed Dean of Students in 1963.

In 1968 he was elected to the U.S. House of Representatives from the 2nd District of Virginia and held that seat until his retirement from the Congress in 1986. During his congressional service, he was a member of the House Armed Services Committee, the House Select Committee on Intelligence, and the Committee on Standards of Official Conduct (Ethics Committee). Dr. Whitehurst kept a diary of his 18 years in the Congress and published two volumes of excerpts from the diary, *Diary Of A Congressman* and *Diary Of A Congressman: Abscam And Beyond*. The original volumes of the diary he left to the Leyburn Library at Washington and Lee, along with his official papers. They are available for research purposes.

In 1987, Dr. Whitehurst returned to Old Dominion University to resume his academic career and holds the George and Linda Kaufman Chair as Lecturer in Public Affairs. He teaches courses in both history and political science. For ten years he also served as news and political commentator for WVEC-TV in Norfolk.

Dr. Whitehurst has been married for over 60 years to the former Jennette Franks of Plymouth, Massachusetts. They have a daughter, Frances, and a son, Cal, who is a graduate of Washington and Lee, class of 1971. Dr. and Mrs. Whitehurst have two grandsons and two great-grandsons.

Randolph G. Whittle, Jr.

Randy Whittle graduated from W&L in 1952 majoring in history. Pursuing a career as a city manager, he received a masters degree in governmental administration from the University of Pennsylvania. Following three years active duty with the Navy, his public career included service as City Manager of Bluefield, WV, Assistant Director of the Regional Planning Council in Baltimore, MD, Florida state Planning Director, and Executive Director of the Greater Johnstown Committee. When he retired in 1998, he had been filling in for nearly a year as interim City Manager of Johnstown, PA.

Believing that every community should have a written local history, and knowing that Johnstown had a fascinating past that had gone neglected—except for a spate of works dealing with its great flood of 1889—he set about to author *Johnstown, Pennsylvania—A History*. The span of the two-volume work begins just after the recovery from the 1889 disaster and continues until about 1980. The books were published in 2006 and 2007 by the History Press, Inc. of Charleston, SC. In the "Preface and Acknowledgements" section of his work, Whittle stated that while researching and writing the book, "More than once I sought the wisdom of my mentor, William A. Jenks, a professor emeritus of history at Washington and Lee University.

The W&L History Department, 1969. Back Row: Jarrett, Sensabaugh, Futch, Wagner, Turner, McAhren. Front Row: Moger, Crenshaw, Jenks.

Printed in the United States
90443LV00005B/184-279/A